D1806840

COURTYARD HOUSING FOR HEALTH AND HAPPINESS

This is a unique book that traverses a wide range of topics including philosophy, oriental wisdom, psychology, and modern housing design. It aims to answer a central question – how to design a healthy house and a happy home – so practical and yet so eternally important for us all. The study proposes courtyard garden houses as a paradigmatic model. It promotes multiculturalism in architecture and in social life as a whole, which is so central to a new global sensitivity on the rise in North America and elsewhere.

In a word, this book has masterfully integrated a range of topics from philosophy to building design, addressed a profound yet practical issue of housing for a healthy and happy life, and promoted cross-cultural thinking so central to a new sensitivity on the rise in the twenty-first century.

It is a great book that addresses issues practical yet central to life for everyone – a book everyone should read – for reorganizing your interior, building a new home, debating for a neighbourhood, or simply pursuing harmony in your personal and social life.

Jianfei Zhu, Associate Professor,
Faculty of Architecture, Building and Planning, University of Melbourne, Australia

Courtyard Housing for Health and Happiness

Architectural Multiculturalism in North America

Donia Zhang
York University, Canada

ASHGATE

© Donia Zhang 2015

All rights reserved. No part of this publication may be reproduced, stored in a retrieval system or transmitted in any form or by any means, electronic, mechanical, photocopying, recording or otherwise without the prior permission of the publisher.

Donia Zhang has asserted her right under the Copyright, Designs and Patents Act, 1988, to be identified as the author of this work.

Published by
Ashgate Publishing Limited
Wey Court East
Union Road
Farnham
Surrey, GU9 7PT
England

Ashgate Publishing Company
110 Cherry Street
Suite 3-1
Burlington, VT 05401-3818
USA

www.ashgate.com

British Library Cataloguing in Publication Data
A catalogue record for this book is available from the British Library.

Library of Congress Cataloging-in-Publication Data
Zhang, Donia, 1967-
  Courtyard housing for health and happiness : architectural multiculturalism in North America / By Donia Zhang.
    pages cm
  Includes bibliographical references and index.
  ISBN 978-1-4724-4911-5 (hardback) -- ISBN 978-1-4724-4912-2 (ebook) -- ISBN 978-1-4724-4913-9 (epub) 1. Courtyard houses. 2. Architecture--Human factors. 3. Architecture and philosophy--China. 4. Architecture and globalization--North America. I. Title.
  NA7523.Z495 2015
  728'.31--dc23
                                                                    2014041039
ISBN 9781472449115 (hbk)
ISBN 9781472449122 (ebk – PDF)
ISBN 9781472449139 (ebk – ePUB)

Printed in the United Kingdom by Henry Ling Limited,
at the Dorset Press, Dorchester, DT1 1HD

Contents

List of Figures   *vii*
List of Tables   *xi*
Foreword   *xiii*
Preface   *xv*
Acknowledgments   *xix*

1   Introduction: Health and Happiness in Housing   1

2   Four Key Themes in Chinese Philosophy to
     Promote Health and Happiness at Home   23

3   Health as Balancing *Yin Yang*:
     Form and Environmental Quality of the Housing   39

4   Health as Gathering *Qi*:
     Space and Construction Quality of the Housing   61

5   Happiness as Attaining Oneness:
     Matters of Social Cohesion in the Homes   75

6   Happiness as Knowing the Dao:
     Time and Cultural Activities in the Homes   91

7   Four Keystones of Courtyard Housing Design   105

8   Conclusion: Courtyard Housing for Health and Happiness   119

Appendix: Survey Questionnaire   *137*
Bibliography   *159*
Index   *177*

List of Figures

P.1 The stamp collection set features the eight Gates of Chinatown
     across Canada, arranged in rows representing the typical urban
     planning system in North America (top). The same stamp collection
     set is arranged in the "Nine Squares" planning system in imperial
     China (bottom)   xvi
P.2 Chinese Archway built in 2008–2009 in Toronto's East Chinatown,
     with gray granite walls covered with dark green glazed tiles   xvii

1.1 Plan of a standard or typical classical Beijing courtyard house
     (*siheyuan*)   7
1.2 A generic plan of Suzhou traditional courtyard house with lightwells   7
1.3 Granada Court inner courtyard, Pasadena, California   8
1.4 Site plan of the Harper Court:
     Seven Fountains, West Hollywood, California   9
1.5 Harper Court: Seven Fountains,
     north courtyard viewed from the east, West Hollywood, California   10
1.6 Site plan of the Meridian Court, Pasadena, California   11
1.7 Meridian Court main courtyard, Pasadena, California   12
1.8 Gartz Court entrance, Pasadena, California   12
1.9 Bain Apartments Co-operative South Lindens courtyard,
     Toronto, Ontario, Canada   13
1.10 Spruce Court Housing Co-operative, Toronto, Ontario, Canada   14
1.11 Bristol Court housing courtyard with garages, Richmond Hill,
     Ontario, Canada   14
1.12 Jenny Green Co-operative Homes courtyard, Toronto, Ontario,
     Canada   15
1.13 Kingsmere housing courtyard, Thornhill, Ontario, Canada   15
1.14 Windward Co-operative Homes courtyard, Toronto, Ontario, Canada   16
1.15 Map of the world showing the locations of the USA and Canada
     in relation to China, to indicate the similarities in their climatic
     conditions and geographies that affect housing design   17

2.1   Map of North America showing the land and surrounding seas where
      possible wind directions can be generated   26
2.2   A conceptual model of a typical classical Beijing courtyard house for
      a single extended family   30
2.3   A generic model of a classical Suzhou courtyard house compound
      for a single extended family   31

3.1   A typical subdivision suburban housing pattern in Canada,
      with single-detached houses as the main housing form   42
3.2   A typical single-detached house in Richmond Hill, Ontario, Canada,
      with a two-car garage   43
3.3   Typical semi-detached suburban houses in Richmond Hill,
      Ontario, Canada   45
3.4   A front view of row/town houses in Richmond Hill, Ontario, Canada   45
3.5   The back of the row/town houses with garages and a driveway for
      vehicle access but not designed for human activities   46
3.6   A single-storey house/bungalow in Richmond Hill, Ontario, Canada   47
3.7   An apartment building of fewer than five storeys in Richmond Hill,
      Ontario, Canada   48
3.8   An apartment building of more than five storeys in Richmond Hill,
      Ontario, Canada   48
3.9   Site plan of the Bain Apartments Co-operative showing the
      nine communal courtyards, Toronto, Ontario, Canada   53
3.10 Bain Apartments Co-operative North Maples courtyard,
      Toronto, Ontario, Canada   53
3.11 The Courtyard House, Toronto, Ontario, Canada   55
3.12 The courtyard of the Courtyard House, Toronto, Ontario, Canada   55
3.13 House with a front balcony as decoration, Richmond Hill,
      Ontario, Canada   56
3.14 Balconies at the back of housing for sunlight and fresh air,
      Richmond Hill, Ontario, Canada   56
3.15 A garage roof terrace that can be used for various activities in
      warm seasons, Richmond Hill, Ontario, Canada   58

4.1   Single-detached suburban houses pattern in the US   62
4.2   Single-detached suburban houses pattern in Canada   62
4.3   Living room of a single-detached house, Richmond Hill, Ontario,
      Canada   63
4.4   Family room of a single-detached house, Richmond Hill, Ontario,
      Canada   64
4.5   Dining room of a single-detached house, Richmond Hill, Ontario,
      Canada   64
4.6   Kitchen of a single-detached house, Richmond Hill, Ontario, Canada   65

5.1   Back yard fences hinder neighborly interaction, Richmond Hill,
      Ontario, Canada   77
5.2   Children watching a puppet show at Bain Apartments Co-operative
      North Maples courtyard, Toronto, Ontario, Canada   80

5.3   Courtyard as landscaped garden at Bain Apartments Co-operative
      North Maples courtyard, Toronto, Ontario, Canada   81
5.4   Courtyard as landscaped garden at Church-Isabella Residence
      Co-operative, Toronto, Ontario, Canada   81
5.5   Courtyard as social space at Bain Apartments Co-operative
      North Oaks courtyard, Toronto, Ontario, Canada   83

6.1   During the warm seasons, a group of seniors do exercise every
      morning in a community park, Richmond Hill, Ontario, Canada   95
6.2   A group of women dancing at lunchtime at College Park,
      Toronto, Ontario, Canada   98
6.3   Children playing at Withrow Park, Toronto, Ontario, Canada   98
6.4   People talking at Little Norway Park, Toronto, Ontario, Canada   99
6.5   View of autumn leaves at Heath Street Corner Park, Toronto,
      Ontario, Canada   99
6.6   Centennial celebrations at
      Bain Apartments Co-operative North Maples courtyard,
      Toronto, Ontario, Canada   103
6.7   Centennial celebrations by the children at
      Bain Apartments Co-operative North Maples courtyard,
      Toronto, Ontario, Canada   103

7.1   Four keystones of courtyard housing design to promote health and
      happiness in accordance with traditional Chinese philosophy   106

8.1   Proposed North American courtyard garden house system for
      Scheme A based on the "Nine Squares" system   122
8.2   Proposed North American courtyard garden house system for
      Scheme B based on the "Six Squares" system   122
8.3   Scheme A of the proposed courtyard garden house compound
      housing eight nuclear families   123
8.4   Scheme B of the proposed courtyard garden house compound
      housing four nuclear families   123
8.5   Scheme A of the proposed courtyard garden house compound site plan   124
8.6   The pattern of Scheme A of the proposed courtyard garden
      house compound   124
8.7   Scheme B of the proposed courtyard garden house compound site plan   125
8.8   Scheme A courtyard garden house elevations with three sets of
      different window patterns   126
8.9   Scheme B courtyard garden house elevations with three sets of
      different window patterns   126
8.10 Scheme A courtyard garden house compound ground/first-floor plan   127
8.11 Scheme B courtyard garden house compound ground/first-floor plan   128
8.12 Courtyard garden house roof plan   129
8.13 Proposed courtyard garden house semi-basement plan   130

8.14 Scheme A of the proposed courtyard garden house
     ground/first-floor plan   131
8.15 Scheme B of the proposed courtyard garden house ground/first-floor
     plan   132
8.16 Proposed courtyard garden house second-floor plan   133

List of Tables

3.1 Location considerations for ethnic Chinese in North America when
    buying/renting a home   40
3.2 Summary of ethnic Chinese preferences for the form of the housing   59

4.1 Color connotations associated with emotion   65
4.2 Color connotations associated with orientation   66
4.3 Facility provision at home to promote health   71
4.4 Summary of ethnic Chinese preferences for the space of the housing   73

6.1 Respondents' daily activities at home to promote happiness   93
6.2 Respondents' daily activities at home on an ordinary day   96
6.3 Public places where respondents conduct their favorite activities   97
6.4 Cultural festivals celebrated by ethnic Chinese in North America   100

7.1 Matrix of measurement for courtyard housing to
    promote health and happiness   107
7.2 Four keystones of courtyard housing design for
    health and happiness   116

8.1 Scheme A courtyard garden house density and plot ratio   134
8.2 Scheme B courtyard garden house density and plot ratio   134
8.3 Summary of the proposed new courtyard garden houses   135

Foreword

When speaking about housing, North Americans still claim to subscribe to a singular myth, often referred to as either the American or the Canadian "dream." It consists of an owner-occupied dwelling, free-standing on its own plot of land, which supposedly guarantees personal privacy, independence and, on some accounts, democracy itself. It is no secret that this has never described the way that many people actually lived. More to the point, there has always been a significant minority for whom this was not even an ideal. Until the 1920s, for example, many middle-class families were perfectly happy to remain as renters, even though they could easily have afforded to buy.

More relevant to the present, since the 1960s a growing proportion of North American households have embraced alternate forms of housing. In terms of design, the widespread acceptance and adoption of Planned Unit Developments produced neighborhoods with a mixture of dwelling types and various configurations of small-scale open spaces. The influence of New Urbanism has reinforced this trend, complicating it by re-introducing some old combinations of land uses that have been made new again. The proliferation of gated communities, condominiums, and other types of Common Interest Developments, has demonstrated that tens of millions of households are pleased to relinquish some privacy, and limit their rights of ownership, if neighbours do likewise. North Americans may never have been more open to unconventional ideas about housing and neighborhood design than the present. Among these, the residential courtyard is an attractive option.

As Donia Zhang shows in this book, courtyards come in various shapes and sizes but all tend to bring people into closer relation with one another than the conventional single-family home. Some will welcome this, while others baulk. One of the problems that advocates of courtyards must confront is the fact that, largely by chance, in North America "courts" have negative connotations. They may conjure black-and-white images of overcrowded, late nineteenth-century tenements or, more likely, of low- and medium-rise public housing projects dating from the 1930s through the 1960s. The poor physical and social conditions that prevailed—and sometimes still exist—in such "projects" have everything to do with poverty and nothing to do with design. As Zhang shows us, courtyards have a long, respectable and indeed impressive tradition in China, especially Beijing. In principle, they have much to recommend them. In practice, given the large and growing number of ethnic Chinese in North America, we are likely to see more of this type of housing. But courtyards have not been, and need not be, a mark of cultural origin. To be sure, Zhang suggests that courtyards effectively express long-standing ideals in Chinese philosophy and society, but she also indicates that one need not subscribe to those ideals in order to enjoy the physical and social benefits. They are a valuable, new-old design choice in a society that is increasingly multicultural and which no longer buys wholesale into a particular version of the ideal home.

Professor Richard Harris,
School of Geography and Earth Sciences, McMaster University, Canada

Preface

A tree, swaying in the wind,
eastward, westward, southward, northward,
but her root is deeply embedded in the world.
Without wind, a tree cannot bring us cool,
yet no matter which direction the wind blew,
a tree always knew her root.

Donia Zhang, 2004, *A Tree in the Wind*

North America is showing an increased interest in Chinese culture. This phenomenon is partly due to China's rising economic power, as according to the International Monetary Fund (IMF), China has overtaken the USA to become the world's largest economy by the end of 2014;[1] and partly due to the timeless wisdom in some areas of traditional Chinese philosophy brought by a growing number of immigrants.

At the time of writing (2013–2014), there are 44 national and state acupuncture and traditional Chinese medicine associations with their 103 affiliated colleges and universities, and over 40 Daoist organizations and 80 Confucius institutes across the USA and Canada. There is also an incomplete list of 111 Chinese language schools and cultural centers and 13 *Feng Shui* schools along the east and west coasts of North America. These cultural and educational establishments have undoubtedly helped spread traditional Chinese culture to the people in the "New World."

Today, in most American cities with a large Chinese population, the Spring Festival (Chinese New Year) is celebrated with parties. In Seattle, the Chinese Culture and Arts Festival and other important festivals such as the Dragon Boat Festival and the Mid-Autumn Festival, are held every year. On every Spring Festival, the Canadian prime minister would deliver a speech to acknowledge

---

[1] Arends, 2014; Gorman, 2014.

P.1   The stamp collection set features the eight Gates of Chinatown across Canada, arranged in rows representing the typical urban planning system in North America (top). The same stamp collection set is arranged in the "Nine Squares" planning system in imperial China (bottom)
Source: Canada Post, 2013.

Chinese immigrants' significant contributions to every sector of the Canadian society, and British Columbia recently (May 2014) apologized for their historical racist and discriminatory policies, such as the 1914 head-tax, against Chinese immigrants. Developed from the Vancouver International Dragon Boat Festival, since 1988, the Toronto International Dragon Boat Race Festival is an annual event that brings Chinese and other Asian communities to the Toronto Center Island.

In addition to Canada Post's well-known Chinese New Year stamp series featuring the 12 Chinese zodiac signs, in May 2013, they issued a new collection dedicated to the eight Gates of Chinatown across Canada, which are "symbolic of cooperation between various levels of Canadian and Chinese governments, businesses, and citizens" (Canada Post, 2013).

The local Chinese business community, in cooperation with the Toronto Municipality, Toronto Public Library, and other businesses, in 2008–2009, erected the China Gate (Toronto Chinese Archway, 中华门) in East Chinatown. It is the first of its kind constructed in Toronto, and it took 10 years to finally get it built. The engraved couplet on each side of the middle arch reads: "弘扬中华建筑艺术铭记千秋" ("Expanding Chinese architectural art to be remembered by generations to come") and "丰富加国多元文化流芳万代" ("Enriching Canadian multiculturalism to leave a good name for generations to come"). It is a symbol of "East-meets-West," and an icon of Chinese cultural heritage transplanted in the North American soil.

P.2 Chinese Archway built in 2008–2009 in Toronto's East Chinatown, with gray granite walls covered with dark green glazed tiles
Source: Photo by Donia Zhang, 2013.

The eighteenth century witnessed the influence of classical Chinese gardens on the design of French and English landscape gardens. One may well predict that the twenty-first century will see the impact of traditional Chinese courtyard houses on Western housing development. In fact this is already happening in several American cities as you will read in Chapter 1 of the book.

Donia Zhang

Acknowledgments

I gratefully acknowledge Ashgate Publishing in the UK that has kindly accepted my second book for publication; in particular Valerie Rose, Charlotte Edwards, Caroline Spender, Carolyn Court, and their editorial team for improving and managing the production of the book. This study has received institutional support from the York Centre for Asian Research (YCAR) and the City Institute (CITY) at York University in Canada.

I would like to express my sincere gratitude to SUNY Distinguished Professor Emeritus Ronald G. Knapp for his initial encouragement, sustenance in supplying resources, careful review, and valuable suggestions. I am also grateful to Professor Richard Harris at McMaster University who has provided clear, detailed, and constructive comments, and the book foreword. As well, my genuine appreciation goes to Dr Marcel Vellinga at Oxford Brookes University whose critique of Chapter 1 has helped shape the content's direction in its initial stage.

Dr Aylin Orbasli, Pete Smith, Professor Emeritus Mike Jenks, Professor Emeritus Richard Hayward, Professor Emeritus Michael Humphreys (all from Oxford Brookes University), Dr Yunqing (Lynn) Xu at Xi'an Jiaotong-Liverpool University in China, and Becky Mak and Naomi Lau in Canada, have all offered valuable suggestions after pilot testing the online survey. The staff at the China Center of the University of Minnesota, the Asian Affairs Center of the University of Missouri, and Marina Hill at AIA Central Valley have assisted me in disseminating the survey.

Thanks for the data input from North American Chinese students and scholars associations at universities and colleges; Confucius institutes; Daoist and Buddhist associations; *Feng Shui* schools; *Yi Jing* groups; acupuncture and traditional Chinese medicine colleges and universities; Chinese language schools and cultural centers; Chinese Christian churches; Chinese architects in the American Institute of Architects and the Royal Architectural Institute of Canada; Chinese architectural students from universities and colleges; Chinese realtors from the National Association of Realtors, California Association of Realtors, and the Canadian Real Estate Association; and Chinese embassies and consulate generals in North America. I am also thankful to the property management and residents of three housing co-operatives in Toronto and three cohousing estates across Canada for their contributions. Without their enthusiastic support, the study could not be completed.

Thanks also go to Jarod Dobson at Statistics Canada for extracting and providing relevant data from the 2006 Census of Canada; Sara Sutachan at California Association of Realtors and Stephanie Singer at the National Association of Realtors for sending me useful materials; the staff at the Canadian Housing Information Centre for searching and sending references; and Professor Emeritus Robert Murdie from York University for recommending a relevant thesis.

I should not forget to acknowledge that Professor Emeritus Ronald Jeram taught me Revit Architecture and helped fine-tune some details of the first computer model in Chapter 8.

At last but not least, I am indebted to my parents Junmin Zhang and Suzan Li for their unconditional support throughout the project. I would also like to acknowledge my special friend, Dr Mark R. Harrigan (M.D.), a neurosurgeon who initially inspired me to pursue the topic, and who has morally sustained me to complete the study.

1

Introduction: Health and Happiness in Housing

If you want to be happy for a year, plant a garden.
If you want to be happy for life, plant a tree.

English proverb

If you want happiness for a year, inherit a fortune.
If you want happiness for a lifetime, help others.

Chinese proverb

THE PURSUIT OF HEALTH AND HAPPINESS

Health and happiness are fundamental to people's livelihoods and the continuity of humankind; together they form one of humanity's perpetual pursuits. The *World Health Report*, first published in 1995, is the leading publication of the World Health Organization (WHO), and the United Nations' *World Happiness Report 2012* reflects a new worldwide call for more attention to happiness as a criterion for government policies.

Health is a holistic condition. The *Concise Oxford Dictionary* defines health as "the state of being well in body or mind," it describes "a person's mental or physical condition" (1911/1995, p. 626). In 1946, the World Health Organization defined that "Health is a state of complete physical, mental and social well-being and not merely the absence of disease or infirmity" (2006, p. 1). This definition, although controversial because of the use of the word "complete," has remained the most enduring. WHO's Ottawa Charter for Health Promotion (1986) further declares that "Health is a positive concept emphasizing social and personal resources, as well as physical capacities" (p. 1). Besides healthcare interventions, a number of other factors are known to influence the health status of individuals, including their environments, lifestyles, and socio-economic conditions.

Happiness as important to society is not new. To enlightenment thinkers, the fundamental driving force for humanity is the quest for happiness. Many biological, psychological, philosophical, and religious approaches have striven to define happiness and identify its sources. Ancient Greek philosophers such as Plato (424–348 BCE) in *Protagoras* (1924) argued that happiness is the harmony of the soul, whereas Aristotle (384–322 BCE) in *"Art" of Rhetoric* (1926) and *Nicomachean Ethics* (1999) maintained that happiness consists of lifetime activity in the pursuit of highest virtue. Likewise, Roman philosopher Seneca (ca. 4 BCE –65 CE) in a dialogue *On Happy Life* (2012) advocated virtue against pleasure. A contemporary definition of happiness is the "subjective enjoyment of one's life as-a-whole" (Veenhoven, 2011, p. 17).

In his *Declaration of Independence*, Thomas Jefferson (1743–1826) regarded "the pursuit of happiness" as important as life and liberty in the United States. Utilitarian thinkers, notably English philosopher Jeremy Bentham (1748–1832), demanded public policy to promote "the greatest happiness of the greatest number" (Bentham, 1789).

Since the twentieth century, various research groups have endeavored to apply scientific methods to discover what "happiness" is, and how people might attain it. In particular, happiness economics is a quantitative inquiry, typically combining with other fields such as psychology, sociology, or its related subjects, for instance, quality of life, life satisfaction, positive and negative effects, wellbeing, and so on, to study happiness.

Although most happiness economics research findings show that on average, wealthier countries are happier than poor ones, and that within countries wealthier people are happier than poor ones,[1] the studies conducted by Richard Easterlin in 1974 and Charles Kenny in 1999 indicate that once a certain standard of living is achieved, there is no clear link between increased wealth and happiness.[2] Yet even among the poorer countries, there is no obvious relationship between average income and happiness, suggesting many other factors, including cultural traits, is at work (Easterlin, 2003). This result indicates that constant craving for more economic gains at the expense of environmental poverty will *not* lead humanity to greater happiness.

Happiness is therefore a holistic state that needs to be assessed using more than economic measures. Bhutan's Gross National Happiness (GNH) Index established in 1972 is the first of its kind not relying on the Gross National Product (GNP) Index to evaluate happiness, and China's Happiness Index enacted at the end of 2007 is part of its campaign to create a harmonious society.

Studies have shown that sunny weather makes people happier than gloomy days,[3] so do genes and personality.[4] There is a variation of happiness: having a sense of goal or purpose in life (in Greek terms, *"eudaimonia"* or *"eudaimonism"*[5]),

---

[1]   Frey and Stutzer, 2000; Graham, 2005; Pew Research Center, 2006.

[2]   Easterlin, 2003; Kenny, 2001; Kenny and Kenny, 2006; Nias, 2001.

[3]   Kenny and Kenny, 2006; Nias, 2001.

[4]   Argyle, 2001; Bartlett, 2014; Kenny and Kenny, 2006; Layard, Clark, and Senik, 2012.

[5]   *Eudaimonia* or *eudaimonism* can be translated as "to be inhabited or accompanied by a good *daimon*, or guiding spirit" (Montegomery, 2013, p. 18).

enjoying short-term pleasure (in Greek words, "*hedonia*" or "*hedonism*"[6]), having a religion or spirituality, gaining wisdom, or having companions.[7] Health and happiness are reciprocal; health affects happiness and happiness impacts on health.[8] There also found a strong correlation between education, health, and happiness. Individuals with higher levels of educational attainment tend to be healthier and happier than those with lower ones.[9] Nevertheless, Michalos (2007) argued that the complexity in the definition of "education" (formal, non-formal, and informal) have both direct and indirect effects on the scenario.

Thus, happiness is due to a combination of internal factors such as personality, health, and education, and external factors such as economics and the environments.

HEALTHY CITIES AND HAPPY CITIES

The environments (natural, built, and social) are often cited as an important factor influencing the health status of individuals. Thus the term "healthy" is also widely applied in the context of non-living organisms such as healthy cities, healthy communities, or healthy environments.

Contemporary public health concern can be traced back to Edwin Chadwick, secretary to the Health in Towns Commission in the UK, who, in 1843, reported about workers' poor living conditions in British cities and towns in the early nineteenth century. Subsequently, the British government established the Health of Towns Association to address public health issues.[10]

The revival of public interest in environmental health can be attributed to the Healthy Toronto 2000 Convention in 1984. Thereafter, WHO (1994, 2003) endorsed the "Healthy Cities," and later "Healthy Communities" movement, whose principles are set in the Ottawa Charter in 1986 to promote a holistic approach to *Health For All*, using its broad definition to include the social and environmental determinants of health, and the interrelationship of health with issues such as housing, education, peace, equity, social justice, stable ecosystem, and sustainable resources.[11]

---

[6]   *Hedonia* or *hedonism* is a school of thought that argues that pleasure is the only intrinsic good (*Stanford Encyclopedia of Philosophy*, 2004).

[7]   Argyle, 2001; Bartlett, 2014; Bergsma and Ardelt, 2012; Bergsma, Poot, and Liefbroer, 2008; Biswas-Diener, Kashdan, and King, 2009; Huta and Ryan, 2010; Kasser and Sheldon, 2002; Kenny and Kenny, 2006; Peterson, Park, and Seligman, 2005; Ryff and Singer, 2008; Veenhoven, 2003; Waterman, Schwartz, and Conti, 2008.

[8]   Bergsma, Poot, and Liefbroer, 2008; Cravit, 2006–2009; Layard, Clark, and Senik, 2012; Pew Research Center, 2006; Sabatini, 2011; Veenhoven, 2008.

[9]   Argyle, 2001; Bergsma and Ardelt, 2012; Frey and Stutzer, 2000; Hayward, Pannozzo, and Colman, 2005; Sabatini, 2011.

[10]   Awofeso, 2003; Hancock, 1993, 1997.

[11]   Awofeso, 2003; Ashton, Grey, and Barnard, 1986; de Leeuw, 1999, 2009; Duhl, 2005; Hancock, 1993, 1997; Toronto Public Health, 2011; Kenzer, 1999; Kickbusch, 2003, 2007; Masuda, Poland, and Baxter, 2010; National Center for Environmental Health, 2008; Taylor, 2010; Wigle, 1998; Wolff, 2003.

The Healthy Cities and Healthy Communities is a global movement aimed at solving a number of critical urban health issues, such as toxic environments, poor housing, lack of public transportation, violence, crime, substance abuse, shortage of childcare, and racial discrimination as young people in contemporary cities are increasingly experiencing unhealthy conditions.[12]

The Toronto Healthy City Office (1991) stated that a healthy city should provide, among other things, "a clean, safe physical environment of high quality (including housing quality) … the encouragement of connectedness with the past, with the cultural and biological heritage of city dwellers and with other groups and individuals … a form that is compatible with and enhances the preceding characteristics" (p. 20). WHO (1998) likewise defined a healthy city as one that is "continually creating and improving those physical and social environments and expanding those community resources which enable people to mutually support each other in performing all the functions of life and in developing to their maximum potential" (p. 13). In the above definitions, the healthy development of social and cultural environments is considered as important as that of the natural and built environments.

The second General Healthy Cities Alliance Assembly and Conference was held in Suzhou (China) in 2006, with the theme of "Healthy Cities in the Globalizing World." Moreover, the principle of the Phase Five (2009–2013) of the Health Cities project is "health and health equity in all local policies," covering three core areas: caring and supporting environments, healthy living, and healthy urban environments and design.[13]

A healthy community is a critical part of a healthy city, and it has various definitions each applicable to its locality. The University of British Columbia defined a healthy community as a "community in which all organizations—from informal groups to governments—are working effectively together to improve the quality of all people's lives" (Boothroyd and Eberle, 1990, p. 7). However, there remain no universal indicators of measuring the effectiveness of Healthy Cities or Healthy Communities projects, not only because the results can only be observable locally,[14] but also because, to some extent, it varies by culture and level of technology.

The Happy City movement that is changing the structure and soul of cities around the world is documented by Charles Montgomery in his book *Happy City* (2013), where he states that "The City Has Always Been a Happiness Project" since ancient Greek and Roman times. Drawn from the insights of philosophers, psychologists, neuroscientists, and happiness economists, Montgomery summarizes a set of happy city principles as follows:

---

[12] Wolff, 2003; World Health Organization, 2003.

[13] WHO Regional Office for Europe, 2009, p. 2.

[14] Boonekamp et al., 1999; Ison, 2009; O'Neill and Simard, 2006; Ouellet, Durand, and Forget, 1994; Plümer, Kennedy, and Trojan, 2010; Poland, 1996a, 1996b.

1. The city should strive to maximize joy and minimize hardship.
2. The city should lead people towards health rather than sickness.
3. The city should offer people real freedom to live, move, and build our lives as we wish.
4. The city should build resilience against economic and environmental shocks.
5. The city should be fair in the way it allocates space, services, mobility, joys, hardships, and costs.
6. The city should, most of all, enable people to build and strengthen the bonds between friends, families, and strangers that give life meaning, bonds that represent the city's greatest achievement and opportunity.
7. The city that acknowledges and celebrates humanity's common fate, that opens doors to empathy and cooperation, will help people tackle the great challenges of the twenty-first century (Montgomery, 2013, p. 43).

His outline demands that a society should have democracy, human rights, environmental health, economic stability, and strong social ties as the basis for building a happy city. Well-designed cities are just one of the elements that contribute to happiness, though design may have big impacts on the above aspects, as Winston Churchill's famous quote goes: "We shape our buildings; thereafter they shape us."

HEALTHY HOUSING AND HAPPY HOMES

Healthy housing and a happy home is a vital component of a healthy city and a happy city, and the concept has revived internationally. Countries such as Canada, the USA, the UK, Australia, China, among others, have all incorporated health and happiness criteria into their new housing designs or old housing renovations.[15]

Since the modern era, Fleeming Jenkin's *Healthy Houses* (1879/2010) could be the first book that concerns sanitary principles of house drainage and ventilation in the nineteenth century. Canada Mortgage and Housing Corporation (1996–2012) recently gave it a relatively more comprehensive definition:

> *A healthy house is a house that is healthy for its occupants as well as for the global environment. Healthy homes provide healthy indoor environments, use resources such as water and energy efficiently, and are affordable. They respond to evolving household needs using a simple, sensible approach to building, renovation and day-to-day operations. And they are located in communities that are planned and managed to enhance quality of life, protect the environment and encourage economic prosperity. (p. 1)*

---

[15]   Baker-Laporte, Elliott, and Banta, 2008; Berman, 2001; Bower, 2000; Canada Mortgage and Housing Corporation, 1994/2009; Chiras, 2000; Healthy House, 2007; Healthy-House.co.uk, n.d.; Healthy House Institute, 2006–2012; Luò, 2006; Morley, Mickalide, and Mack, 2011; Ranson, 1991; Schneider-Skalska, 2011; Trulove, 2006.

Previous research findings reveal that there is a correlation between occupants' socio-economic status and health, because expenditures on housing may mean that the money cannot be spent on other things that influence health, such as recreation, education, nutrition, and health services uncovered by insurance.[16] Good quality housing has positive influences on health which can reduce healthcare costs and improve participation, productivity, and performance in workplace.[17]

Several studies have also shown that high household occupancy density, poor air quality, and inadequate ventilation are clearly associated with the incidence of respiratory and contagious diseases, notably asthma, tuberculosis, lead poisoning, injuries, and mental health.[18] Children are particularly vulnerable to hazardous physical conditions, such as lead, mould, damp and cold conditions, vermin, cockroach allergen, and overcrowding. Conversely, stable, safe, and secure housing is linked to healthy child development.[19]

James Hamilton's *Happy Home: Affectionately Inscribed to the Working People* (1860/2009) is a historic account on how to live a happy life by following God's Way according to the Christian Bible. Marion Harland's *Secret of a Happy Home* (1896/2011) is another classic on how to maintain harmonious family relations. And D. James Kennedy's *Secret to a Happy Home* (1997) sets the principles for a successful marriage and educating children. Other volumes on the topic offer practical guidance on interior decorations to make homes visual delight.[20]

As early as 1945, prominent Chinese architect Liang Sicheng (1998) had pointed out that residential design must take people's lives as the priority. To satisfy their living requirements, architects must pay attention to the impacts of the physical environment on occupants' healthy development of body, mind, and spirit, making the living space elevate their cultural expressions. Therefore, it is not enough for a house to be physically comfortable; it has to be spiritually pleasant because a happy spirit can promote a healthy body. Moreover, every house must be designed to help create harmonious neighborly relations. Planners and architects must establish an urban "form-order" to sustain the "social-order" because there is a mutual influence on one another (pp. 219–20).

Housing is multidimensional which includes the physical structure with design features (house), the social and psychological aspects (home), the areas surrounding the building and the planning characteristics and services (neighborhood) (Moloughney, 2004).

---

[16]   Conference Board of Canada, 2010; Dunn, 2002; Hwang et al., 1999; Toronto Public Health, 2011, 2012.

[17]   Conference Board of Canada, 2010.

[18]   Canadian Tuberculosis Committee, 2007; Krieger and Higgins, 2002; Sternberg, 2009.

[19]   Bashir, 2002; Cooper, 2001.

[20]   See Nayar, 2011; Paganelli, 2012; Winward, 2012.

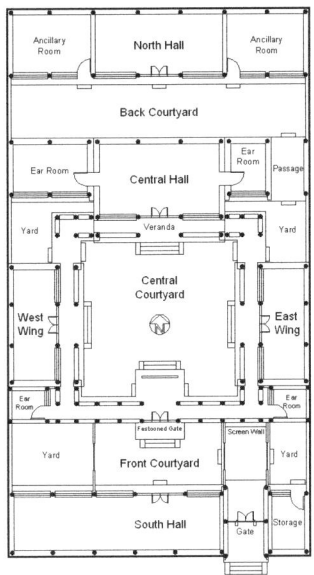

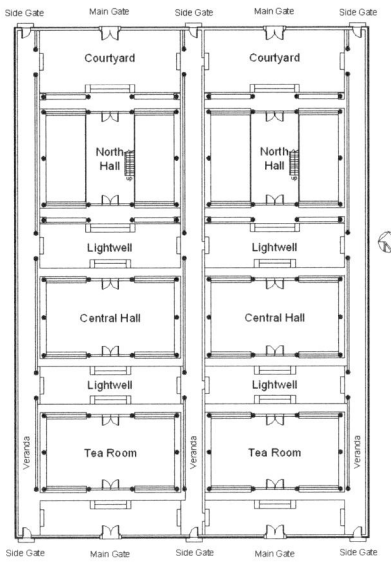

1.1   Plan of a standard or typical classical Beijing courtyard house (*siheyuan*)
Source: Drawing by Donia Zhang after Ma, 1999, p. 17.

1.2   A generic plan of Suzhou traditional courtyard house with lightwells
Source: Drawing by Donia Zhang, 2013–2014.

Professor Lóu Yulie at Peking/Beijing University has identified three levels of health preservation: physiological, psychological, and philosophical. The physiological dimension refers to the body, the psychological denotes the mood or emotion associated with social relations, and the philosophical implies the understanding of the law of the universe and the essence of life.[21] At present, human demand for health is often more psychological and philosophical than physiological, and the quest for meaning in residential design has extended to include social and cultural (Luò, 2006, p. 6).

COURTYARD HOUSING AND ARCHITECTURAL MULTICULTURALISM

My previous doctoral research findings indicate that courtyard housing in China not only facilitates residents' physical health and natural healing, it is also conducive to their social interaction and cultural activities (Zhang, 2013). This study aims to verify those findings and to test a set of housing design indicators developed in my earlier study in a different setting so that it may have wider validity.

This book is original; it focuses on courtyard housing in North America. It defines a courtyard as a pedestrian, communal, outdoor space enclosed on three or four sides by buildings or walls, in which residents/tenants can sit, talk, and socialize with one another.

However, in North America, the most common housing types are single-detached, semi-detached, row/town house, and apartment buildings; courtyard housing is rare but the number is rising.

---

21   *Journey of Civilization*, 2013.

1.3   Granada
Court inner
courtyard,
Pasadena,
California
Source: *Moule and
Polyzoides, Architects and
Urbanists.*

In California, courtyard housing was adapted from Spanish precedents[22] by American architects, notably the husband-and-wife team Nina and Arthur Zwebell, who designed and built it in the 1920s–1930s.[23] It then spread to the city of New Orleans, and some other places in the USA. Two books document these projects: *Courtyard*

---

[22]   The courtyard house arrived in Spain with the first wave of Arab Muslim conquest from North Africa in about 750 CE. Spain, having been occupied by the Arabs for over 500 years, incorporated many Arab cultural patterns (Hall, 1976, p. 159). The concept took root and its development began. Spanish conquest in America was followed by settlements patterned after Iberian models influenced by Arab Muslim culture. The basic house type of the new towns and cities in Latin/Hispanic America was the courtyard house (Land, 2006, pp. 235–6).

[23]   Hawthorne, 2005; Leigh, 2004.

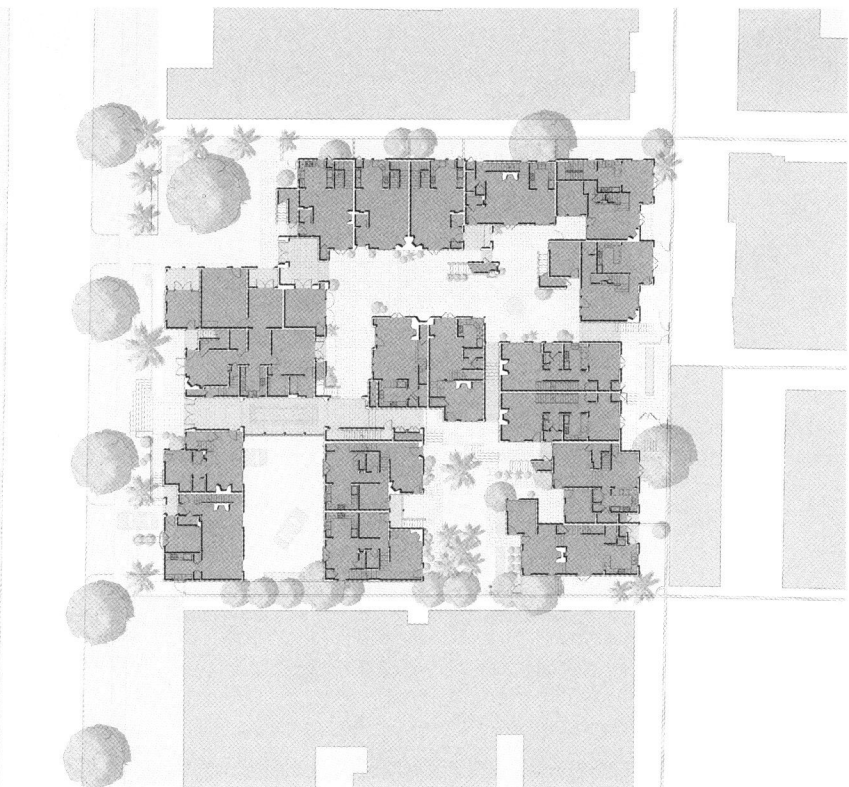

1.4   Site plan of the Harper Court: Seven Fountains, West Hollywood, California
Source: *Moule and Polyzoides, Architects and Urbanists.*

Housing in Los Angeles: A Typological Analysis by Polyzoides, Sherwood, and Tice (1982/1992), and *Courtyards: Aesthetic, Social, and Thermal Delight* by John S. Reynolds (2002). See also the book *High Life: Condo Living in the Suburban Century* by Matthew Lasner (2012) which touches upon the subject.

Beginning in the 1960s, new courtyard-style housing was constructed in American cities, such as the atrium houses in Madison Park (b. 1961) and Hyde Park (b. 1967) in Chicago (Blaser, 1995), Sunnyside Gardens in New York, and Rivermont House Carrfour Supportive Housing in Miami, Florida (Enterprise Foundation, 2002). The courtyard style revived in the form of bungalow courts as part of the New Urbanism movement in the 1990s, and courtyards are often at the top of an American homebuyer's wish list (Keister, 2005, p. 23). The examples include Fair Oaks Court and Vista del Arroyo Bungalows (restored 2007–2008), Gartz Court, Granada Court, the award-winning Harper Court (b. 2002), Laurel Court (b. 2004), Meridian Court (b. 2004), Mission Meridian Village (b. 2002), Silver Spur Court (b. 2008), among others. Most of these courtyard housing projects are in Mediterranean style, designed or restored by American architects Stefanos Polyzoides and his wife and partner Elizabeth Moule, who attempted to reconnect with Los Angeles history and improve the urbanism of the city.[24]

---

[24]   Broffman, 2008; Jarmusch, 2004; Kellogg, 2006; Leigh, 2004; McDonald, 2005; Newman, 2002.

1.5   Harper
Court: Seven
Fountains, north
courtyard viewed
from the east,
West Hollywood,
California
Source: *Moule and
Polyzoides, Architects and
Urbanists.*

The State of Oregon also has a heritage of courtyard housing, often built in English cottage style in Portland's streetcar-served neighborhoods during 1900– 1950. To honor this tradition, the City of Portland (2008) organized a courtyard housing design competition in 2007 with 257 entries, and published a subsequent report entitled *Courtyard Housing: A Catalogue of Designs and Design Principles*, showcasing their four winning schemes. This event signaled a strong support of the continuity of courtyard housing in America today.

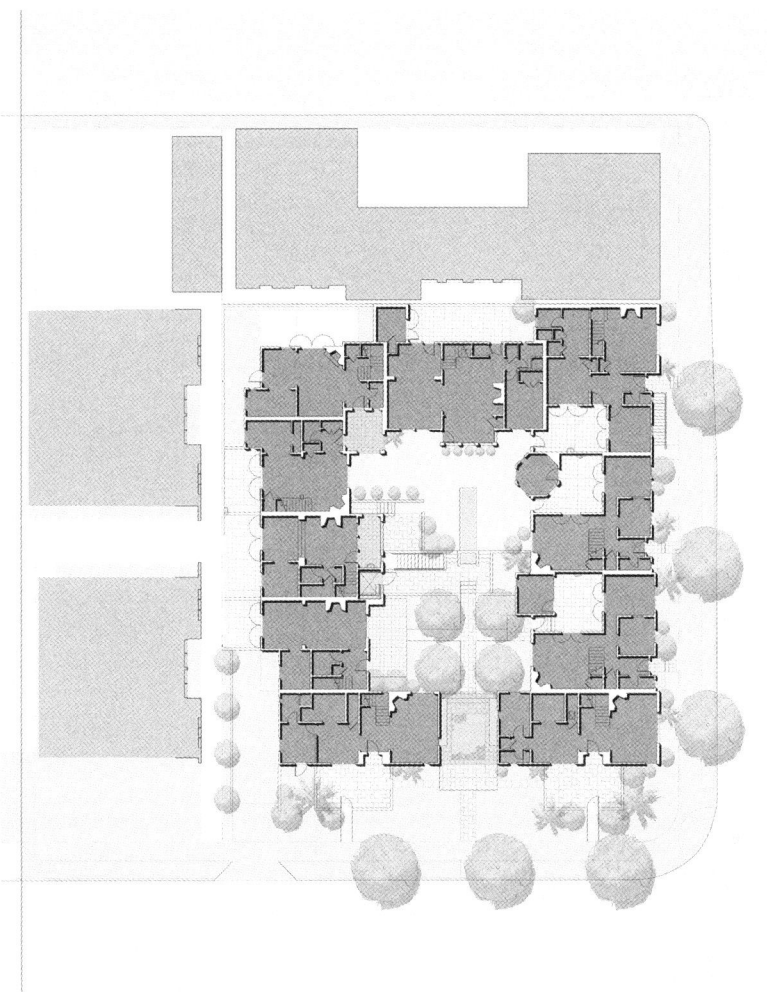

1.6   Site plan of the Meridian Court, Pasadena, California
Source: *Moule and Polyzoides, Architects and Urbanists.*

Influenced by the "Garden City" movement[25] initiated by Sir Ebenezer Howard in 1898 in the UK, courtyard housing started in Toronto, Ontario, Canada as early as 1910. The examples are the Three Streets Housing Co-operative (b. 1910), Bain Apartments Co-operative (former Riverdale Courts, b. 1913–1920s), and Spruce Court Housing Co-operative (b. 1913–1926). The latter two projects were designed in English Tudor style by Toronto architect Eden Smith (1858–1949). This unique set of buildings was the first social housing in Canada constructed by the Toronto Housing Authority. The Bain Apartments Co-operative was incorporated in 1977 as one of the first housing co-operatives in Ontario (Austin, 2013).

---

[25]   The Garden City movement was a response to the congested and unhealthy conditions of working-class housing constructed during the industrial revolution. A key concept of the movement was the inclusion of green space into urban districts through appropriate site planning.

1.7   Meridian
Court main
courtyard,
Pasadena,
California
Source: *Moule and
Polyzoides, Architects and
Urbanists.*

1.8   Gartz
Court entrance,
Pasadena,
California
Source: *Moule and
Polyzoides, Architects and
Urbanists.*

In Winnipeg, Southwood Village (b. 1967) was also designed in the courtyard style by architect Les Stechesen.

Since the 1980s, courtyard-style housing revived in Canada, typically in the name of "co-operative housing" built by the Co-operative Housing Federation of Canada. At the time of the survey (2013), 16 of 53 (30 percent) co-operative housing in Toronto have identified with one or more courtyards.

1.9   Bain Apartments Co-operative South Lindens courtyard, Toronto, Ontario, Canada
Source: Photo by Donia Zhang, 2013.

The Toronto co-operative housing with communal courtyards include Arcadia Housing Co-operative, Church-Isabella Residence Co-operative (b. 1917), Courtyard Housing Co-operative (b. 1993), Hugh Garner Housing Co-operative (b. 1982), Jenny Green Co-operative Homes, New Hibret Co-operative Homes (b. 1996), Oak Street Housing Co-operative (b. 1987), Peggy and Andrew Brewin Housing Co-operative (b. 1995), Windward Co-operative Homes (b. 1986), among others. Bristol Court (b. 2003) and Kingsmere (b. 1998) are non-co-operative housing with courtyards. The award-winning Toronto Courtyard House (b. 2006) designed by ethnic Chinese architects Christine Ho Ping Kong and Peter Tan is their home and studio. This list suggests that courtyard housing already exists and has proven to be acceptable in North America.

Inspired by Danish models in 1964, the Canadian Cohousing Network (CCN, formed in 1992) is part of a global cohousing initiative and courtyard spaces are fundamental to the cohousing design concept. At the time of the study (2013–2014), CCN endorsed 28 cohousing projects across Canada, although some are still in the planning and development stages. For example, Cranberry Commons Cohousing in Vancouver suburb Burnaby, WindSong Cohousing Community in Langley (British Columbia), and Wolf Willow Cohousing in downtown Saskatoon, all incorporated communal courtyards. In 2013, the Cohousing Association of the United States listed 213 cohousing communities on their website, and in 2014, the number increased to 234.

1.10   Spruce Court Housing Co-operative, Toronto, Ontario, Canada
Source: Photo by Donia Zhang, 2013.

1.11   Bristol Court housing courtyard with garages, Richmond Hill, Ontario, Canada
Source: Photo by Donia Zhang, 2013.

1.12   Jenny Green Co-operative Homes courtyard, Toronto, Ontario, Canada
Source: Photo by Donia Zhang, 2013.

1.13   Kingsmere housing courtyard, Thornhill, Ontario, Canada
Source: Photo by Donia Zhang, 2013.

1.14   Windward Co-operative Homes courtyard, Toronto, Ontario, Canada
Source: Photo by Donia Zhang, 2013.

These discoveries show that the trend of North American housing development is to incorporate common areas indoors and outdoors to achieve better social integration and cultural vitality.

Chinese Housing in North America

This study primarily concerns ethnic Chinese perceptions of health and happiness in housing in North America, with findings that may have implications for other ethnic groups in different parts of the world.

In search of wealth, the California Gold Rush drew the first significant number of laborers from China to the United States in 1820. In the 1860s, a greater number of ethnic Chinese were recruited to help build the Central Pacific Railroad, known as the Transcontinental Railroad. After the railway construction was completed, many of them joined the Californian agriculture or fishery industries.

Nowadays, Chinese-Americans form the largest Chinese community in North America, including those with partial Chinese ancestry, constituting 1.2 percent of the US population, or approximately 3.8 million people (US Census Bureau, 2010a). In 2010, half of Chinese-Americans lived either in the states of California or New York. The three metropolitan areas with the highest Chinese-American population are the Greater New York Area, the San Jose–San Francisco–Oakland Area, and the Greater Los Angeles Area (US Census Bureau, 2010b, 2010c).

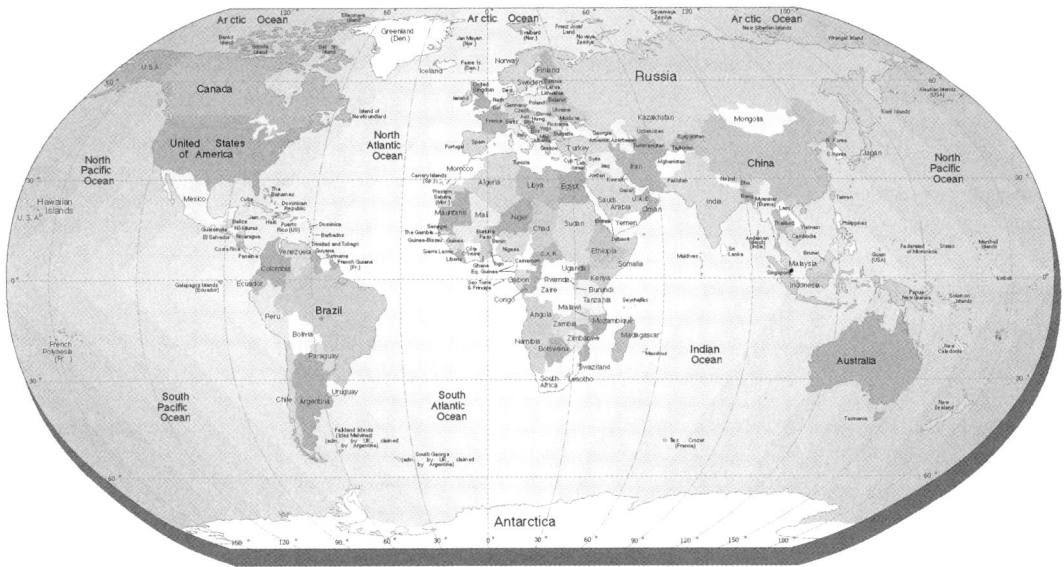

Income and social status of Chinese-Americans vary widely in locations. Many Chinese-Americans in Chinatowns of large cities are often members of a poor working class; others are well-educated upper-class people living in affluent suburbs. Although some of the upper- and lower-class Chinese live geographically close, they are often divided by a large socio-economic and income gap (Tickner, 2008; US Census Bureau, 2010c).

The first group of Chinese workers came to the west coast of Canada in 1788 to help build a ship. Then they ventured into the Gold Rush (1858–1880) and were recruited to construct the railway (1881–1885). The ethnic Chinese made invaluable contributions to the construction of the New World, yet they endured persistent institutional racial discrimination from the head tax (1885–1923) to the exclusion era (1923–1947).

Today, Chinese-Canadians are the second largest Chinese community in North America after the United States, including mixed Chinese and other ethnic origins, constituting 4.3 percent of the Canadian population, or 1.3 million people (Statistics Canada, 2006). Most Chinese-Canadians reside in the provinces of Ontario and British Columbia. Canada 2001 Census shows that 72 percent of Chinese-Canadians lived either in metropolitan Vancouver[26] or the Greater Toronto Area.

Chinese coming to North America brought with them many of their cultural values, such as Daoism and Buddhism, Confucian respect for elders and filial piety, strong family ties, honesty as entrepreneurs, and high value on education.[27]

Often referred to as a "Model Minority," Chinese-Americans are highly educated and earn higher incomes compared with other demographic groups in the United

1.15   Map of the world showing the locations of the USA and Canada in relation to China, to indicate the similarities in their climatic conditions and geographies that affect housing design
Source: Magellan Geographix, 1994.

---

[26]   Vancouver has the highest proportion of Chinese-origin people of any North American city.

[27]   Committee of 100, 2006; Liu, 2005.

States (US Census Bureau, 2000a). With their above average educational attainment rates, Chinese-Americans have a higher homeownership rate of 65 percent than the national average of 54 percent.[28]

Likewise, Chinese-Canadians are among the best-educated groups in Canada, holding records of high educational attainment, making up a high percentage of Canada's educated class, and maintaining one of the highest household incomes among most visible minority demographic groups in the nation. Since 2001, the Chinese-Canadian homeownership rate remained stagnant at 78 percent, compared to a national average of 68 percent.[29]

With China's fast economic development since the 1990s, ethnic Chinese have become the second largest foreign buyers of homes in the USA, behind Canadians; accounting for $7.4 billion of sales in the 12 months ending March 2011 and increased 24 percent from the previous 12 months. In California, China was the top first country of foreign home-buyers, followed by India and Canada. Moreover, 53 percent of Chinese home-purchases in the United States were made in California; Illinois came in a distant second with 5 percent, followed by Massachusetts, North Carolina, and Texas, all at 4 percent; New York had 3 percent.[30] Regrettably, there are no comparable data for Canada.

Since 2012, there have been reports about a proposed large project of "China City of America" (CCOA) across New York's Mamakating-Thompson town line, with various culturally-themed parks, a school, a medical center, and 1,000 housing units in both Chinese courtyard and Western villa styles, among other things. According to Sherry Li, CCOA's Chief Executive Officer, it is becoming reality in the Sullivan County, NY over multiple years. Similar concepts have been proposed in Michigan and Idaho. This project has aroused heated debates as to whether such large-scale Chinese "cities" should be built in America.[31] The answer does not lie in the realm of architectural design; the deeper problems are cultural and political.

Architectural Multiculturalism

Because the USA and Canada are countries with diverse cultural groups, with examples of courtyard housing emerged out of varied cultural traditions— British, Spanish, Mediterranean, etc., and also because such housing encourages interaction among neighbors who may be from different cultural backgrounds, these courtyard housing projects point to the critical question of multicultural planning and design.

---

[28]   Borjas, 2002; Cruz-Viesca and Chiu, 2008; Dooley, 2003; Painter, Yang, and Yu, 2002; US Census Bureau, 2000a, 2000b.

[29]   Government of Canada, 2009; Ipsos Reid, 2007; Medianu, 2007; Somerville, Li, and Teller, 2007.

[30]   California Association of Realtors, 2011; National Association of Realtors, 2012, 2013.

[31]   China City of America, 2014; Hust, 2013; Mattern, 2013; Vickery, 2012; Zheng, 2012.

Traditional planning primarily focused on the relations among physical forms of objects rather than people, let alone diverse people (Milroy and Wallace, 2002). There is an increasing pressure on the planning profession to address public concerns of culturally diverse groups in immigrant-receiving countries where designing and building multicultural housing has become essential to facilitate cultural vitality.[32]

Cultural vitality refers to human wellbeing, creativity, diversity, and innovation. Heritage and distinctiveness play a major role in facilitating cultural vitality because meaning and symbolism and its landscape contribute to the health and happiness of the people.[33] Canada was the first country in the world to establish a national policy of multiculturalism in 1971, and protects it in the Canadian *Multiculturalism Act of 1988*.

In his essay "Architectural Ethics, Multiculturalism, and Globalization," Michael E. Zimmerman (2003, p. 5) contended that to create a world of harmony that works for everyone, *genuine* multiculturalism entails that one is able to recognize the limits of one's own culture and draw insights from other cultures.

The construction of a city as a "landscape of difference" (Sandercock, 2000) is shared by some in the planning profession. In his article "What is This Thing Called Multicultural Planning?," Mohammad A. Qadeer (2009) offered 20 entries in a Multicultural Planning Policy and Practice Index, three of which are relevant and cited as follows:

1. Policies/projects for ethnic heritage preservation (clause 14);
2. Guidelines for housing to suit diverse groups (clause 15);
3. Promoting ethnic community initiatives for housing and neighborhood development (clause 16) (Qadeer, 2009, p. 13).

In his paper "Architecture, Multiculturalism and Cultural Sustainability in Australian Cities," David Beynon (2009) observed that the way the built environment represents and accommodates people of different cultures is an important aspect of developing a sustainable society. He remarks that because architecture constructs space and helps to shape social relations and cultural identities, a most significant part of diasporic health is their capacity of participating in building communities that represent themselves. Since the 1950s, the buildings constructed by a wide variety of immigrant groups have contributed greatly to the changing nature of Australian cities and the development of Australian urban culture. Beynon (2009) asserts that increased understanding and knowledge of the impact of immigration and multiculturalism on the built environment will facilitate planners and architects to create inclusive and dynamic cities and communities that deserve celebration.

Ronald G. Knapp's (2010) *Chinese Houses of Southeast Asia* is a masterpiece on Architectural Multiculturalism. The book beautifully documents 37 private

---

[32]   Achugbue, 2005; Agrawal, 2012; Agyeman, 2011; Fincher, 2003; Goonewardena, Rankin, and Weinstock, 2004; Lee, 2002; Milroy and Wallace, 2002, 2004a, 2004b; Sandercock, 2000.

[33]   Hargreaves and Webster, 2000; Hawkes, 2001; O'Brien, 2008.

residences of overseas Chinese in Southeast Asia and vividly demonstrates that cultural diffusion, interaction, and assimilation have resulted in these hybrid houses combining Chinese, European, as well as indigenous architectural styles and features.

Aims and Objectives

The aims of the research are to investigate what factors contribute to ethnic Chinese perceptions of health and happiness in housing in North America, and why. Furthermore, it explores what makes residents (regardless of their ethnic origins) happy or unhappy in the communal courtyards. As such, the objectives are as follows:

1. To synthesize the literature on health and happiness in the built environment;
2. To identify key themes in Chinese philosophy that promote health and happiness at home;
3. To investigate what design elements, if any, promote health and happiness in housing in North America;
4. To suggest courtyard housing design principles based on the findings.

Significance of the Study

The design of ethnic Chinese housing in North America to promote health and happiness is an untapped area of research, although there is a vast literature on the history and sociology of ethnic Chinese in North America.[34] There is also a wealth of research on the meanings of home for immigrants in Western countries.[35]

A Canadian study is found on housing policy and immigration in Montreal focusing on the Chinese community, with the data largely drawn from the 1986 Census (Aterman, 1993). Another piece is a post-occupancy evaluation of the social integration of Chinese elderly in Metro Toronto Housing Company (Canada Mortgage and Housing Corporation, 1996). There is also a specially compiled survey on the Chinese community in Canada from the 2001 Census (Lindsay, 2001). However, these studies did not address the architectural design of Chinese immigrant housing and its role in Chinese diaspora living experiences.[36] This research attempts to bridge the knowledge gap.

---

[34]   For example, Abada, Hou, and Ram, 2008; Chang, 2003; S. Chen, 2002; W. Chen, 2006; DeVoretz, 2009; Huang, 2006; Lai, 2010; J. Li, 2001; P.S. Li, 1999; W. Li, 1998, 2005; Lindsay, 2001; Louie, 2004; Mar, 2010; Meng, 1981; Miscevic and Kwong, 2000, 2007; Pon, 2005; Preston and Lo, 2000; Roy, 2007; See, 1996; Tian, 1999; Tung, 2000; Worrall, 2006; Wu, 2001.

[35]   Ahmed et al., 2003; Blunt and Dowling, 2006; Fortier, 2001; Logan, 2010; Rapport and Dawson, 1998.

[36]   Hsu, 2002; Jacobs, 2004; King, 1997; Levin, 2012; Ley, 1995; Mitchell, 2004; Thomas, 1997.

Four key themes in Chinese philosophy to promote health and happiness are identified: Health as Balancing *Yin Yang*, Health as Gathering *Qi*, Happiness as Attaining Oneness, and Happiness as Knowing the Dao, which are used as benchmarks for measuring ethnic Chinese housing in North America regards to their form and environmental quality, space and construction quality, matters of social cohesion, and time and cultural activities. Chinese philosophical principles are consistent with courtyard housing design, and therefore are the guiding theory in my previous (Zhang, 2013) and the current study.

This new online survey (Appendix) was built on the structure of my onsite survey carried out in China in 2007, with additional variables to investigate the health and happiness in housing occupied by ethnic Chinese in North America. The online survey was conducted in 2013 that involved 360 participants who were 16 years or older, residing in the USA (65 percent, excluding Alaska and Hawaii) and Canada (35 percent).[37]

Limitations and Delimitations of the Study

In-depth interviews (Appendix) were conducted with 60 informants: three planning professionals, 37 ethnic Chinese residents, and 20 non-Chinese residents living in courtyard-style housing in North America. This sample structure indicates that the findings may have broader implications beyond Chinese ethnicity.

The majority of the survey participants are first-generation Chinese (81 percent; n = 160), having lived in North America for an average of 16 years (n = 156). Second generation is much less (13 percent; n = 160), only a few are third-generation Chinese (1 percent). The average age of the survey participants is 39 years old (n = 154), with more females (55 percent; n = 163) than males (45 percent).

The four key themes identified in Chinese philosophy cover both Daoism and Confucianism because they both revere the Dao—the Way of Nature (including human nature). Like Daoism, Confucianism emphasizes the "unity of humans and the universe" in the Confucian *Doctrine of the Mean*, as well as family unity.

The study does not, however, attempt to prove the validity of the Chinese cultural themes because they are time-tested and have been proved legitimate in Chinese medical theory and practice for at least 5,000 years. The scientific evidence or effects

---

[37]   The ethnic Chinese participated in the online survey were from Toronto (28 percent), New York (12 percent), Los Angeles (8 percent), San Francisco (7 percent), and Vancouver, BC (4 percent). Moreover, 41 percent were from other parts of the USA and Canada, including Chicago (18), Dallas (9), Houston (9), Miami (9), Denver (8), Atlanta (5), Orlando (5), Washington DC (5), Columbus (4), Memphis (4), Seattle (4), College Station (3), Boston (3), Halifax (3), Louisville (3), Montreal (3), Philadelphia (3), Tallahassee (3), Dayton (2), Fairfax (2), Fort Lauderdale (2), Kansas City (2), Saskatoon (2), Arlington (Texas) (1), Bloomington (1), Calgary (1), Champaign (1), Charlotte (1), Eugene (1), Evergreen (1), Iowa City (1), Jackson (1), Kingston (1), Lafayette (1), Las Cruces (1), Lexington (1), Lodi (1), Morgantown (1), New Orleans (1), North Carolina (1), Oakville (Ontario) (1) Oklahoma City (1), Omaha (1), Ottawa (1), Palm Beach (1), Portland (1), Pullman (1), Sacramento (1), San Diego (1), St. Louis (1), Tucson (Phoenix) (1), Twin Cities (1), Virginia Beach (1), Wilmington (1), Winnipeg (1), Worcester (Massachusetts) (1).

of electromagnetic fields on human health, which is largely what *Feng Shui* theory contests, have been discussed elsewhere,[38] which is not the focus of the study. Moreover, there is an emerging interdisciplinary field combining neuroscience with architecture, called "neuroarchitecture," which closely correlates with *Feng Shui*, and which investigates how such factors as space, layout, orientation, light, color, etc. affect the physical and psychological health and happiness of occupants, concerning their stress, emotion, memory, behavior, and so on.[39] This facet has been touched on briefly in Chapter 4 of the book, and it can be explored further in another volume.

STRUCTURE OF THE FOLLOWING CHAPTERS

Chapter 2 identifies four key themes in Chinese philosophy and explains how they promote health and happiness at home. Chapter 3 evaluates the environmental and architectural design aspects of the North American housing in relation to the residents' physical health. Chapter 4 examines the spatial and constructional aspects of the housing to see how it elevates physical and psychological health and happiness of the occupants. Chapter 5 investigates the economic and social aspects of the occupants and their happiness about their homes. Chapter 6 reveals their cultural beliefs and behavioral patterns in their homes. Chapter 7 synthesizes the findings and suggests principles of courtyard housing design. To conclude the study, Chapter 8 emphasizes the contributions to the tree of knowledge and to the tree of life, and proposes courtyard garden house design models that may have universal implications.

---

[38]   See Becker and Selden, 1998; Case Adams Naturopath, 2012; Maxim, 2010.
[39]   See Eberhard, 2007, 2009; Kayan, 2011; Sternberg and Wilson, 2006; Zeisel, 2006.

2

Four Key Themes in Chinese Philosophy to Promote Health and Happiness at Home

All things have their backs to the *Yin*,
and stand facing the *Yang*.

When all things are filled with *Qi*,
they achieve harmony.

Laozi, c. 571–471 BCE, *Dao De Jing*, verse 42

This chapter identifies four key themes in Chinese philosophy to promote health and happiness at home. They are Health as Balancing *Yin Yang*, Health as Gathering *Qi*, Happiness as Attaining Oneness, and Happiness as Knowing the Dao. This premise sets a framework for analysis of the empirical findings in Chapters 3–6.

HEALTH AS BALANCING *YIN YANG*

The Chinese characters for health include 健康 (*jiankang*), 康宁 (*kangning*), or simply 康 (*kang*), with its associated words such as 长寿 (*changshou*, "longevity") or 寿 (*shou*). Traditional Chinese philosophy holds that every living organism in the universe is derived from the endless cycle of the sun fire and earth water, thus fire and water constitute the basic substance of life. This idea establishes *Yin Yang* theory, and *Yin Yang* balance and harmony is a fundamental concept applied to both nature and human affairs.

Yin Yang (阴阳) literally means "shade and light" with the word *Yin* (阴) derived from the word for "moon" (月) and *Yang* (阳) for "sun" (日). *Zhou Yi* (*Yi Jing*, "The Book of Changes") suggests that polar opposites created Heaven and Earth, and *Yin* and *Yang*. When Heaven and Earth intersect and *Yin* and *Yang* unite, it gives life to all things. When *Yin* and *Yang* separate, all things perish. When *Yin* and *Yang* are in disorder, all things change. When *Yin* and *Yang* are in balance, all things are constant.[1] The mutual interdependence of *Yin* and *Yang* is called 和合 (*hehe*). The first 和 signifies "harmony" or "peace," and the second 合 denotes "union" or "enclosure." The combined words imply that harmonious union of *Yin* and *Yang* will result in good fortune, and that any conflict is viewed only as a means to eventual harmony.[2]

The Chinese view is that only when the *Yin Yang* complementary forces are in perfect balance can it create a healthy home where *qi*, which can be translated as "cosmic breath," "life force," or "matter-energy," can flow smoothly and harmoniously to nourish the occupants. This notion is expressed in the Confucian *Doctrine of the Mean* and manifested in Daoist interplay of open/courtyard (*yin*) and closed/building (*yang*), or solid/building (*shi*) and void/courtyard (*xu*)[3] spaces in classical Chinese courtyard houses.[4]

Chinese *Feng Shui* ("wind and water") theory advocates buildings to be "sitting north and facing south" (坐北朝南), or "carrying *Yin* at the back and encompassing *Yang* in the front" or "having hills behind and river in front."[5] This site requirement relates to sunlight quality. Since China and North America are situated in the northern hemisphere of the globe, where most parts are north of the Tropic of Cancer, sunlight comes from the south all year round. South orientation is thus thought to be an important factor in house design because sunlight can offer people many benefits:

1. In the northern hemisphere, sunlight can warm people in winter, and the temperature of south-facing rooms is higher than north-facing ones (in the southern hemisphere, north and south reverses);
2. Sunlight participates in the synthesis of vitamin D in human bodies that can prevent rickets in children and help elderly people strengthen their bones;
3. A moderate amount of ultraviolet rays in sunlight can kill bacteria, which is especially good for people with respiratory diseases; and
4. Sunlight can improve human immunity (Kou, 2005; Luò, 2006).

Feng Shui masters further suggest that a house site should ideally be "surrounded by mountains (*yang*) and encircled by water (*yin*)" (山环水抱). It is especially auspicious if the site contour corresponds to the four gods: Green[6] Dragon in the

---

[1]   阴阳合则生, 阴阳离则灭; 阴阳错则变, 阴阳平则恒。

[2]   Lau, 1991, p. 214; Yu, 1991, pp. 51–2.

[3]   *Xu* (虚) and *shi* (实) is Chinese aesthetic concept that can be interpreted in numerous ways. *Xu* may denote "void, virtual, potential, unreal, intangible, formless, or deficient" and *shi* may mean "solid, actual, real, tangible, formed, or full."

[4]   Knapp, 2005b, 2005c; Kou, 2005; Li, 2008; Luó, 2006; Luò, 2006; Lupone, 1999; Ma, 1999; Wang, 1997; Zi, 2006.

[5]   负阴抱阳, 背山面水。

[6]   In classic Chinese, there was no differentiation between green and blue, the word 青 (*qing*) could mean either green or blue, or even black in some cases.

east, Red Bird in the south, White Tiger in the west, and Black Tortoise in the north.[7] Moreover, the Green Dragon in the east should be higher than the White Tiger in the west to block the northeast winds.

This arrangement is propitious because Green Dragon represents masculine *Yang* strength, whereas White Tiger signifies feminine *Yin* power. As such, Chinese people historically preferred living in a three-sided or four-sided enclosure of classical courtyard houses where *Yin* and *Yang* forces are both present and in balance.[8] If the house form is complete and symmetrical, it psychologically fulfils human desire for perfection. With mountains at the back and two buildings (as supports) on the left and right, it would make inhabitants feel safe and stable.

Feng Shui theory regards a house exterior as the "tree trunk" and its interior as the "branches," and this relationship should not be reversed. *The Ten Books on Houses for the Living* (《阳宅十书》) states: "If the external form of the building is inauspicious, no matter how proper the internal spaces are arranged, it is still inauspicious. Thus the exterior form of a house should be of primary importance."[9]

Feng Shui differentiates wind as *Yin* wind and *Yang* wind. East and south winds are warm winds, which are *Yang* winds and harmless. West and north winds are cold winds, which are *Yin* winds that should be avoided; otherwise they could chill to the bone. The prevailing easterly trade winds in portions of southeast North America, and a dominant seasonal monsoon wind during May through July, are *Yang* winds. The westward-moving trade winds expanding northwestward from the Caribbean Sea into southeast North America during July are also *Yang* winds. The Chinook winds in the interior west of North America in winter are *Yin* winds to be sheltered from.[10]

A house site should be ideally in a reversed U-shape and has concealed terrain slightly higher in the north, enclosed by mountains on three sides (north, east, and west), and facing a broad open land with a river and vista in the south. In *Feng Shui* terms, this outward-looking space is called "outer bright hall" (外明堂 *wai mingtang*), and a relatively flat plain in the middle that can "hide wind and gather *qi*" is named "inner bright hall" (内明堂 *nei mingtang*), which is the *Feng Shui* spot (穴 *xue*).[11] This kind of site condition is termed "*Feng Shui* treasure land" (风水宝地).

---

[7]   左青龙, 右白虎, 前朱雀, 后玄武。It is unknown why there is this belief in the Han dynasty that the dragon has a special relationship with the eastern quadrant of the earth, and the tiger with the western quadrant (Liu, 2002).

[8]   Li, 2008, p. 196.

[9]   若大形不善, 总内形得法, 终不全吉, 故论宅外形第一。

[10]   *The Yellow Emperor's Canon of Internal Medicine* (《黄帝内经》) has specific regulations regarding what kind of wind is good for health.

[11]   *Xue* (穴) is also used to describe critical acupuncture points in Chinese medicine.

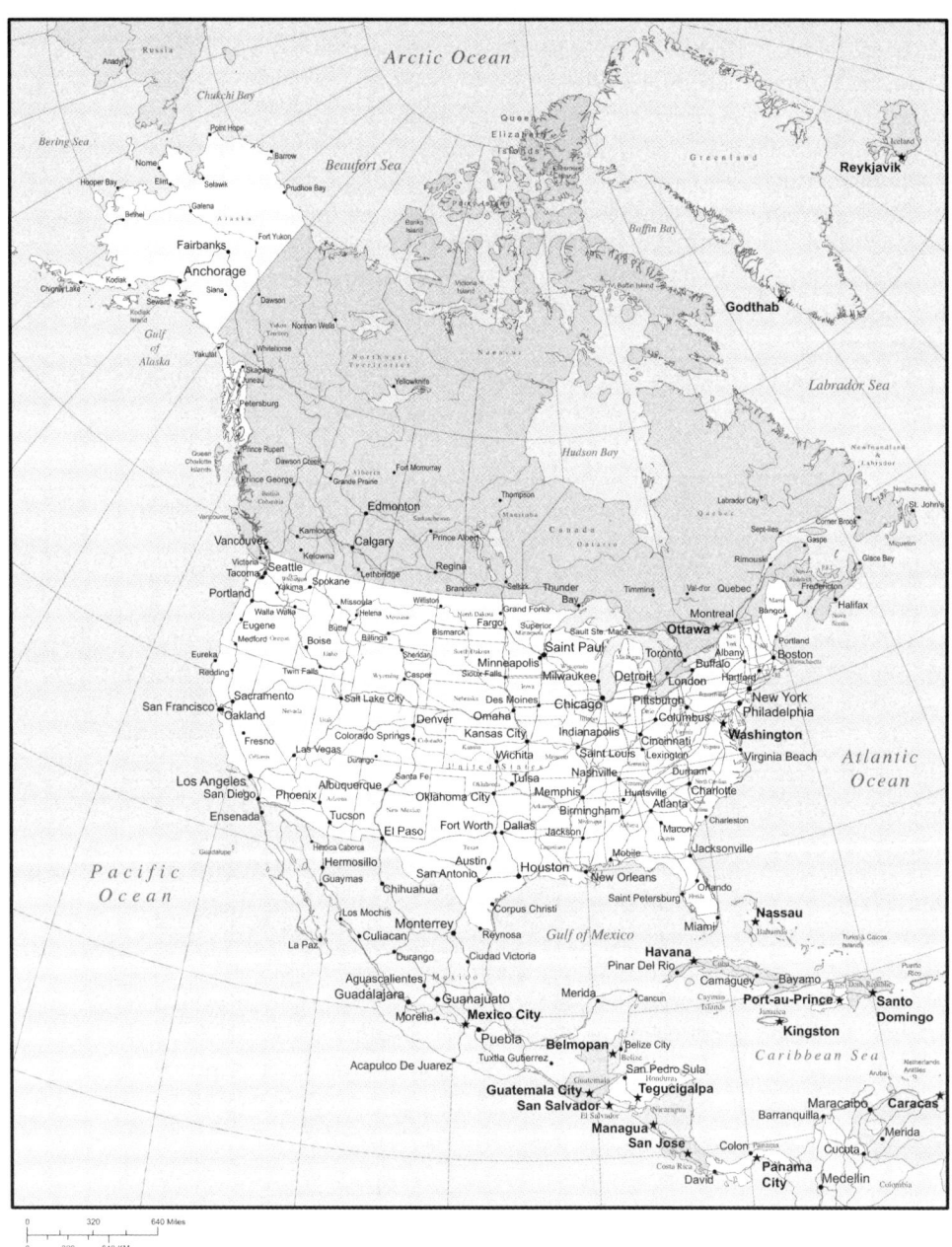

2.1   Map of North America showing the land and surrounding seas
where possible wind directions can be generated
Source: MapResources.com, 2014.

Feng Shui site specifications have scientific basis. Adjacent to water can bring convenience to life (e.g., irrigation, transportation, aquatics, etc.). A gently sloped site can help avoid flooding and make drainage easy. The luxuriant vegetation on the mountain may conserve water and soil, modify microclimate, and provide fuel and other resources. This natural environment of relatively enclosed space is reminiscent of the "Land of Peach Blossoms."[12] It will undoubtedly contribute to forming an ecologically good life to its occupants.

For urban sites where there are no mountains or river, the surrounding roads can be regarded as the waterways, and the roofs opposite to the house as the mountains. These extended meanings make *Feng Shui* theory more widely applicable.

HEALTH AS GATHERING *QI*

Qi (气), which can be translated as "cosmic breath," "life force," or "matter-energy," is the central kernel in Chinese philosophy. *Qi* has been differentiated as heaven *qi*, earth *qi*, yin *qi*, yang *qi*, wind *qi*, water *qi*, smoke *qi*, and human breathing *qi*, all of which relate to living organisms.

Nowadays, *qi* is perceived as the microwave radiation and celestial electromagnetic radiation from the sun that is constantly changing to become mountains and water, and is moving above the air and below the earth to nourish all things.[13] Land is very much like an aerial receiving microwave, and a large amount of this microwave forms a special gas field. *Feng Shui* theory thus advocates that a favorable site should be able to "hide wind and gather *qi*" (藏风聚气).

The Chinese have long recognized a closed circulatory system among groundwater, wind, cloud, and rain, as groundwater evaporates into wind, wind rises up to become cloud, cloud turns into rain, rain penetrates the ground to become groundwater again, and water collects cosmic *qi*. When selecting a site, *Feng Shui* masters pay particular attention to the relationship between water and *qi* and consider that, a site surrounded by mountains and encircled by water must have *qi* because water absorbs microwaves easily, and when *qi* meets water it creates an enclosure conducive to human health.[14] Thus, the goal is to enable *qi* to enter and flow smoothly and circulate around the house to nourish the occupants.[15] This is partly why water is a favorable feature near a house or in a city.

Feng Shui masters suggest: "Before looking at the mountains, first examine the water. If there are only mountains without water, the site is not pursuable."[16] Water is often likened to dragon's blood, called "water dragon." Just like "mountain

---

[12] "Land of Peach Blossoms" (世外桃源) is commonly translated into English as "The Peach Blossom Spring;" it is an idealized place envisioned by Tao Qian (also known as Tao Yuanming, 365–427) in the Jin dynasty.

[13] Kou, 2005; Luò, 2006; Ma, 1999.

[14] Luò, 2006; Ma, 1999.

[15] Lupone, 1999.

[16] 未看山, 先看水, 有山无水休寻地。 (Li, 2008, p. 202; my translation).

dragon," wherever there is meandering water surrounding a mountain, it becomes the major determining factor for the selection of a house site.

The Daoist founder Laozi (c. 571–471 BCE) observed: "Nothing in the world is as soft and yielding as water. Yet for dissolving the hard and inflexible, nothing can surpass it" (*Dao De Jing*, verse 78).[17] It shows that the ancient Chinese had already realized water's dual character and summarized site selection methods and flood prevention techniques.

Water in different regions contains different chemicals and minerals, some with radioactive element of nitrogen may cure diseases, whereas others containing hydrocyanic acid or hydrochloride may cause illnesses. It is therefore not recommended to build houses near poor water sources. The general principle of discerning water quality is to judge the quality of *qi* of the surrounding mountains, to recognize positive *qi* and search for water, as the saying goes: "The higher the mountains, the longer the watercourse, and the better quality the water is."[18]

That is to say that the watercourse should come from a long way so that its dragon *qi* is vigorous and the occupants' wealth will stay. If the dragon *qi* is short, the wealth of the residents may not accumulate. Moreover, if the incoming water source is short and its outgoing route is long, the water is deemed weak. Thus a Chinese proverb says: "Mountain forms the dwellers' characters while water shapes their properties,"[19] suggesting that living water may bring good fortune whereas dead water may cause bad luck.

Feng Shui masters select water also based on its form, as the Chinese phrase reveals: "Splashing water makes *qi* disperse whereas serene water helps *qi* gather."[20] This rule indicates that the incoming water should be winding and encircling, while the outgoing water should be lingering and tranquil. If the water is dashing, swift, or bouncing, it is held inauspicious.

Another way of discerning the water quality is by its color, taste, and smell. As Huang Miaoying in *Bo Shan Pian* (《博山篇》) advises:

> If the color of the water is blue, it tastes sweet and smells fragrant, this is excellent. If the color of the water is white, it tastes clear and feels warm, this is mediocre. If the color of the water is opaque and it tastes strong, this is lowest quality. If the water tastes sour and smells acerbic, the site is not worth pursuing.

Thus the Chinese proverbs say: "One place of water nurtures one place of people,"[21] and "green mountains and clear water generate scholars; while barren mountains and unruly water produce slyboots."[22] Although some of the words may sound exaggerated, they caution people that water quality *does* affect inhabitants.

---

[17]   天下莫柔弱于水，而攻坚强者莫之能胜。

[18]   水源于山，山高则水好，山有多高，水有多长。(Yang, 2008, p. 284; my translation).

[19]   山管人丁水管财。

[20]   水飞走则生气散，水融注则内气聚。(Li, 2008, p. 202; my translation).

[21]   一方水土养育一方人。

[22]   山清水秀出秀才，穷山恶水出刁民。

Besides water, earth *qi* (地气) is considered highly important in *Feng Shui* theory. Earth *qi* refers to the site's soil quality, size, level, temperature, and humidity. If the earth *qi* is too strong or too weak, the residents may feel uncomfortable. *Feng Shui* masters hold that soil quality affects occupants' health in at least four ways:

1. soil containing minerals such as zinc, molybdenum, selenium, fluorine, and so on, will radiate into the air through photosynthesis, which may affect human health;
2. damp or rotten soil may cause arthritis, rheumatic heart disease, skin disease, and so on, because this kind of earth condition nurtures bacteria— the source of all diseases, which is not suitable for a building site;
3. planet earth is a heavenly body surrounded by magnetic fields; humans do not feel their existence but are constantly affected by them; strong magnetic fields can either cure or harm a person, they may cause dizziness, sleepiness, or neurasthenia;
4. if there are caves or water more than three meters below the ground, or if there is a complex geological composition, it may emit a long seismic wave, polluted radiation, or particle flow, which may cause headaches, dizziness, endocrinopathy, and so on.[23]

Hence, when selecting a site, one should look for good quality soil such as red soil or a little mixed with black soil. The best quality soil is not too dry and is conducive to growing trees and vegetation. Ancient *Feng Shui* texts suggest that "There should be no trees to hide the front gate of the house, but at the back of the house, it is ideal to plant trees that are dense all year round in order that the occupants can live there long and tranquilly."[24] Only if the trees and grass surrounding the house is luxuriant, can the *qi* around the house be vigorous to penetrate through the earth channel and make the homeowner wealthy and honorable.

Qu qi (衢气) refers to the orientations of the roads around the house, which may also affect the occupants' health. Moderate *qu qi* not only could facilitate transportation, but also avoid interference beyond the roads. *Feng Shui* masters however do not recommend having too many roads surrounding the house, or having a road directly facing the gate; otherwise the *qu qi* would be too strong to cause illnesses. The house should also be far from places where there is a high concentration of people or traffic for fire prevention, theft precaution, environmental hygiene, children's safety, and so on, which all relate to human physical needs.

Qiao qi (峤气) refers to the space enclosed by high walls. If the enclosure is moderate and the courtyard size proportional to the height of the surrounding buildings, the residents would feel comfortable. If it is out of proportion, the inhabitants would feel either distant or constrained. Then the microclimate needs to be adjusted by creating returning wind and *qi* (回风反气) through high walls to improve the air circulation in the courtyard, drain the humidity, lower the temperature, and prevent the cold air.[25]

---

[23] Luò, 2006; Ma, 1999.

[24] 门前净无遮蔽, 宅后偏宜绿树。浓茂四时形不露, 安居久远露千钟。(Li, 2008, p. 180; my translation).

[25] Ma, 1999, p. 30.

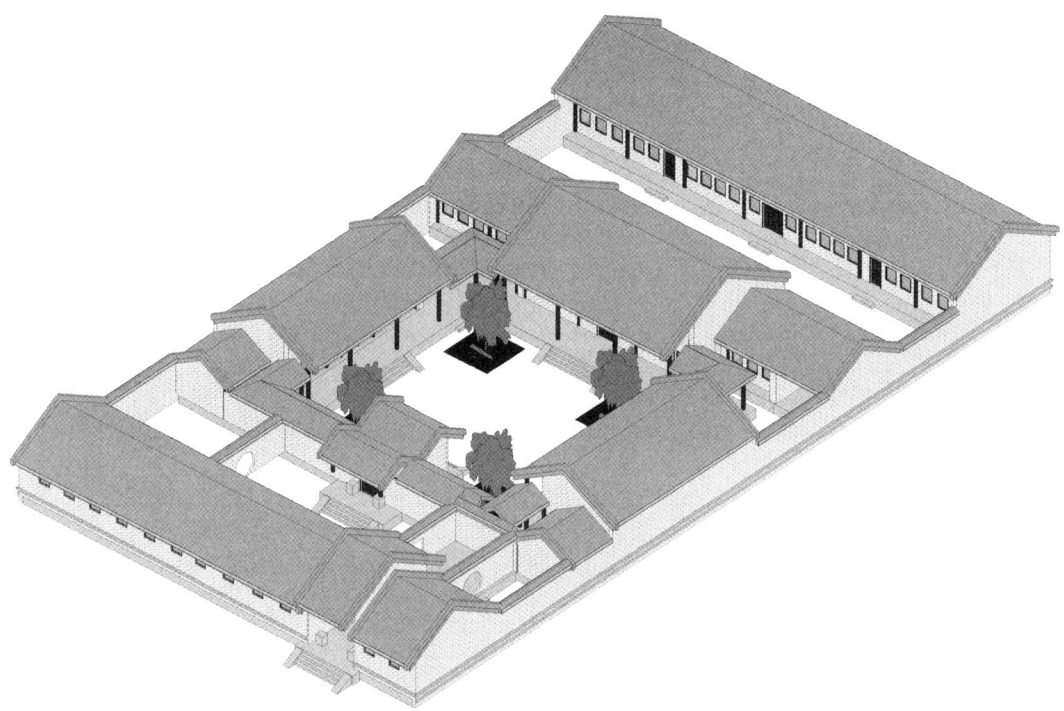

2.2   A conceptual model of a typical classical Beijing courtyard house for a single extended family
Source: Computer model by Donia Zhang, 2014.

When designing a courtyard house, the *Yellow Emperor's Canon of Internal Medicine* (《黄帝内经》) advises that five *xu* (虚 "deficiency") would make its occupants poor and five *shi* (实 "fullness") would make them rich. The five *xu* include: a big house with fewer people; a small house with a big gate; incomplete enclosing walls; the well and stove in wrong places; and a big plot with large courtyards but fewer rooms. The five *shi* include: a small house with many people; a large house with a small gate; complete enclosing walls; a small house with many livestock; and ditch water flowing to the southeast.[26] Thus in traditional Chinese philosophy, it is important to match the size of a house with the size of a household.

The outdoor space in front of the gate of a classical Chinese courtyard house, called *mingtang* (明堂), is where earth *qi* gathers. *Mingtang* is best to be clean, wide, bright, flat, and square-shaped. It should avoid being narrow or slanted, or piled with stones or rocks, or filled with thorns plants. *Mingtang*'s most important function is to "hide wind and gather *qi*" to establish auspiciousness and eschew inauspiciousness. Moreover, a spacious central hall with an exquisite garden view would make occupants happier than a crammed room with a barren view.

---

26   Kou, 2005, pp. 59, 89–90; Ma, 1999, p. 38.

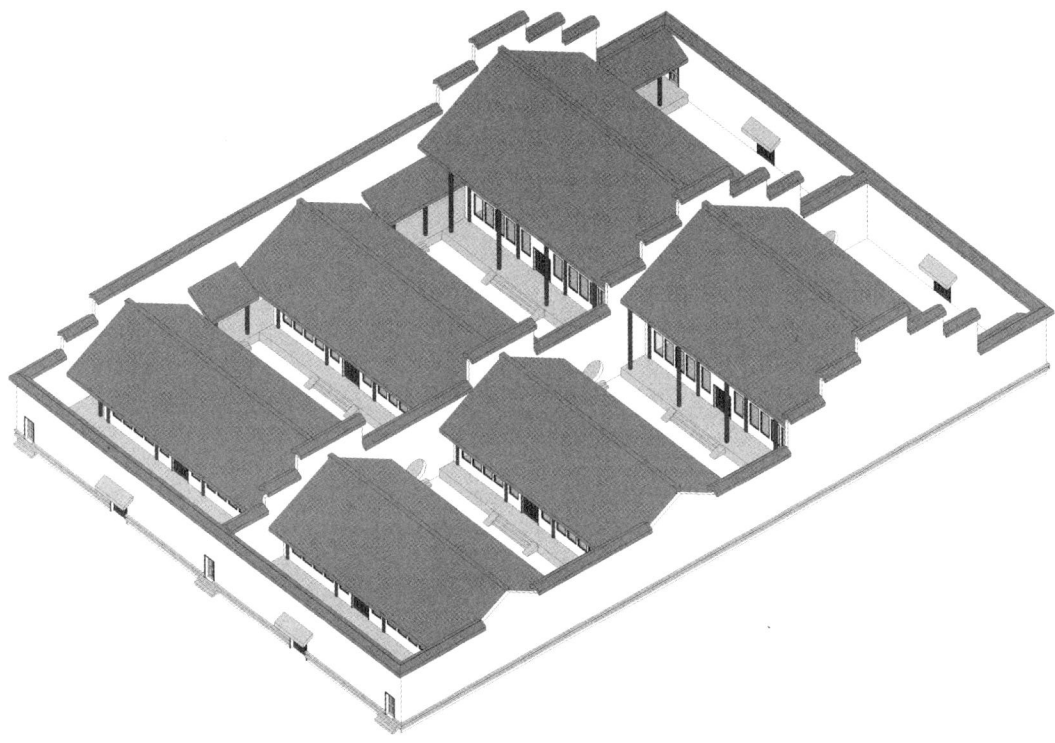

The gate location is most important in *Feng Shui* theory because it is the "mouth of the *qi*" (气口), through which *qi* enters or exits. Its orientation and size of opening has direct impact on the communication between the inside (sacred) and the outside (profane), and the modification of microclimate. If there is a road or waterway encircling the gate, it will gain *qi* and exchange information with the cosmos, which is thought to be conducive to the occupants' health. Classical courtyard houses of Beijing (meaning "Northern Capital") situated on the northern side of the east–west lanes normally have their gates in the southeast corners, preferably facing east to greet the morning sun. Whereas Beijing courtyard houses situated on the southern side of the lanes often have their gates in the northwest corners, because southeast and northwest are considered by *Feng Shui* masters to be auspicious orientations for a gate.

In a Beijing courtyard house, the kitchen is normally located in the east in accordance with the desire of the Kitchen (or Stove) God. Later, for those households that have a designated dining room, the kitchen is also placed in the east hall. Latrines and storages are often located in the inauspicious southwest or northeast corners.

Suzhou courtyard houses in southern China normally have their gates in the middle of the south or north enclosing walls. If the gate is in a wrong place or too big, it will weaken the earth *qi* and destroy the intimate ambiance of the household.

2.3   A generic model of a classical Suzhou courtyard house compound for a single extended family
Source: Computer model by Donia Zhang, 2014.

Feng Shui masters sometimes draw parallels between a house site and a human body, as the *Yellow Emperor's Canon on Houses* (《黄帝宅经》) states: "Take the mountain as your body, the spring river as your blood, the soil as your skin and flesh, the grass as your hair, the house as your clothes, and the door as your hat. If one can do so, it is extremely auspicious."[27] Thus, the concept of *qi* is also widely used in Chinese medicine when we examine how it transmits, flows, and functions in humans. *Qi* may as well be understood as people's feelings, which differ from time to time, from location to location, and from individual to individual.

Feng Shui practice avoids having broken, decayed, ruined, divided, or incomplete things in a house because these objects could give rise to unhealthy imaginations. For example, if there are two ponds in front of a house gate, its shape looks like the Chinese character 哭 ("cry"), evoking sadness.

Placing plants and flowers in and around a house will not only add aesthetics, but also reduce one's mental pressure and provide a little taste of nature in an otherwise boring environment to minimize the effects of noise and air pollution on humans. *Feng Shui* masters regard flora as the most attractive and relatively inexpensive method of therapeutic treatment, as it has been found that when placing flowers in interior space, it can activate *qi* and offer an invisible healing effect. Regardless of geographic region, living plantation can exert positive influence on the flow of *qi*, as well as helping *qi* to return to its balance.[28]

The natural *qi* created by flora may also prevent air stagnation in dim corners and harmonize *qi* passing through circulation corridors. In special circumstances, for example, near radioactive electronic equipment, flora can produce energy counterbalancing static electricity. While in polluted air, flora can generate fresh air to produce a purifying effect. Thus, when flora is placed properly indoors, it is an important source of *qi*.[29]

Daoist second founder Zhuangzi (c. 369–286 BCE) contended that humans and everything in the universe are created by *yin qi* and *yang qi*. In his chapter 6 "The Great and Venerable Teacher" (大宗师), Zhuangzi states that, "they have joined with the Creator as [humans/]men to wander in the single *qi* of heaven and earth."[30] In his chapter 22 "Knowledge Wandered North" (知北游), Zhuangzi declares that "[Hu]man's life is a coming-together of *qi*. If it comes together, there is life; if it scatters, there is death."[31] These sentences reveal that *qi* is the critical life-giving force in traditional Chinese philosophy.

---

27   以形势为身体, 以泉水为血脉, 以土地为皮肉, 以草木为毛发, 以舍室为衣服, 以门户为冠带, 若得如斯, 是事严雅, 乃为上吉。

28   Li, 2008, p. 288.

29   Li, 2008, p. 288.

30   彼方且与造物者为人, 而游乎天地之一气。

31   人之生, 气之聚也; 聚则为生, 散则为死。

HAPPINESS AS ATTAINING ONENESS

Chinese philosophy considers humans as part of nature and the universe, hence the expression "unity of heaven and humans" (天人合一). When selecting a building site, Daoist or *Feng Shui* masters would advise that one must carefully and thoroughly observe the surrounding natural environment, be in harmony with nature, and modify and utilize nature to create favorable conditions for human happiness.

The Chinese characters closest to the Western notion of happiness include 福 (*fu*, "good fortune"), 乐 (*le*, "pleasure"), and 喜 (*xi*, "joy"). The concepts of 福 and 乐 are frequently examined in Chinese schools of thought, while 喜 is a word more commonly used for traditional Chinese weddings when 喜 is pasted on walls, doors, or windows in its twofold form 喜喜 to denote "double happiness."

The Chinese concept of 福 or good fortune was manifested in its historically favored social collectivism rather than individualism. Chinese collectivism demanded an extended family to live in the same courtyard house compound, and the family members would often pool their income together to accumulate wealth and to establish private enterprise. From a socio-economic perspective, this practice was conducive to achieving family unity and to contribute to China's flourishing economy in its feudal society.

Confucius (551–479 BCE) stated that having friends is 乐 or a pleasure, as he asked in the beginning of his *Analects*: "Is it not delightful to have friends coming from distant quarters?" (book 1, chapter 1, section 2).[32] A Chinese proverb likewise says that "A thousand glasses of wine is not enough when bosom friends meet; using wine to eliminate worry will cause even more worries,"[33] suggesting that having a companion is better than being alone while drinking wine.

Confucius then recommended doing three things in life to bring happiness: learning etiquettes and music, speaking of the goodness of others, and having many worthy friends (*Analects*, book 16, chapter 5). Conversely, Confucius pointed out three things in life that are unhealthy and harmful: taking pleasure in extravagance, sauntering and inactivity, and finding joy in feasting (*Analects*, book 16, chapter 5).

To Confucius, happiness is being able to savor the simplest things in life, as he said: "With coarse rice to eat, with water to drink, and my bended arm for a pillow. I find joy in them" (*Analects*, book 7, chapter 15). In a similar vein, Confucius praised his disciple Yan Hui: "Admirable indeed was the virtue of Hui! With a single bamboo dish of rice, a single gourd dish of drink, and living in his mean narrow lane, while others could not have endured the distress, he did not allow his joy to be affected by it. Admirable indeed was the virtue of Hui!" (*Analects*, book 6, chapter 9).

Likewise, Mengzi (Mencius, 372–289 BCE) suggested that a gentleman should have three delights. The first is that his parents are both alive and that his brothers have no troubles. The second is that he has no shame to face the heaven above and

---

32   有朋自远方來、不亦乐乎?
33   酒逢知己千杯少, 借酒消愁愁更愁。

no deceit to people on the earth below. The third is that he has the most talented students to teach in the kingdom (*The Complete Works*, book 7, part 1, chapter 20).

Thus Confucian concept of happiness is to continuously improve one's virtue, to care for others, and to obtain social unity. While Daoist happiness lies in remaining one's natural instinct and returning to their primary state. But for Buddhists, happiness requires extinguishing three causes of human suffering: greed, hatred, and illusion. Mozi (c. 470–391 BCE) then developed a unique Chinese school of thought and argued that the world disorders are caused by a lack of "universal love," which he defined as such:

> It is to regard the state of others as one's own, the houses of others as one's own, [and] the persons of others as one's self. When feudal lords love one another there will be no more war; when heads of houses love one another there will be no more mutual usurpation; when individuals love one another there will be no more mutual injury. When ruler and ruled love each other they will be gracious and loyal; when father and son love each other they will be affectionate and filial; when older and younger brothers love each other they will be harmonious. When all the people in the world love one another, then the strong will not overpower the weak, the many will not oppress the few, the wealthy will not mock the poor, the honored will not disdain the humble, and the cunning will not deceive the simple. And it is all due to mutual love that calamities, strife, complaints, and hatred are prevented from arising. Therefore the benevolent exalt it. (Book 4: Universal Love II)

Although Mozi's universal love may sound idealistic, he had indeed touched on a fundamental issue and called for humanity's unification as "One" to establish world peace, harmony, and happiness. For Mozi, universal love is a reciprocal reaction because he observed that "Whoever loves others is loved by others; whoever benefits others is benefited by others; whoever hates others is hated by others; whoever injures others is injured by others" (book 4: *Universal Love II*). When universal love is viewed this way, it should not be too difficult to implement it.

HAPPINESS AS KNOWING THE DAO

Chinese philosophical view is that the eternal cycle of the four seasons helps sustain life. This way of nature is the 道 (Dao). Similar to Christian belief that the ultimate bliss is to know God,[34] the Chinese are convinced that happiness is to know the Dao.

The Chinese word 道 or Dao can be translated as "way," "path," "route," or sometimes more loosely referred to as "doctrine" or "principle," which was later also adopted in Confucianism. Within these contexts, Dao signifies the primordial essence or fundamental nature of the universe.

Laozi (c. 571–471 BCE) in his timeless guide on the art of living, *Dao De Jing* ("The Book of the Way"), explained that Dao is not a "name" for a "thing," but the

---

[34]   Hamilton, 1860/2009; Kraye, 2001; McCready, 2001; Smith, 2001.

underlying natural order of the universe whose ultimate essence is hard to define. Dao is thus "eternally nameless" (*Dao De Jing*, verse 1) and is distinguished from the countless "named" things which are considered to be its manifestations. In Daoism and Confucianism, the objective of spiritual practice is to "become one with the Dao" (*Dao De Jing*, verse 23), or to harmonize one's desire with nature in order to achieve "inaction contrary to nature" (无为, *wuwei*). Although it cannot be easily defined, Dao can be known or experienced, and its principles can be discerned by observing nature's cycle. In Daoism and Confucianism, Dao often explicitly refers to moral or ethical conducts and their natural outcomes.

Dao is intrinsically related to the concept of *Yin Yang*, where every action creates its counteraction as inevitable movements within the Dao, and proper practices involve accepting, conforming to, or working with these natural developments. Dao is an active and holistic view of nature rather than a static and atomistic one.

Confucius (551–479 BCE) focused his life on the pursuit of the Dao of 仁 (*ren*, "benevolence" or "virtue") rather than material goods,[35] as he confessed in his *Analects*: "If a [hu]man in the morning hears the Dao, [s/]he may die in the evening without regret" (book 4, chapter 8).

Mengzi (372–289 BCE) likewise suggested that a virtuous person should uphold the Dao of *ren*, as he maintained: "Honor virtue and delight in righteousness, and so you may always be perfectly satisfied. Therefore, a scholar, though poor, does not let go his righteousness; though prosperous, he does not leave his Dao. Poor and not letting righteousness go, thus the scholar holds possession of himself" (*The Complete Works*, book 7, part 1, chapter 9).

Because Chinese people look at things as having *Yin Yang* dialectic duality, they perceive good fortune (happiness) and misfortune (unhappiness) as two ends of a pendulum that are interchangeable and can be reversed, as expressed in such phrases: "Extreme happiness may turn into sadness" (乐极生悲), and "When bitter experience is over, sweet joy will come" (苦尽甘来). This wisdom may have derived from Laozi's (c. 571–471 BCE) *Dao De Jing* that "Misfortune is beside where fortune lies; fortune is beneath where misfortune lingers" (verse 58).[36] This dialectics is often told in a household tale in China about a farmer who lost his horse, but how do you know that this isn't good fortune?[37] The story goes that,

> *A poor farmer's horse ran off into the country of the barbarians. All his neighbors offered their condolences, but his father said, 'How do you know that this isn't good fortune?' After a few months the horse returned with a barbarian horse of excellent stock. All his neighbors offered congratulations, but his father said, 'How do you know that this isn't a disaster?' The two horses bred, and the family became rich in fine horses. The farmer's son spent much of his time riding them; one day he fell off and broke his hipbone. All his neighbors offered the farmer their condolences, but his father said, 'How do you know that this isn't good fortune?' Another year passed, and the barbarians invaded the frontier. All the*

---

[35]   Wang, 2001, p. 50.
[36]   祸兮福之所倚, 福兮祸之所伏。
[37]   塞翁失马, 焉知非福。

able-bodied young men were conscripted, and nine-tenths of them died in the war. (Translated by S. Mitchell, 1988, p. 109)

The narrative tells that fortune and misfortune can be transformed into one another, and that positive and negative events interact with each other. One should not take any insensitive action to reverse things to its unfavorable side of *huo* (祸 "misfortune").[38] However, just like *Yin* and *Yang*, the inevitable reversal of the two extremes is the Dao (物极必反).

Humans often have many desires, and the fulfillment of one desire tends to lead to temporary satisfaction but more desires to come. To solve this paradox, the Chinese cherish a common idiom: "One who is content with what one has is always happy" (知足者常乐), suggesting that in order to be happy, less desire is essential. This idea may as well be attributed to Laozi (c. 571–471 BCE), as in his *Dao De Jing* he stated that "One who is content is wealthy" (知足者富, verse 33), that "One who is content will not meet disgrace; one who knows when to stop will not encounter danger; thus one may live a long life" (verse 44),[39] that "One who is content with knowing contentment is always content indeed" (verse 46),[40] and that "No misfortune is greater than discontentment, and no misconduct is greater than extravagant desires" (verse 46).[41]

The Chinese concept of contentment coincides with that of French philosopher and mathematician René Descartes (1596–1650), who maintained that happiness is to have a perfectly content mind.[42] A contemporary happiness research likewise shows that Taiwanese people still hold contentment as an important mindset to happiness.[43]

Nevertheless, Sir Anthony Kenny (2001, p. 228) argued that contentment is a necessary but inadequate statement of happiness. This contentment may be due to ignorance, or from a false assessment of options, or from a deficiency of imagination. In Kenny's view, this contentment might be termed "the contentment of the unraised consciousnesses" or "the contentment of the unexamined life," which Socrates considered not worth living. The Chinese contentment is also contrary to Anglo-American culture that advocates humans to always aim for their maximum capacity or capability rather than being complacent over one's occasional success.

Zhuangzi (c. 369–286 BCE), however, observed that because different people have different inborn nature, they should follow their inherent capacity to fully enjoy themselves, and thus contentment is only relative. Zhuangzi distinguished perfect happiness (至乐) from happiness (乐) through his keen observations in life. As for most people, happiness means the possession of such mundane things as wealth, honor, longevity, tasty foods, fine clothes, admirable home, beautiful companions, pleasing music, and the like. To him, these substances are hollow vanity but not true

---

[38]   Wang, 2001.
[39]   知足不辱, 知止不殆, 可以长久。
[40]   知足之足, 常足矣。
[41]   祸莫大于不知足, 咎莫大于欲得。
[42]   Kraye, 2001, p. 151.
[43]   Lu, 2001.

happiness because they are external to the real value of life. Zhuangzi considered perfect happiness as beyond common values; it is a state of mind free from any confinement. This comes to the Daoist notion of *wuwei*—inaction contrary to nature, which is ultimate spiritual relief that transcends the distinction between happiness and unhappiness, and even between life and death.[44]

Similar to Christian humanist notion that real happiness could only be achieved in the afterlife,[45] Zhuangzi (c. 369–286 BCE) viewed death as the "perfect happiness." A well-known story goes that when Zhuangzi's wife died, Huizi went to express his condolences, but he found Zhuangzi sitting with his legs sprawled out, pounding on a tub and singing. Huizi was very surprised and asked: "You lived with her and she brought up your children. It should be enough simply not to weep at her death. But pounding on a tub and singing, isn't it going too far?" Zhuangzi replied:

> You're wrong. When she first died, do you think I didn't grieve like anyone else? But I looked back to her beginning and the time before she was born, before she had a body, before she had a spirit. In the midst of the muddle of wonder and mystery a change happened and she had a spirit, a body, and she was born. Now there is another change and she's dead. It's just like the changing of the four seasons. She's going to lie down peacefully in a vast room. If I were to follow after her bawling and sobbing, it would show that I don't understand anything about fate. So I stopped. (The Complete Works, chapter 18)

Hence in Zhuangzi's view, life and death is a natural cycle. If one sees this true nature and understands the Dao, one is not far from real happiness.[46]

SUMMARY AND CONCLUSION

Through a literature review, this chapter identified four key themes in Chinese philosophy to promote health and happiness at home: Health as Balancing *Yin Yang*, Health as Gathering *Qi*, Happiness as Attaining Oneness, and Happiness as Knowing the Dao.

Derived from the cyclic movements of the sun and the moon, *Yin Yang* dialectic duality is the essence in Chinese philosophy that has been applied in many fields, including Chinese architecture and planning, as well as Chinese medical theory and practice. Binary thinking is also very common in the West, and has been widely criticized for oversimplifying things. Nevertheless, binary thinking is the basis for developing contemporary computer technology, for example, 0 is off and 1 is on.

Qi is the core in Chinese philosophy that is broadly defined as "cosmic breath," "life force," or "matter-energy." It is associated with water cycle in the universe and is used in selecting a site and designing a house to "hide wind and gather *qi*" as well as in Chinese medical theory and practice. D.H. Lawrence observed that water is made of

---

[44]   Wang, 2001, p. 48.
[45]   Kraye, 2001, p. 140; Montgomery, 2013, p. 22.
[46]   Lu, 2001; Wang, 2001.

two parts of hydrogen and one part of oxygen; there is also a third thing that makes it water but nobody knows what that is. In my view, *qi* may be the "third thing."

Daoists and Confucians both advocate the "unity of heaven and humans," and Confucians further stress family unity. Mozi even put forward a "universal love." These social ideologies have contemporary relevance to help establish world peace, harmony, and happiness.

For humans to unify with the universe is to understand the Dao—the way of nature, and to *follow* nature's cycle, rather than acting *against* it. Only by so doing can humans obtain harmony, health, and happiness. Later in the book, I argue that courtyard housing will help humans connect with nature and facilitate residents' activities in line with nature's way.

In Chapter 3 that follows, empirical findings on the architectural form and environmental quality of ethnic Chinese housing in North America will be examined, to see if the housing facilitates the physical health of the occupants living in it.

3

Health as Balancing *Yin Yang*:
Form and Environmental Quality of the Housing

One *Yin* and One *Yang* are called Dao.

Yi Jing, appendix 1, chapter 5

This chapter presents and analyzes the empirical findings on the architectural form and environmental quality of ethnic Chinese housing in North America, to explore whether it facilitates the physical health of the occupants, and whether the concept of balancing *Yin Yang* in traditional Chinese philosophy is reflected in Chinese residents' preferences for their house form. As such, the chapter consists of seven sections: location, exterior form, exterior walls, gate orientation, window orientation, yards and gardens, and roofs.

LOCATION

The survey (appendix) results show that "neighborhood safety" (60 percent; n = 348) is ethnic Chinese residents' primary concern when selecting a house site in North America. "Short walking/driving distance to a good school/college/university" (48 percent) is their second consideration, suggesting that they still place as much emphasis on education as they did traditionally. This result is confirmed by the US Census Bureau's (2000a) finding that Asian-Americans outside the suburbs of large metropolitan areas were typically located near colleges and universities. "Short walking/driving distance to shops/grocery/food stores" (42 percent) and "clean air, land, and water" (42 percent) are their third most crucial considerations.

The above findings concur with UNESCO (2012) and WHO (2012), that clean air and water, and safe cities and communities, all contribute to good health, especially to the health of infants and children. Sternberg (2009) likewise observed that many urban renewal projects with attention to sunlight, fresh air, sanitation, and decreased population density have helped reduce the spread of airborne diseases and improved urban health. However, my finding is contrary to the assertion that Chinese real estate buyers are "not interested in the environment" (Howell, 2014).

The other location factors the respondents considered in the order of importance include: "short walking/driving distance to workplace" (31 percent), "short walking distance to public transit" (30 percent), "walkable neighborhood" (28 percent), "sunny area" (26 percent), "short walking/driving distance to a park/garden/green space" (24 percent), "Chinese community" (21 percent) or "community services" (15 percent), "short walking/driving distance to family/friends" (15 percent), "short walking/driving distance to a hospital" (12 percent), "aesthetics" (9 percent), and "short walking/driving distance to a farmers market" (7 percent). An additional factor they raised is "housing affordability" (4 percent; Table 3.1).

The interview (appendix) respondents particularly mentioned that a walking-friendly environment helps mitigate stress from work and provides easy access to casual sports. Moreover, sidewalk in a neighborhood and good connection with a local park and services can promote physical and mental health. Sternberg (2009) suggested that architecture and urban design should incorporate features that encourage walking so as to control the modern epidemic of obesity. By designing cities, towns, and neighborhoods that encourage walking, people can reduce their reliance on fossil fuels, and thus reduce the negative impact of cities on climate and the environment, and consequently it may improve human health. Björk et al.'s studies (2008) confirm that a lack of neighborhood recreational spaces leads to lower levels of personal satisfaction and higher levels of obesity, and are linked to overall lower health.

Table 3.1   Location considerations for ethnic Chinese in North America when buying/renting a home

Location consideration	Percentage (n = 348)
1. Neighborhood safety	60%
2. Short walking/driving distance to a good school/college/university	48%
3. Short walking/driving distance to shops/grocery/food stores	42%
3. Clean air, land, and water	42%
4. Short walking/driving distance to workplace	31%
5. Short walking distance to public transit	30%
6. Walkable neighborhood	28%
7. Sunny area	26%
8. Short walking/driving distance to a park/garden/green space	24%
9. Chinese community	21%
10. Community services	15%
10. Short walking/driving distance to family/friends	15%
11. Short walking/driving distance to a hospital	12%
12. Aesthetics	9%
13. Short walking/driving distance to a farmers market	7%
14. Housing affordability	4%

Note: My survey results; several elements received the same number of responses and therefore have the same order number.

EXTERIOR FORM

The survey results show that 34 percent (n = 160) of the respondents have lived in a traditional Chinese courtyard house in their country of origin. Most of them currently lived in a single-detached house (42 percent; n = 314), or an apartment in a building that has fewer than five storeys (25 percent), or an apartment in a building that has five or more storeys (13 percent). Very few of them lived in a row/town house (9 percent), or semi-detached house (7 percent), or courtyard house/housing (4 percent). Moreover, the Pearson Correlation shows a moderate, positive correlation between residents' current housing types and their ideal housing types (r = 0.411; n = 297; p < 0.000).

Three city planning professionals, two from Toronto and one from the University of Washington in Seattle, responded to my semi-structured interviews. When asked whether there are any planning restrictions for building courtyard housing in North America, two of them said they were unaware of any such regulations.

An associate professor from the University of Washington's Department of Urban Design and Planning observed that America is a decentralized and free place to build; it has a long tradition of settlers coming to establish ideal new communities of various kinds, including retirement communities, gated communities, religious and spiritual communities, communes, factory towns, and so on, all with their own particular physical and spatial orders. The "China City of America" project, which are new American suburban blocks designed according to Chinese principles, could be placed in this category.

The Toronto chief planner noted that there is not a tradition of building courtyard housing in Toronto or in most municipalities in Canada. The city building tradition here is Anglo-Saxon, and the basic residential building typology include the single-detached house, semi-detached house, row/town house, and walk-up apartment types. This tradition is organizing the primary rooms of the house along the street face, often mediated by a porch and along the rear with interior halls and side stairs for multistory buildings. Open space on the site is planned along the front between the building and the street and in the back yard. Side yard open space is typically narrow due to land costs and mostly useless for much but light and air. In the period after 1945, large-scale apartment towers were built as objects in park-like settings.

As a result, most planning regulations support these housing types, which include official plans and zoning by-laws. The layout of lands for development is for these types and not courtyard types. Each of these regulatory issues supports the status quo and inherently but not explicitly precludes courtyard types, which push the buildings to the property line and organizes the rooms around a central courtyard.

A planning professional in Toronto, however, noted that the current City of Toronto Zoning By-Law limits how close exterior walls of multi-unit buildings can be from each other, which would hinder the courtyard-type configuration. The earlier version of the by-law (No. 438–86) also had limiting distances for exterior walls of single-detached houses.

3.1   A typical subdivision suburban housing pattern in Canada, with single-detached houses as the main housing form
Source: Extract from Town of Richmond Hill webpage map explorer, 2014: http://maps.richmondhill.ca/Public/WebPages/Map/FundyViewer.aspx.

In the United States, building codes and land-use regulations vary from locality to locality. Generally, the more rural the area, the less regulation there is. For more built-up areas, or areas where there is more regulation, one needs to look out for the setback and lot coverage rules. Any place that allows zero-lot-line[1] construction or shared party walls should be amenable to courtyard housing, at least with respect to the side lot lines. Yet, there are not many places that would dispense with the front and back yards altogether.

When asked "What can planning authorities do to better facilitate Chinese residential cultural tradition in North America?," the Toronto planning professional suggested that perhaps by providing more flexibility to accommodate cultural norms, not just for housing but for urban planning in general. There may be a need to address rules for fire and emergency egress, site planning, and servicing standards. These questions may be comparable with the site planning issues related to laneway housing in Toronto. Another comparable situation is urban design standards relating to infill housing, specifically for sites that feature open private space surrounded by housing units.

This planner in Toronto also observed that one key change in the last decade or so is the introduction of common elements, which allows a cluster of property owners to share ownership of a common parcel, such as a driveway or courtyard. The common element is tied legally to each of their own properties. This is called "planned unit developments" (PUDs) and has made it easier to provide services and access needed to build clusters of in-fill housing.

The same planner continually argued that the matter of courtyard housing may also require moving from a model of houses for nuclear families, to planning housing that accommodates multi-generational households. Vancouver, for example, has allowed accessory buildings to be constructed behind single-detached houses in order to provide affordable housing options for seniors ("granny flats" or "garden suites"). The current planning rules in Ontario for such accessory buildings or suites seem to be rather complex and ambiguous.

---

[1]   A zero-lot-line home is built very close to the property lines, which reduces or eliminates the space available for front and backyards (see: http://topics.wisegeek.com/topics.htm?zero-lot-line#).

3.2   A typical single-detached house in Richmond Hill, Ontario, Canada, with a two-car garage
Source: Photo by Donia Zhang, 2013.

The Toronto chief planner claimed that at this point in time, there is little pressure to introduce the courtyard type in Toronto. No developers are proposing the type, and no residents come forward in public meetings on zoning or official planning to ask for this type. Nevertheless, in North America in the 1970s, there was some interest in the courtyard house (sometimes called the "carpet house"). Several significant projects were constructed, such as Mies Van Der Rohe's Laffeyette Park in Detroit, which included blocks of courtyard houses.

The associate professor at the University of Washington observed that southwestern USA, like Mexico, has its own tradition of courtyard houses. However, he felt that transplanting classic Beijing *siheyuan* (courtyard houses) blocks to America may sound like quite a stretch.

Single-Detached House

Single-detached houses represent most (60 percent; n = 314) of the surveyed ethnic Chinese residents' aspirations, and 24 of 37 interviewees (65 percent) preferred a single-detached house with a front and back yard/garden. This finding reflects market economists' observations and the National Association of Realtors' 2011 Community Preference Survey (Montgomery, 2013, pp. 29, 278).

The interviewees' reasons are that a single-detached house has windows in all four directions that offer abundant sunlight and fresh air. A single-detached house is a place of privacy, relatively independent, and usually has plenty of spaces to foster close family relations. It has more indoor and outdoor spaces than row/town house for conducting physical activities in a convenient way. Parents and children can do many things together in and out of their house. Meanwhile, it can offer more personal space to avoid conflict among family members. House chores and maintenance activities keep the occupants mentally and physically active. Also, when buying a house, one is also acquiring land—something more tangible than apartments.

It should be of no surprise that ethnic Chinese in North America predominantly preferred a single-detached house because a classical Chinese courtyard house is usually comprised of a cluster of independent buildings, and each building (or hallroom) accommodated a nuclear family within an extended family living in the same courtyard house compound.

Courtyard House/Housing

About one in five (21 percent; n = 314) surveyed ethnic Chinese and 4 of 37 (11 percent) ethnic Chinese interviewees wished to live in a courtyard house/housing, but 26 of 37 (70 percent) of them wanted a communal courtyard. They argued that this housing form brings in sunshine, fresh air, broad view, and a feeling of ease, which are conducive to the physical and mental health of the occupants. Since communication with fellow human beings is essential to good health, a courtyard house/housing can provide plenty of meeting spaces for social interaction to take place. As in a traditional Chinese courtyard house (*siheyuan*), the form is also ideal for offering private spaces to host a three-generation family.

This result echoes that of the Choices Surveys conducted by Lee (2002) in the Victoria-Fraserview/Killarney (VFK) and Sunset communities in Vancouver, BC that Chinese residents desired courtyard housing (pp. 73, 76, 116, 120–21). One of my survey respondents explains:

> In 2006 I wanted to have a courtyard house custom built in the town of Chico, about 150 miles northeast of San Francisco. The building codes and square-foot minimums wouldn't allow me to have the house built on an affordable sized lot. The larger lots were much larger, such as five acres, and had living area square-foot minimums making the house too large and expensive for me to build as a single-family home. So I ended up buying a house that only has a fenced yard. My idea of building a courtyard house only remains a 'dream,' because I'd need about 1.5 million dollars to build such a home, and I still doubt the local building codes and other restrictions would allow me to build such a home. I don't know why in California it's impossible to find a home where I could have a private courtyard as a place to get exercise and enjoyment working in the garden and grow food. I also want my home to be energy-efficient. I hope to encourage residential real estate developers to start building siheyuan [Beijing courtyard house] type of homes.

Semi-Detached and Row/Town House

Only five percent (n = 314) of the surveyed ethnic Chinese favored a semi-detached house, and three percent preferred a row/town house. Two of 37 (5 percent) interviewees wanted a row/town house. They maintained that a row/town house can create alleys or walkways for people to interact with one another, and that the interior space is wider where the kitchen and the living room are not on the same floor. Among the 37 interviewees, no one preferred a semi-detached house. However, in *The New York Times* (August 8, 2013), Hughes reported that semi-detached, two-family houses with a small front yard in Queens of New York is hot for Chinese home buyers.

My interview informants criticized the downside of a semi-detached or row/town house that it shares a party wall with neighbors. The party wall insulation is often poor as one can hear the noise from the neighbors that may cause tensions, although it also depends on the neighborly relations.

3.3   Typical semi-detached suburban houses in Richmond Hill, Ontario, Canada
Source: Photo by Donia Zhang, 2013.

3.4   A front view of row/town houses in Richmond Hill, Ontario, Canada
Source: Photo by Donia Zhang, 2013.

3.5   The back
of the row/town
houses with
garages and a
driveway for
vehicle access but
not designed for
human activities
Source: Photo by Donia
Zhang, 2013.

Single-Storey House/Bungalow

Two of 37 (5 percent) interviewees preferred a single-storey house or a bungalow because it normally has wide frontage and no stairs. As such, it is easier for people to walk in and out, which is convenient especially for the elderly as they may easily fall down the stairs.

Apartment Building

Only 7 percent (n = 314) of the surveyed ethnic Chinese preferred an apartment in a building that has fewer than five storeys, and 5 percent favored an apartment in a building that has five or more storeys. Two of 37 (5 percent) interviewees favored an apartment either higher or lower than five storeys. They commented that such a mixed-income building with structures appropriate for shelter, light, air, view, and communal green space may offer closer neighborly relations and respectful social interaction than single-detached houses, thus it may promote more mental and physical health. They noted that in most cases, the environment of an apartment building can be maintained tidy and clean by the property management. Certainly, it also depends on the *quality* of the people living there. Because of the low number of respondents who chose this housing type, the finding is only indicative.

EXTERIOR WALLS

Brick (46 percent; n = 310) is reported as the most common exterior wall material of the dwellings currently occupied by the survey respondents, followed by wood (30 percent), concrete (12 percent), stone (9 percent), and prefabricated panel (7 percent).

When asked "What material of exterior walls may ideally promote healthy environment?," brick is again their first choice (37 percent; n = 307), followed by stone (26 percent), wood (21 percent), concrete (15 percent), and prefabricated panel (4 percent). Nevertheless, over one third (36 percent) of the participants was unsure or did not know. This finding reveals that natural or traditional building materials for exterior walls are still favored over modern or synthetic materials for better environmental health.

In response to the interview question "Will you be happier if your house exterior is in a traditional Chinese architectural style, and why?," 16 of 37 (43 percent) interviewees said they would be happy or happier because they found traditional Chinese architectural style beautiful, earthy, tranquil, and harmonious, and that it would be soothing since traditional Chinese architecture emphasizes harmonious combinations of nature with architecture. Two informants specifically mentioned Beijing *siheyuan* (courtyard house) because of their nostalgia and longing for their homeland.

3.6   A single-storey house/bungalow in Richmond Hill, Ontario, Canada
Source: Photo by Donia Zhang, 2013.

3.7　An apartment building of fewer than five storeys in Richmond Hill, Ontario, Canada
Source: Photo by Donia Zhang, 2013.

3.8　An apartment building of more than five storeys in Richmond Hill, Ontario, Canada
Source: Photo by Donia Zhang, 2013.

They felt that Chinese courtyard houses, if built in North America, would be special compared with other housing styles. They considered Chinese architectural style reflects their cultural background and roots, helps maintain their cultural identity, and it is a means of cultural recognition. It would make them aware that they are Chinese, and that they should not forget their culture of origin. It would let their children and other ethnic groups know about Chinese architectural culture, and it may attract other ethnic groups who are interested in Chinese culture.

Six of 37 (16 percent) interviewees felt that depending on how well the Chinese theme is incorporated into the design, it would be nice to have some tastes of Chinese architectural characteristics in North America. Other interviewees observed that the grey-colored traditional Chinese exterior brick walls look better and last longer than the wood fences here, which do not weather well as they change color in a few years and look deteriorated very quickly. Some found the red brick walls enclosing traditional Chinese courtyard houses are better-looking, and the yard fences here should match the material and color of the exterior walls of the house. Several interviewees felt that if their homes were built for aesthetic reasons, a Chinese architectural style can be an option but not a necessity.

Sixteen of 37 (43 percent) interviewees said they would *not* necessarily be happier if their house exterior is in a traditional Chinese style because they want to "do in Rome as the Romans do." Being in North America, they would like to blend in with the American or Canadian community. They fear that if their house is in a traditional Chinese style, it may look strange in the neighborhood, or it may cost more to build, or it may not suit the climate here, or it may not fit the needs for the US/Canadian markets, since anything too uncommon may incur unnecessary attention and impact resale value of their homes. Some even said they prefer Western-style exteriors, either English or French style.

Three respondents said they did not prefer a traditional Chinese-style house because they had no prior living experience in it, and therefore they did not know what it is like. For example, a respondent described:

> I lived in an old and shabby country house in China, which was not as nice-looking as this Western-style house in Florida. Although some Western-style houses are not as good-looking as Chinese-style houses in southern China, they are more practical with car garages.

Other respondents contended that material durability triumphs over architectural style. Still others said they felt very happy and comfortable living in a Western-style home. As this informant recalled:

> I like the Western-style house here because it is timber-structured and has good thermal insulation. Southern China's climate is wet and humid; travertine stone veneer or tiled exterior walls of the house in Guangzhou can make the interior very humid in the rainy season in spring. Moreover, the unsystematic planning of Guangzhou made some houses in the low lying lands flooded, and people had to raise their ground level by adding an extra layer of floor material to avoid flooding.

Three interviewees claimed that their house interior is more important than the exterior, and that the architectural style does not matter to them.

GATE ORIENTATION

Regarding the orientation of their existing home's front gate (or front entrance in the case of an apartment building), south (23 percent; n = 247) and north (22 percent) share almost an equal state, so do east (15 percent) and west (14 percent). Other directions such as southeast (5 percent), northeast (5 percent), southwest (3 percent), and northwest (3 percent), are reported as uncommon gate orientations.

For their ideal home's front gate (or front entrance in the case of an apartment building), south (30 percent; n = 243) is more preferred than north (14 percent), and east (8 percent) more than west (4 percent). These choices comply with *Feng Shui* theory. However, traditional Chinese gate orientations of southeast (2 percent) and northwest (2 percent) did not receive good responses, nor did southwest (3 percent) or northeast (0 percent). Notably, a significant 37 percent of the survey participants were unsure or did not know about their ideal gate orientations, indicating that gate orientation did not matter to them. Overall, south gate orientation is ideal to the surveyed ethnic Chinese in North America.

WINDOW ORIENTATION

To promote physical health, south window orientation preference has surpassed all other directions for the living room (36 percent; n = 242), bedroom (34 percent; n = 241), family room (34 percent; n = 237), study room (24 percent; n = 230), dining room (18 percent; n = 236), kitchen (17 percent; n = 239), and bathroom (14 percent; n = 237). However, for the kitchen, north (13 percent) and east (10 percent) are also preferred orientations, but not so much of the west (5 percent), perhaps due to the hot summer suns in the afternoons. More than half (56 percent) of them were unsure or did not know, suggesting window orientation did not matter to them.

This finding is consistent with that of Hughes (2013) and Satow (2015) that southern exposure tops a list of important factors among Chinese home buyers in New York, showing their continued cultural trait of ideal *Feng Shui*. South-facing windows allow for substantial heating from the sun, however, exterior shades are often needed to prevent summer overheating (Canada Mortgage and Housing Corporation, 1994/2009, p. 6).

The survey findings also indicate that to promote physical health, south–north (33 percent; n = 243) window cross-ventilation orientation is much more preferred than east–west (9 percent), or northeast–southwest (5 percent), or northwest–southeast (4 percent) directions. Significantly, nearly half (49 percent) of the participants were unsure or did not know, suggesting that cross-ventilation orientation did not matter to them. Overall, south–north cross-ventilation is desired by the surveyed ethnic Chinese in North America, reflecting Chinese tradition.

YARDS AND GARDENS

Regarding their homes' existing outdoor spaces, the respondents reported that they have more front yards/gardens (65 percent; n = 217) than back yards/gardens (60 percent), and more balconies or decks (34 percent) than patios (23 percent). Yet courtyards/gardens are unusual (12 percent).

When the participants were offered with multiple choices which outdoor spaces around their homes may ideally promote physical health, back yards/gardens were reported as most commonly health-promoting (76 percent; n = 224), followed by front yards/gardens (67 percent), balconies/decks (42 percent), patios (38 percent), and courtyards/gardens (32 percent). Because courtyards/gardens are rare spaces in North American house buildings, this may explain why they received lower responses.

The respondents claimed that their front and back yards are conducive to physical and mental health because these spaces are where one can plant flowers, vegetables, and fruit trees, and where children can play and adults can do fitness exercises or gather with friends. The green grasses are also comfortable to the eyes. This finding confirms the account by Montgomery (2013, pp. 108–11) that the last few decades have generated ample empirical evidence that being in touch with nature (trees, grass, vegetation, etc.) or viewing nature makes people happier and healthier. Ulrich (1984) found that hospital patients need less pain medication and recover faster when their windows face views of nature rather than brick walls.

For bigger houses with an outdoor swimming pool in the back yard, the pool can offer health exercises and cool sensations when swimming in the summer. An ethnic Chinese living in Florida described her yards with satisfaction:

> We have big and beautiful front and back yards, and the back yard faces a canal surrounding the city. We also have a screened porch and sunspace facing the back yard that we use often, such as resting or doing exercises on treadmill. From the house, to the sunspace, and to the outside, there are three sets of glass sliding doors for viewing the scenery and canal. We like it when seeing the dark blue night sky through the glass doors while lying on the bed. It is visually pleasing and comfortable.

One in three surveyed respondents (33 percent; n = 240) grow food, vegetables, or fruits in the outdoor spaces around their homes. It is common knowledge that home produce is often healthier to eat than market-purchased ones because we usually do not apply chemicals to stimulate growth.

Communal Courtyard

Many more (26 of 37, or 70 percent)[2] of the ethnic Chinese interviewees, as opposed to the survey respondents (21 percent; n = 314), said they would like to have a communal courtyard near their homes. This discrepancy could be that they liked

---

2   These 37 interviewees exclude the 20 non-Chinese participants living in co-operative housing or cohousing in Canada.

both a single-detached house and a communal courtyard. But when the survey participants were asked to choose only one answer, 60 percent of them selected single-detached house.

The ethnic Chinese interviewees stated that a communal courtyard is usually a large open space with trees and grasses that help improve the air quality and landscape. Communal courtyards can offer a platform for community activities, such as doing morning exercises, after-dinner walk, leisure activities, and talking with neighbors, which are all conducive to the physical and mental health of the occupants.

They further noted that communal courtyards can promote better social interaction and neighborly communication that will result in more human care for one another. Communal courtyards can also foster liveliness and excitement of social gathering that some residents would like. Living in a communal courtyard was the way some respondents grew up with, it can remind them of their childhood memories. Through festival celebrations and weddings in a communal courtyard, neighbors can get to know and befriend with one another as people ought to learn to share and interact cordially. A communal courtyard can be great as long as the neighbors all have similar living habits, for instance, no late night parties or noisy teenagers hanging out at night.

My fieldwork shows that 16 of 53 (30 percent) housing co-operatives in Toronto have communal courtyards. A good example is the 260-unit Bain Apartments Co-operative (former "Riverdale Courts") built in east Toronto in 1913. The units range from one to four bedrooms, in 25 three-storey buildings, as well as two small semi-detached houses, scattered over two large city blocks, and arranged around nine communal courtyards. When I visited the neighborhood in a July afternoon in 2013, I found four courtyards had groups of residents seated around a table, chatting and enjoying lively conversations. A resident told me that this place is like a "village within the city"—it creates a sense of *community* and each courtyard has its own *culture*. The residents living in the same courtyard take care of one another and share things with their neighbors. Although the courtyards can get noisy at times, they are constantly striving to find new ways to live together in harmony, and develop and strengthen their cooperative life. The Bain Apartments Co-operative is a vibrant community with thriving arts and cultural events that allow residents to meet new friends and feel safe in the courtyards. Montgomery (2013, p. 134) likewise observed that town houses' courtyards draw people closer.

However, 9 of 37 (24 percent) interviewees would *not* want a communal courtyard near their homes as they feared that it would compromise their privacy. Some respondents were uncomfortable with the idea that their neighbor's front door was placed directly in front of theirs. Others worried that people might get drunk and make noise in the courtyard, or they have to share responsibility with their neighbors for taking care of the courtyard. If their neighbors want to plant some flowers that they dislike, or that they are allergic to, it may trigger tension or cause conflict. Some also speculated that communal courtyards can be difficult to establish relationship with neighbors if they are not open-minded.

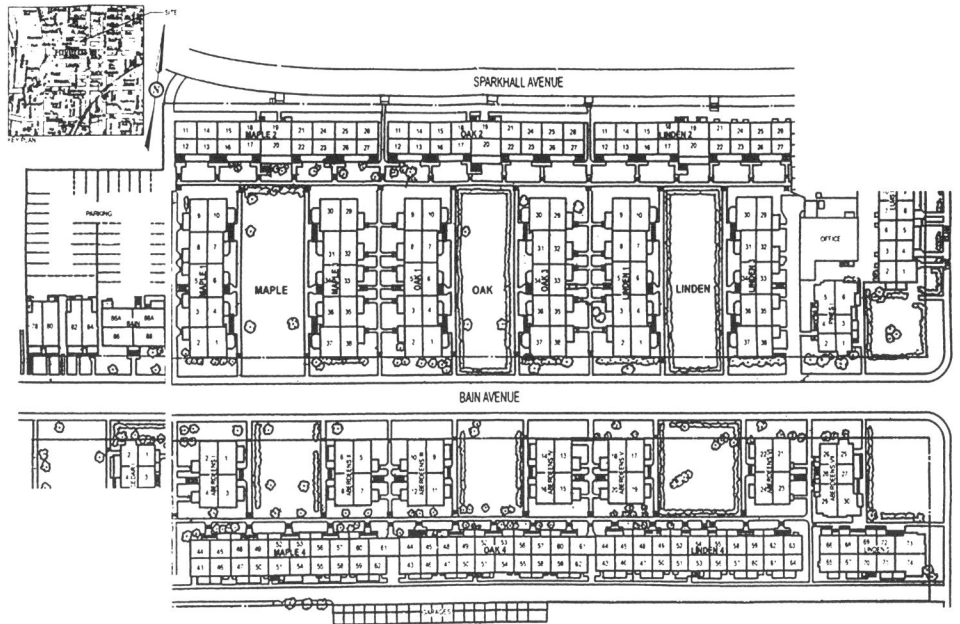

3.9 Site plan of the Bain Apartments Co-operative showing the
nine communal courtyards, Toronto, Ontario, Canada
Source: Flyer from Bain Apartments Co-operative, 2013.

3.10 Bain Apartments Co-operative North Maples courtyard, Toronto, Ontario, Canada
Source: Photo by Donia Zhang, 2013.

Single-Family Courtyard

Two of 37 (5 percent) ethnic Chinese interviewees preferred a single-family courtyard as opposed to a communal courtyard. There is such a project constructed in Toronto at 2087 Davenport Road (rear). This infill site was originally a contractor's warehouse with a storage yard in a mixed-use industrial neighborhood. The ethnic Chinese architects' couple, Christine Ho Ping Kong and Peter Tan, bought the land in 2001 and designed and built a 200-sqm (2,200-sqf), two-storey courtyard house as their home and studio. The project was completed in 2006 and has won several residential design awards in 2007 and 2008 by the City of Toronto and the Ontario Association of Architects, among others. They have participated in Toronto's annual "Doors Open" event four years since its inception, to present their courtyard home to the general public because of a growing interest in this housing type. Christine said that their courtyard is highly used for family activities almost all year round. In the warm seasons, they would eat, drink, and accommodate visitors in the courtyard. Their daughter especially liked to sit in the courtyard to read books and do painting.

During the "Doors Open" event in 2013, another ethnic Chinese couple also expressed that they would like to have their own custom-designed courtyard house built in Toronto because they found the ordinary single-detached houses boring and lacking spatial interests.

Balconies

Twenty-seven of 37 (73 percent) interviewees would like to have balconies or decks for getting sunlight, fresh air, and natural views. They found that balconies or decks offer open spaces where people can place a table and chairs for breakfast and afternoon tea, to enjoy the summer breeze, to have sunbath, to have social gathering and parties, to dry laundry, and to grow pot plants, food, and things.

They further expressed that balconies can provide a platform for seeing and talking to neighbors, and for providing a community watch over the things going on below. Some respondents recalled having balconies was the way they grew up with; it reminds them of their childhood memories. When they grow older, they can put a rocking chair in the balcony, sit in it, and take a nap. These descriptions reveal that a balcony is a place where people can relax and enjoy an outdoor life, especially for people living in apartments. A Toronto resident described her balcony with pride: "We live at a housing co-operative with 63 other households [...] Our unit is in a southwestern direction with a balcony that I call my 'treehouse.'"

Three of 37 (8 percent) interviewees felt that a balcony would be a welcoming addition but not an essential, if they live in a two-storey house with a back yard. Another three interviewees disliked a balcony as it would require too much maintenance work. Some respondent felt that a balcony gives a dangerous feeling if in a nineteenth-floor high-rise apartment; a sunroom or solarium would be better.

3.11　The Courtyard House, Toronto, Ontario, Canada
Source: Photo by Donia Zhang, 2013.

3.12　The courtyard of the Courtyard House, Toronto, Ontario, Canada
Source: Photo by Donia Zhang, 2013.

3.13　House with a front balcony as decoration, Richmond Hill, Ontario, Canada
Source: Photo by Donia Zhang, 2013.

3.14　Balconies at the back of housing for sunlight and fresh air, Richmond Hill, Ontario, Canada
Source: Photo by Donia Zhang, 2013.

ROOFS

Regarding their existing roof shapes, more than half (54 percent; n = 232) of the survey respondents had pitched roofs, and one in five (20 percent) had flat ones, only a small number (8 percent) of them had semi-pitched and semi-flat roofs.

To promote physical health, the survey participants much preferred pitched roofs (36 percent; n = 232) than flat ones (8 percent), while others also indicated semi-pitched and semi-flat roofs (10 percent).[3] The interview findings show that 19 of 37 (51 percent) participants preferred a pitched, or sloped, or gabled roof. They found that pitched roofs with large overhangs provide protection from the sun, and that a pitched roof will allow water from rain and snow to run off easily without pooling to cause leaks like a flat roof would. When a pitched roof installed with a skylight, it allows more sunlight into the house, although it will also increase the possibility of rainwater leakage and noisy sound of heavy rainstorms. Moreover, the respondents observed that pitched roofs with volume ceilings (high ceilings) are beneficial for indoor air circulation, reducing heat, and the interior will be cooler in the summer. Thus it is more suitable for North American climate. They also considered a pitched roof with multi angles as better-looking than other roof shapes because it gives the house a sense of three dimensions.

Nevertheless, three of 37 (8 percent) interviewees thought that a flat roof may promote physical health because it gives an open space that enables one to relax and breathe freely. Moreover, a flat roof can offer roof terrace/garden where one can grow foods and vegetables, a potential for greening the environment, although the waterproofing can be expensive. There may be new ways to reduce the cost of it.

Four of 37 (11 percent) interviewees said they did not know physical health and roof shape have any correlation. Two (5 percent) of them reasonably argued that roof shapes should depend on the climate of the region. A significant number (32 percent) of them were unsure or had no preference for their roof shapes.

Asphalt shingles is the most popular existing roof material (20 percent; n = 233) of the survey participants, compared with clay tile (13 percent), concrete (9 percent), slate (8 percent), vinyl (5 percent), cedar (3 percent), metal/copper (1 percent), and thatch (0.4 percent). The residents considered clay tile (23 percent; n = 227) (a Chinese tradition) as the healthiest roof material for the environment, followed by cedar (8 percent), slate (6 percent), and concrete (5 percent). Metal/copper (4 percent) and asphalt shingles (4 percent) were thought to be less healthy roof materials, and thatch (2 percent) and vinyl (1 percent) were considered the least healthy roof materials. The respondents seemed to think that natural roof materials are the healthiest for the environment. However, the majority (62 percent) of them was unsure or did not know, suggesting that the question is perhaps too technical for them.

---

[3]   A significant number (44 percent; n = 232) of the survey participants were unsure or did not know, suggesting that roof shape is perhaps a technical question beyond the general public's knowledge.

3.15   A garage roof terrace that can be used for various activities in warm seasons, Richmond Hill, Ontario, Canada
Source: Photo by Donia Zhang, 2013.

When comparing Western roofs with traditional Chinese titled roofs, a Chinese resident in Florida noted that the asphalt roofs here have better thermal insulation; although Chinese titled roofs look better, they can be easily blown off in case of windstorms, and therefore, are perceived more dangerous.

Roof Terrace/Garden

Roof terraces/gardens are rare (5 percent; n = 217) among the surveyed ethnic Chinese homes in North America. However, to promote physical health, 25 percent (n = 224) of the survey respondents and 54 percent (n = 37) of the interviewees would like to have a roof terrace/garden, as they found it eco-friendly, where people can plant vegetables, flowers, creepers and vines, air clothes, and have BBQs, or simply sit and enjoy the outdoor life. It is good to have a roof terrace/ garden also because the interior space can be cooler in the summer since green spaces can protect a building from excessive heat by absorbing and filtering it. On summer nights, one can sleep on a roof terrace/garden and enjoy the cool outside as long as it would not pose privacy issues to the neighbors or vice versa. A roof terrace/garden is a space for relaxation, particularly for people living in apartments or high-rise buildings.

Nine of 37 (24 percent) interviewees would dislike a roof terrace/garden. They argued that although a roof terrace/garden can be a nice space, it will create more work and will be difficult to maintain. It may leak in the rain or when the snow melts, which may cause problems for the room below. It may also make the room below hotter in the summer and colder in the winter.

Two of 37 (5 percent) interviewees felt that a roof terrace/garden is impractical in cold climate such as Canada.

SUMMARY AND CONCLUSION

This chapter presented and analyzed the empirical findings on the architectural form and environmental quality of ethnic Chinese housing in North America. The results show that the *Yin Yang* concept in traditional Chinese philosophy is somewhat reflected in their choice of housing forms, as 21 percent (n = 314) of the ethnic Chinese survey respondents preferred a courtyard house/housing; although only 11 percent (n = 37) of the ethnic Chinese interviewees wanted a courtyard house, 70 percent of them favored a communal courtyard, because the courtyard space facilitates social interaction and is conducive to the health of the occupants. However, my interview with the Toronto chief planner reveals that the present municipal government is unaware of this housing demand as there is no previous research tackling this issue.

The survey results further show that residents' preference for south window orientation in each room surpasses all other directions for better sunlight quality. This finding complies with *Feng Shui* theory and Chinese cultural trait. This finding also reflects the preference of many people of the backgrounds who know nothing of *Feng Shui*. The significance of the fact is that *Feng Shui* theory may have universal implications.

The research findings also indicate that pitched roofs are favored more than flat ones because of their attractive appearance and better thermal performance. Balconies/decks, roof terraces/gardens are welcoming additions to a house since they can offer sunlight, fresh air, ventilation, as well as outdoor spaces that have the potential to accommodate various social and cultural activities.

Table 3.2   Summary of ethnic Chinese preferences for the form of the housing

Design Elements	Preference (n = 360)
Exterior form	Single-detached house: 60% Courtyard house/housing: 21%
Exterior walls	Chinese architectural style: 43% Non-Chinese architectural style: 43%
Gate orientation	South: 30%
Window orientation	South: 36% (for living room)
Yards and gardens	Communal courtyard: 70% (n = 37)
Roofs	Pitched: 36%

Source: My summary.

In Chapter 4 that follows, the space and construction quality of ethnic Chinese housing in North America will be explored, to see whether it helps gather *qi* (cosmic energy) to promote the health of the occupants.

4

Health as Gathering *Qi*:
Space and Construction Quality of the Housing

> You have only to comprehend the one *qi* that unites the world.
> Zhuangzi, c. 369–286 BCE, *The Complete Works*, chapter 22

This chapter examines the space and construction quality of the housing occupied by ethnic Chinese in North America, to see whether it promotes physical health of the occupants, and whether it complies with traditional Chinese philosophy in gathering *qi*. The chapter consists of eight sections: interior space, interior colors, floor levels, furniture styles and materials, facility provision, construction quality, maintenance and management, and car park spaces.

INTERIOR SPACE

Interior space is very important for a home design because previous research finding indicates that people spend 90 percent of their time indoors (Eberhard, 2009; Lyle, 1994). In North America, single-detached and semi-detached houses are prevalent. A land surveyor who has worked all over the US for over 40 years estimated that the average lot size for a single-detached American home is approximately 22 m × 36 m = 792 sqm (75 ft × 120 ft = 9,000 sqf). Whereas Jim Adair (2003) projected that the average lot size for a single-detached Canadian home is about 15 m × 34 m = 510 sqm (50 ft × 110 ft = 5,500 sqf). As such, the average site area of a Canadian house is roughly 64 percent of an American one.

The online survey on residents' home interior space and room sizes did not yield sensible results due to the questions asked in square meters—the metric (international) system widely used in China; however in North America, the imperial system of square feet is prevalent. Some of the survey respondents probably have entered metric measurements while others input imperial figures. Thus their average home interior space is 503 sqm (n = 177), and their ideal home interior space is 616 sqm (n = 166).

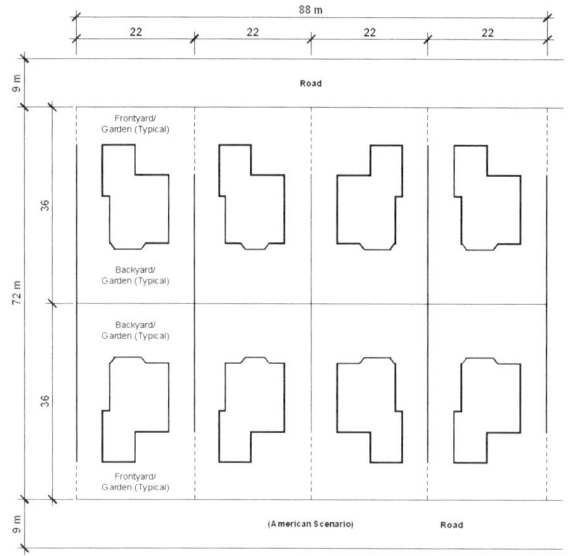

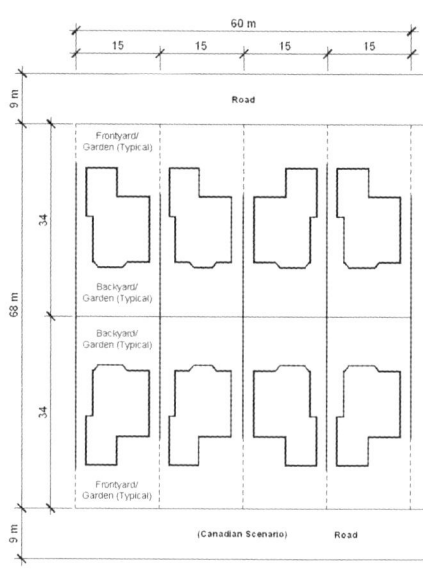

4.1   Single-detached suburban houses pattern in the US
Source: Conception and drawing by Donia Zhang, 2013.

4.2   Single-detached suburban houses pattern in Canada
Source: Conception and drawing by Donia Zhang, 2013.

These numbers are much larger than reality can afford; the results do not make sense. As a survey respondent explained: "Not sure at all which size of each room that will be healthy—the numbers put in there are randomly selected." Nevertheless, the data reveals a preference for larger interior space than the residents have had.

The interview data have in fact generated some sensible results. The respondents wanted an average interior space of 195 sqm (2,093 sqf; n = 24) for a family of three to four members. They commented that depending on the household size, 50–60 sqm per person seems to be appropriate.

Existing literature also offers some clues about home interior space in North America. According to the US Census Bureau (2006), the average size of an American single-detached house is about 230 sqm (2,470 sqf, excluding basement), which has three bedrooms, two bathrooms, and a two-car garage. Based on the *Pulse Survey* conducted by the Canadian Home Builders' Association (2013, p. 11), the average size of a Canadian single-family home is 186 sqm (2,000 sqf).

Some of my interview respondents expressed that their interior space is "the bigger, the better." While others indicated that the interior space should be appropriate to the household size because they do not want to spend more time to clean extra rooms not being used, a finding that reflects that of Montgomery (2013, p. 80). To facilitate family communication, the house size has to be just about right. If the house is too big, everyone goes to their own rooms without seeing much of their family members, which will not be conducive to family interaction. If the house is smaller, it may facilitate family members' contact.

Generally, the respondents desired a large living room with a high ceiling (as low ceilings would make one feel oppressed), a family room, a dining room, a kitchen, one bedroom per person, two bathrooms, an office, a fitness room, a garage,

and a storage space. Each room should be at least 10–15 sqm to allow people and fresh air to move freely to promote physical health. Others argued that a healthy interior space should create a happy atmosphere and warm ambience to make the occupants feel comfortable. Still others maintained that it is more about the state of mind than physical measurement. To promote health, all rooms should have a window leading to the outside to offer natural ventilation and avoid overheating in the summer.

4.3   Living room of a single-detached house, Richmond Hill, Ontario, Canada
Source: Photo by Donia Zhang, 2013.

INTERIOR COLORS

The informants felt that the colors of their interior walls also affect their mood and happiness. In an earlier (unpublished) survey by the author on color connotations associated with orientation and emotion (appendix), which involved 264 participants from various countries of origin, the results show that their top color choice for happiness is yellow (36 percent), followed by green (16 percent), red (15 percent), or blue (13 percent). Whereas for grief, their top color is grey (31 percent), followed by black (25 percent), or blue (17 percent). The color for love is red (50 percent), followed by pink (24 percent). Among them, 229 respondents offered justifications for their color choices as presented in Table 4.1.

4.4   Family room of a single-detached house, Richmond Hill, Ontario, Canada
Source: Photo by Donia Zhang, 2013.

4.5   Dining room of a single-detached house, Richmond Hill, Ontario, Canada
Source: Photo by Donia Zhang, 2013.

4.6   Kitchen of a single-detached house, Richmond Hill, Ontario, Canada
Source: Photo by Donia Zhang, 2013.

Table 4.1   Color connotations associated with emotion

Emotion	Color	Connotations (n = 264)
Happiness	Yellow (36%)	It represents brightness (25 responses), smiley face (13), sun/sunshine (13), warmth (6), cheerfulness (6), delightfulness (4), flowers (3), liveliness (2), or hope (2).
	Green (16%)	It symbolizes nature (4 responses), life (4), or wealth (3).
	Red (15%)	It relates to Chinese tradition (7 responses), brightness (4), warmth (2), excitement (2), fun (2), or joy (2).
	Blue (13%)	It signifies brightness/light (3 responses), sky (2), peace (2), calmness (2), or relaxation (2).
Grief	Grey (31%)	It is linked to dullness (11 responses), sadness (11), gloom (11), depression (6), cool/cold (3), lifeless/colorless (3), despair (3), darkness (2), or ugliness (2).
	Black (25%)	It denotes darkness (10 responses), funeral (7), death (6), depression (6), sadness/sorrow (5), or mourning (2).
	Blue (17%)	It is associated with the saying "feeling blue" (7 responses), sadness (6), cold (4), somberness (3), depression (2), or darkness (2).
Love	Red (50%)	It stands for passion/intense emotions (31 responses), heart (19), roses (10), Valentines (5), fire/heat (5), brightness (5), warmth (4), or sunny days (2).
	Pink (24%)	It signifies softness/tenderness (6 responses), warmth (5), romance (4), roses (4), brightness (3), heart (3), or happiness (2).

Note: My survey results; the color blue is for both happiness and grief. It indicates that different people have different interpretations of colors.

In her book *Healing Spaces: The Science of Place and Wellbeing*, Esther Sternberg (2009, pp. 39–40) observed that the color green is perhaps the "default mode for our brains. It was the background we were weaned on in primordial times, the background that told us we were safe, [and] the background that lulled us to sleep against a darkening sky." Sternberg (2009, p. 48) further recounted that in another study, researchers exposed healthy patients to 10 minutes of light of red, green, or blue wavelengths and measured their heart-rate variability. They found that the red and green wavelengths had a stimulating effect, and that the blue ones were calming. This finding echoed the patients' report that the blue light is relaxing, and the red and green lights are energizing. However, Semir Zeki (1999) in his book *Inner Vision* discovered the color reverse in the visual system: the cells that are excited by red are inhibited by green, those provoked by yellow are calmed by blue, and those animated by white are repressed by black. In his ground-breaking book *Brain Landscape: The Coexistence of Neuroscience and Architecture*, John Eberhard (2009, p. 48) noted that besides emotional associations, things that affect color perception include the viewer's age, disposition, and mental health; people who have similar personality traits often share color perceptions and preferences; but there are general perceptions that blues and greens are restful, and reds are alerting (e.g., red lights, red flags, etc.).

This study also reveals that the color for east is represented by yellow (25 percent), red (22 percent), or green (21 percent). The color for south is symbolized by red (23 percent) or green (23 percent). The color for west is signified by orange (17 percent), green (16 percent), blue (15 percent), or yellow (15 percent). And the color for north is embodied by blue (40 percent) or white (21 percent). When the survey participants were asked "Do you think there is a correlation between emotion and orientation?," nearly half (49 percent; n = 264) of them answered "yes." Of the 264 survey respondents, 229 offered explanations for their color choices as presented in Table 4.2. These findings reveal that the sun, being the source of light, is the most important factor for respondents' association of color and orientation.

Table 4.2   Color connotations associated with orientation

Orientation	Color	Connotations (n = 264)
East	Yellow (25%)	It represents sunrise (38 responses), Asians (3), or sand (3).
	Red (22%)	It symbolizes sunrise (32 responses), fire (5), warmth (5), or life (2).
	Green (21%)	It stands for forest/trees (6 responses), plants/vegetation (4), grass (4), spring (3), growth (3), nature (3), peace (2), or temperate climate (2).
South	Red (23%)	It denotes hot/tropical climate (24 responses), bright sun (5), warmth (5), or fire (2).
	Green (23%)	It represents plants/vegetation (10 responses), grass/garden (10), forest/trees (8), warmth (7), good weather (2), farmland (2), life (2), growth (2), peace (2), freshness (2), or spring (2).

	Orange (17%)	It signifies sunset (30 responses), fall season (2), or the American Grand Canyon (2).
West	Green (16%)	It represents prairie/farmland (5 responses), forest (5), sunset (4), spring (3), life (3), growth (2), or peace (2).
	Blue (15%)	It denotes ocean/sea (9 responses), sunset (6), sky (4), tranquility (2), Paradise in Buddhism (2), or air/atmosphere/breeze (2).
	Yellow (15%)	It symbolizes sunset (15 responses), brightness (2), sand/desert (2), or the Western world (2).
North	Blue (40%)	It is associated with cool/cold (52 responses), sky (19), North Pole (6), sea/water (3), snow (3), ice/glacier (3), or calmness (2).
	White (21%)	It is linked to cold/snow (37 responses), North Pole (9), ice (4), or infinite space (2).

Note: My survey results.

East

The survey respondents contended that if they live in an east-facing room and see the sunrise (14 responses) in the morning, they would feel happy (14), energetic (5), warm (4), positive (4), hopeful (3), loving (3), excited (2), peaceful (2), and comfortable (2). Nevertheless, two respondents said east represents grief to them.

South

The survey participants said when their bedroom faces south, or when they go to south, they see bright (5 responses) sunshine/sunlight (8) and greeneries (4), they would feel happy (20), warm (10), positive (2), excited (2), peaceful (2), relaxed (2), or comfortable (2). However, six of them associated south with grief or feeling down.

West

The survey informants expressed that if the orientation of their bedroom faces west, when they see the sunset (10 responses) in the afternoon, they would feel happy (4), as their home would be full of life (3) or love (3). While others contended that west orientation conveys the end of a day that makes them feel depressed (3), hot (3), or uncomfortable (2). Still others associated west with freedom (2) or openness (2).

North

The survey respondents revealed that if they go to north, seeing leafless trees and dried grass, they would feel cold (13 responses), depressed (7), dark (5), grief (4), wintery (3), lazy (2), or lonely (2). Others associated north with happiness (3) or positive emotions (3) because north arrow is usually pointing upwards (2) that represents looking up and anticipating good things to come (2). North to some is also associated with solitude and reflection (2).

Feng Shui and Orientation

Four of 264 (2 percent) survey respondents mentioned *Feng Shui*, and contended that each person's birth year, month, and date have special orientations that would give them happiness, love, and energy; certain direction they sit at work or sleep at night has an effect on them. Generally, a person's environment has influences on how s/he feels. For example, living on a street without greeneries may make one feel down, whereas on a street with beautiful sceneries may make one feel happy. The sun is also the basis of human physical orientation. When people face the sun and bathe in its warmth, they would feel happy. A medical student from the University of Toronto speculated that just like how electricity affects the nervous system, the neurons, and neurotransmitters, the earth's magnetic field may have an effect on human central nervous system and their emotions. With the huge magnetic field surrounding the earth, people may feel something when synaptic charges communicate with the brains.

Nevertheless, 51 percent of 264 survey respondents assumed *no* correlation between emotion and orientation. Four of them argued that it is based on individual interpretations and their life experiences, while three others held that it is derived from nature or geography rather than emotion.

FLOOR LEVELS

The surveyed ethnic Chinese residents in North America considered the ground/ first floor (52 percent; n = 190) would promote physical health, followed by second floor (38 percent), and third floor (17 percent). Rooftop (10 percent) and basement (6 percent) are less favorable for health. These findings to a large extent are coherent with my previous research findings in China (see Zhang, 2013).

The interview results confirm the survey findings, as 17 of 37 (46 percent) interviewees considered the first floor as conducive to their physical health. They argued that the first floor is safe and convenient to get in and out for many physical activities. Children and seniors are especially suitable to live on the first floor to avoid the danger of getting up and down the stairs. The first floor has more space and easy access to the kitchen and main activity areas to make them feel relaxed. The first floor is close to the earth and greeneries that are refreshing and good for the eyes. The first floor is also better sheltered from the rooftop, which can be hot in the summer and cold in the winter.

Nonetheless, 9 of 37 (24 percent) interviewees thought that the second floor would promote physical health because walking up and down the stairs is a good exercise that helps keep them fit. The second floor does not have as much moisture as the first floor, the air is fresher, and it is quieter and less associated with traffic, noise, or pollution from the streets. It provides a sense of security without feeling constrained. These factors may help prevent diseases.

Five of 37 (14 percent) interviewees argued that the third floor is beneficial to physical health, and three respondents indicated the fourth floor or above. They maintained that the third floor can receive plenty of sunlight and avoid moisture.

Meanwhile, mosquitoes and bugs are relatively fewer than in the lower levels. The third or fourth floor stairways also give them a fair amount of physical exercise.

Six of 37 (16 percent) interviewees had no preference for floor levels. They contended that any floor would help with physical health as long as it is readily accessible. They argued that the higher the floor level, the better it is for physical health because of cleaner air and less dust. They further maintained that the factors affecting people's mental and physical health lie in their psyche. Ideally, all floors including basement, should be bright and spacious with free airflow. Basement overall is less desirable because of a lack of sunlight, inferior air quality, humidity, and cold in winter if thermal insulation is not properly installed. The floor to ceiling height is better to be 2.8 m–3 m to allow enough sunlight and fresh air to come in to promote physical health.

First Floor Open Plan

Twenty-four of 36 (67 percent) interviewees preferred an open plan for the ground/ first floor. They observed that an open plan with more windows is good for sunlight and air circulation; it gives the illusion of a bigger space that looks brighter and better. Since they use the kitchen often, an open plan would offer a bigger kitchen for cooking and gatherings. An open plan would also make one feel less crowded or constrained so that the body can move more freely and feel more relaxed and comfortable. As well, it provides more room for decorations and distant views to the outside. Nonetheless, household appliances and furniture are still necessary. Hypothetically, any floor with a small space and a narrow hallway used by everyone in the household is beneficial to have an open plan to promote more air flow and physical activities.

Three of 36 (8 percent) interviewed respondents favored a semi-open plan to have at least the kitchen separate from the rest of the rooms so that the cooking smell from it will not penetrate everywhere in the home.

Five of 36 (14 percent) interviewees disliked an open plan because it is not good for sound or thermal insulation. They preferred having walls or screens to separate individual rooms.

FURNITURE STYLES AND MATERIALS

The interior furniture styles of ethnic Chinese in North America are varied, with mixed style (41 percent; n = 190) being the most common, followed by modern Western style (36 percent), classical Western style (10 percent), modern Chinese style (9.5 percent), and classical Chinese style (6 percent). Some also mentioned Japanese style. However, 21 percent indicated their furniture had no discernible style, possibly because many of them were students living in lodgings or dormitories, with furniture readily provided.

Wood has been their most common furniture material (88 percent; n = 185), followed by synthetic material (31 percent), glass (23 percent), metal (20 percent), untreated cotton (9 percent), bamboo (6 percent), and cane (4 percent). Leather was not listed as a choice in the survey, but it was mentioned by some respondents.

To promote physical health, wood (92 percent; n = 176) is also their ideal furniture material, followed by bamboo (38 percent), glass (22 percent), metal (14 percent), untreated cotton (14 percent), cane (11 percent), and synthetic material (9 percent). Note synthetic material is their least favored but second most common in their homes. Bamboo is rarely used as a furniture material in North America, but the surveyed ethnic Chinese respondents would like to have bamboo furniture because it is natural and durable and is embedded with Chinese cultural connotations of being upright.

FACILITY PROVISION

The facilities in their homes to promote physical health include: clean running water (82 percent; n = 187), electricity (65 percent), heating system (65 percent), air conditioner (64 percent), smoke detectors (63 percent), green plants (62 percent), carbon monoxide detectors (52 percent), water purification system (51 percent), air humidifier (49 percent), gas (48 percent), Internet cable/digital subscriber line (41 percent), telephone line (34 percent), solar panel (32 percent), television cable (30 percent), swimming pool (24 percent), energy recovery ventilators (24 percent), heat recovery ventilators (23 percent), and whirlpool bathtub/Jacuzzi (22.5 percent). In addition, solar attic fan with remote on–off switch and a built-in gym were sensible suggestions made by some survey participants (Table 4.3).

The result shows that conventional facilities such as running water and electricity are still crucial to have. An Internet cable/digital subscriber line is now considered more necessary than a telephone line or television cable. Green plants are found more important than gas because they emit fresh air conducive to physical health. Solar panels are also in good demand. These findings reveal that although technology has made significant changes to people's lives, incorporating nature into housing design will benefit occupants' health in sustainable ways.

CONSTRUCTION QUALITY

The construction quality of ethnic Chinese housing in North America is generally good (42 percent; n = 187), one third said OK (33 percent), and nearly a quarter said very good (24 percent). Only one percent felt their homes were badly constructed and 0.5 percent thought it was very badly constructed. This finding makes a stark contrast with my previous research findings in China that construction quality was a major issue of the renewed and new courtyard housing in Beijing (see Zhang, 2013).

Construction quality has been considered as paramount important as no matter how well a building was designed, the final product is ultimately judged by the quality of its construction. Moreover, a well-constructed building will last longer and is more economically sustainable, which may also contribute to environmental health. Therefore, construction quality is not a trivial matter to be underestimated.

Table 4.3   Facility provision at home to promote health

Facility provision	Percentage (n = 187)
1. Clean running water	82 %
2. Electricity	65 %
2. Heating system	65 %
3. Air conditioner	64 %
4. Smoke detectors	63 %
5. Green plants	62 %
6. Carbon monoxide detectors	52 %
7. Water purification system	51 %
8. Air humidifier	49 %
9. Gas	48 %
10. Internet cable/digital subscriber line	41 %
11. Telephone line	34 %
12. Solar panel	32 %
13. Television cable	30 %
14. Swimming pool	24 %
14. Energy recovery ventilators	24 %
15. Heat recovery ventilators	23 %
16. Whirlpool bathtub/Jacuzzi	22.5 %
17. Other	
Solar attic fan with remote on–off switch, built-in gym	

Note: My survey results; several elements received the same number of responses and therefore have the same order number.

MAINTENANCE AND MANAGEMENT

The survey respondents indicated that on an average, they renovated their homes once every six years (n = 139), and that their property managements of the apartments renovated their buildings once every four years (n = 115). They considered the renovation should occur at least once every five years (n = 141), which is very close to what they have already had. When rating the quality of maintenance work conducted by their property managements, the respondents thought it was good (28 percent; n = 169), or OK (26 percent), or very good (14 percent). Very few of them found the quality of maintenance work bad (2 percent) or very bad (1 percent). Although the interview questions did not specifically seek their opinions on their home construction quality or maintenance work done, there has been no complaint about it. These findings make a stark contrast with those in Beijing (see Zhang, 2013).

Well-maintained buildings may contribute to occupants' perceptions of healthy homes, as the study finds that the majority of the survey respondents felt their homes healthy (46 percent; n = 178), one-third somewhat healthy (33 percent), and slightly over one-fifth very healthy (21 percent). Only 0.6 percent thought their homes unhealthy or very unhealthy.

CAR PARK SPACES

The majority of the survey respondents preferred two car park spaces (43 percent; n = 179) at home, only a small number of them desired three car park spaces (15 percent), four car park spaces (13 percent), or one car park space (12 percent), although some (4 percent) did not want car park space at all, while a few others wanted as many as 6–8 car park spaces. Nevertheless, in North American suburban single-family homes, two-car garages are the norm, with occasional three-car garages, and these provisions seem to be adequate for most residents. Less car dependency will promote more walking that may contribute to better physical health of the occupants.

SUMMARY AND CONCLUSION

This chapter presented and analyzed the empirical findings on the space and construction quality of ethnic Chinese housing in North America. The findings reveal that their living conditions are generally good, and that their preferred interior space is 195 sqm (2,093 sqf) for a 3–4-person household with good sunlight and natural ventilation to help gather *qi*.

Interior colors also affect occupants' happiness. Earlier unpublished findings by the author show that yellow, green, red, and blue are colors for happiness; whereas grey, black, and blue are colors for grief. It has been noted that the color blue denotes happiness for some but grief for others, suggesting diversity in color interpretations. These findings have implications for interior wall decorations.

To promote health, ethnic Chinese in North America predominantly preferred to live on the ground/first floor, and this result complies with my previous findings in China (see Zhang, 2013), as well as traditional Chinese courtyard living. Open plan for the ground/first floor was also highly favored by most interviewees for better sunlight, air circulation, and daily activities. A courtyard may help achieve all of this.

The interior furniture styles of the ethnic Chinese in North America were varied, with mixed style being the most common. The construction quality of their homes is generally good or very good, which makes a stark contrast with that found in Beijing (see Zhang, 2013). The study has also found that the perceived appropriate time span for conducting maintenance work for a home is once every five years, and a two-car garage for a household is most needed.

Table 4.4   Summary of ethnic Chinese preferences for the space of the housing

Spatial features	Preference (n = 360)
Interior space	50–60 sqm per person, or 195 sqm (2,093 sqf) for a 3–4 person household (n = 24)
Interior colors	Yellow, green, red, and blue are colors for happiness (n = 264)
Floor levels	Ground/first floor with an open plan is most preferred to promote physical health
Furniture styles and materials	Mixed styles and wood is most preferred
Facility provision	Running water and electricity are basic, Internet cable is more important than telephone line or television cable
Construction quality	Generally good
Maintenance and management	Once every 5 years is required
Car park spaces	2-car park spaces per household is mostly desired

Source: My summary.

In Chapter 5 that follows, the social aspect of ethnic Chinese residents in North America will be explored, to see whether the housing in which they live helps with their social relations.

5

Happiness as Attaining Oneness:
Matters of Social Cohesion in the Homes

Those that attained oneness since ancient times:
The sky attained oneness and thus clarity
The earth attained oneness and thus tranquility
The gods attained oneness and thus divinity
The valley attained oneness and thus abundance
The myriad things attained oneness and thus life

Laozi, c. 571–471 BCE, *Dao De Jing*, Verse 39

This chapter examines the social aspect of housing in North America based on the empirical findings. In particular, it seeks to find out what elements, if any, in residential environment facilitate social cohesion and help attain social unity or "oneness." As such, the chapter consists of four sections: education, occupation, and house-purchasing power; social relations with neighbors; marriage/wedding ceremonies/anniversaries; and relations among family members.

EDUCATION, OCCUPATION, AND HOUSE-PURCHASING POWER

The ethnic Chinese survey respondents in North America are highly educated: 88 percent (n = 175) of them have a bachelor's degree, 56 percent have obtained a master's degree, and 26 percent have achieved a doctorate or professional degree. Their high educational profiles could indicate good quality data input.

Although this study was unable to generate a correlation analysis on happiness and education, a research conducted by the Pew Research Center (2006, p. 8) suggests that people with university degrees are happier than those without.

The survey respondents' occupational profiles reflect their high educational profiles as most of them are professionals (53 percent; n = 175) or students (29 percent), although some are technicians and associate professionals (9 percent). A few of them are legislators, senior officials, and managers (3 percent), as well as elementary occupations (1 percent).

These findings somewhat echo the US Census Bureau (2000a) that 48 percent of Chinese-Americans have a bachelor's degree or higher, compared with 24 percent for the total US population; and 52 percent of Chinese-Americans are represented in professional and managerial occupations, compared with 21 percent of Caucasians. The 2001 Census of Canada likewise shows that 27 percent of Canadians of Chinese origin (aged 15 and over) had either a bachelor's degree or higher, compared with 15 percent of the overall Canadian adult population; 7 percent of Chinese-Canadians had a master's degree and nine percent had a doctorate (Lindsay, 2001, pp. 13–14).

Most of the survey participants are employed full-time (61 percent; n = 175), much less part-time (13 percent), unemployed (12 percent), or self-employed (9 percent), and only a small number of them are retired (5 percent). The findings from the Pew Research Center (2006) reveal that retirees and employed are equally likely to be "very happy," and both are happier than those who are unemployed. They also found a significant gender variance among those who are unemployed: women are more likely than men to report being very happy—maybe because for women more than men, not working outside the home is a matter of choice (p. 8).

The ethnic Chinese participants' annual income levels are roughly distributed in four groups: 24 percent (n = 173) are below $30,000; 17 percent between $30,000 and $50,000; 25 percent between $50,000 and $100,000; and 24 percent above $100,000. Those reported having no incomes are likely to be students (10 percent).

More surveyed ethnic Chinese in North America own their homes (58 percent; n = 174) than those who rent it (41 percent). Some others indicated that they live with their parents or family members who own it. Existing literature supports the finding that Chinese-Americans have a higher homeownership rate than the national average. In 2003, the University of Southern California's Lusk Center found that when comparing homeowners with similar income levels in Los Angeles, the Chinese-American homeownership rate is 20 percent higher than Caucasians; in San Francisco, 23 percent higher; and in the New York metropolitan area, 18 percent higher (Dooley, 2003). Likewise, the Asian Real Estate Association of America reported that Chinese-Americans living in the states of Texas, New York, and California all have significantly higher homeownership rates than the national average (Cruz-Viesca and Chiu, 2008).

This result is likely due to the fact that most ethnic Chinese coming to North America in recent decades are top students from Chinese universities who stayed after their graduation from North American universities. This sample population does not represent the average level of the Chinese nation.

SOCIAL RELATIONS WITH NEIGHBORS

Regarding the quality of social interaction between ethnic Chinese and their neighbors in North America, "good" (35 percent; n = 177) and "very good" (19 percent) added together counts for 54 percent of the survey respondents. The interview results also show that 15 of 37 (41 percent) participants have "good" or "very good" social interaction with their neighbors. For those living in single-detached houses, their communications typically occur with the two next-door neighbors, and the neighbor on the other side of the back yard fence.

However, they said the back yard fences hinder neighborly interaction; if there is no fence, it will be easier for them to approach and chat. This finding confirms that of Montgomery (2013, pp. 9, 143, 317). Three of 37 interviewees mentioned that their neighborly relationships are harmonious, but it takes time and efforts to build a deeper one. They felt that if there is a communal courtyard, it will help establish better neighborly relations.

5.1   Back yard fences hinder neighborly interaction, Richmond Hill, Ontario, Canada
Source: Photo by Donia Zhang, 2013.

Montgomery (2013, pp. 38, 41) likewise argued that our trust in neighbors and even total strangers has a big influence on happiness; no matter how much we cherish privacy and solitude, strong and positive relationships are the basis of happiness. Other studies have shown that people who have more types of positive social interactions have better health outcomes, fewer emergency room visits, and fewer and less severe upper-respiratory infections (Sternberg, 2009, pp. 213, 230). Conversely, isolation and lack of social support amplify the risk of depression (Sternberg, 2009, p. 267). A study by Independent Age shows that severe loneliness in England ruins the lives of 700,000 men and 1.1 million women over 50, and this number is rising with astonishing speed. Social isolation is as compelling a cause of early death as smoking 15 cigarettes a day; loneliness is twice as fatal as obesity (Monbiot, 2014).

For detached-house residents, front yards/gardens (42 percent; n = 172) and back yards/gardens (25 percent) are reported as their major places of social interaction. In another study about the way Danish and Canadian people behave in their front yards, Jan Gehl discovered that residents talked most with passersby when the yards are at 3.23 m (10.6 ft) deep to allow for conversation and retreat (Montgomery, 2013, p. 133).

Some respondents indicated the front porch is where they have eye contact with passersby. The garage has been reported as another meeting place for neighbors to sit and discuss things like house repairs, and so on. Moreover, gardening and back yard barbecue facilitate casual communication. For example, the neighbors can share knowledge about how to plant or grow things in the yard. Good neighborly relations are sometimes reflected in situations when a family goes on vacation, their neighbor looks after and waters their plants in the back yard and helps collect their mail, newspapers, and flyers on their driveway.

Compared with detached houses, some respondents felt that row/town houses have allowed the children to play together more easily and the parents to communicate with each other more easily. Whereas others argued that apartment buildings' foyer/lobby/hallway, meeting/common room, laundry room, elevator, corridor, patio, gym, swimming pool, and pedestrian walkway, are the spaces where neighbors can interact and cultivate face-to-face interactions.

Other spaces helping with social interaction include: community/city park/garden (38 percent; n = 172), community center (29 percent), street/lane (23 percent), schoolyard (23 percent), public library (23 percent), health center (20 percent), grocery/food store (16 percent), local café/restaurant (16 percent), shopping mall (13 percent), courtyard/garden (9 percent), farmers market (8 percent), balcony/deck (7 percent), and roof terrace/garden (5 percent).

Because courtyard housing is rare in North America, courtyard did not receive a high score on helping with social interaction. Nevertheless, my interviews with non-Chinese living in co-operative housing and cohousing in Canada indicate that communal courtyards indeed facilitate social relations among neighbors.

The survey findings show that 32 percent (n = 177) of the respondents whose social interaction with their neighbors is "OK," and 7 of 37 (19 percent) interviewees have *some* interaction with their neighbors. They normally exchange greetings when meeting on the sidewalk, but are not particularly close (it will depend on the character of the neighbor as well).

Only 10 percent (n = 177) of the survey respondents have "no interaction" with their neighbors. However, the interview results reveal a much higher rate of 15 of 37 (41 percent) participants who have *no* interaction or *very little* interaction with their neighbors.[1] They indicated that this situation is due to the fact that everybody is busy with their work, and that they like to keep to themselves. There is also a lack of space for social interaction. A Chinese-American living in Florida observed that, unlike the Chinese who always perform dances with neighbors in city/street parks/gardens, the Americans do not conduct social activities outdoors. If they do interact, it is usually in the lobby or hallway of an apartment building, with a couple of simple greetings.

---

[1]   This discrepancy may be that the ones who agreed to participate in the interviews were more "introverted" people, or who saw more need of the study to help increase their social interaction.

A respondent commented: "For people with religious beliefs, they celebrate religious festivals [with their group] in addition to the Chinese festivals." My conversation with an elderly Russian man who had lived in a semi-detached house in Richmond Hill, Ontario, Canada for 14 years told that he got along very well with his next-door neighbor who was an elderly woman living by herself because her children had grown up and left home. He sometimes invited her over for a barbecue on his balcony. However, he did not socialize with other neighbors on the same street, only nodding his head when seeing them passing by. He said he had harmonious social relations with ethnic Chinese residents in the neighborhood that moved away, but he had problems with newer neighbors who belonged to a particular religious group. He found that people from different religious backgrounds might generate disharmony, and that the issue is not privacy but community.

Happiness and Unhappiness in Communal Courtyards

There were 20 non-Chinese residents from three co-operative housing in Toronto and three cohousing across Canada (two in British Columbia and one in Saskatchewan) who participated in my interviews. Their input reveals the things that make them happy and unhappy in the communal courtyards as follows.

Courtyards as Children's Playgrounds
Away from traffic, the courtyards between buildings are safe spaces for children to play together, which is a big benefit for their social development, particularly if it is the only child at home. When the children are playing in the courtyard, they are visible from indoors at all times so that adults can watch over them from time to time, which makes housework and other indoor tasks possible. Whereas for the children, being able to play outside without adults gives them a sense of independence as they can explore the world within the safety of the community. For the courtyard residents, coming home in the summer and seeing the children running through the sprinklers, riding their bikes, and the parents chatting in the courtyard, is a happy experience. Several of them mentioned that they are happy when hearing the sound of children playing in the courtyard.

From talking to parents, it appeared that the children living in communal courtyards spend more time playing outdoors than those who do not have a communal courtyard. Montgomery (2013, p. 188) likewise noted that in an American community, nearly two-thirds of the parents say that there is no place for their children to play within walking distance of their homes, and this is part of the reason that American children are now gaining more weight, leading to obesity.

At another co-operative housing in Toronto where the courtyard is locked from the outside with a pass card, strangers cannot easily wander in, which allows for a greater sense of security for children to play in it. Parents are always nearby, but they do not need to be quite as attentive, knowing that the children are safe, and that there are always adults around who can help if there is any problem arising.

5.2   Children watching a puppet show at Bain Apartments Co-operative North Maples courtyard, Toronto, Ontario, Canada
Source: Photo by Donia Zhang, 2013.

However, some residents complained about people who run daycares out of their units taking over the courtyard regularly with many little children who tear at the plants or eliminate the possibility of a quiet read in the courtyard. Occasionally, the noise from a courtyard gathering or children's riding toys disturbs activities in the surrounding homes. There is also a grievance about bossy neighbors who want to control everything in the courtyard, yelling at the children from their windows.

Courtyards as Landscaped Gardens
The Bain Apartments Co-operative in east Toronto has 26 buildings, of which only a few front onto the street, all the rest face each other across nine semi-enclosed landscaped courtyards that are secluded without being isolated, where residents can enjoy the sunshine in them. The stoops provide a transitional space between private and shared spaces: one can sit out and talk to neighbors and passersby. The residents also have private outdoor spaces overlooking the courtyard, where they can be observers and participants at the same time. The narrow laneways between the buildings create another layer of community. Each household has its own little vegetable patch, where they can do gardening and harvesting together. The green plants and flowers are not only pleasant to look at, some are also edible.

5.3   Courtyard as landscaped garden at Bain Apartments Co-operative
North Maples courtyard, Toronto, Ontario, Canada
Source: Photo by Donia Zhang, 2013.

5.4   Courtyard as landscaped garden at Church-Isabella Residence Co-operative, Toronto, Ontario, Canada
Source: Photo by Donia Zhang, 2013.

The dwellers are both market renters and subsidy-receivers; many have lived there all their lives who take pride in the courtyard surroundings. There is an excellent mix of the built environment with green space for relaxation, which is essential for a healthy lifestyle.

Three residents at Church-Isabella Residence Co-operative in downtown Toronto commented that their bedrooms on the second floor with French doors overlooking the courtyard offer an excellent view and a lovely breeze from the trees and grass that is good for their psyche. Meanwhile, they love the fact that they also have private outdoor spaces where they can relax, enjoy, and interact with others.

The landscape design of the communal courtyards is central to community health and development. Design considerations should come before financial ones because they are vitally important. Some co-operative housing residents suggested reorganizing their courtyard space so that it is truly communal. For instance, have some tables and chairs on a patio for a comfortable visit, or even have an umbrella for sunshade. Better outdoor lighting is also essential so that it will not be too bright when raising their heads to see the night sky while walking around the area. A bib tap for watering the plants is also needed.

Courtyards as Social Spaces
The interviewed residents at co-operative housing and cohousing in Canada felt that living in a communal courtyard strengthens neighborly relations as when they step out their doors, they see a neighbor who is willing to lend a hand, and often there are boxes of vegetables straight from the garden to give to neighbors. The courtyards create a sense of community and encourage interaction among neighbors as people hang out in the courtyards to chat or eat together. Adults not only have immediate friends to talk to, but also share responsibilities with, such as lawn mowing, raking leaves, and shoveling snow, usually on a goodwill, but sometimes as an organized effort resulting from courtyard meetings. When taking a walk around the courtyards, one can see many smiley faces.

At Bain Apartments Co-operative in east Toronto, there is a spirited range of respectful activities to participate in the courtyards, from people watching to stargazing. The courtyards are big enough to find one's own corner, and are ready for potlucks, sales, get-togethers, and "crafternoons."[2] An understanding among the neighbors is that no matter who they are, they deserve respect in the courtyards.

At Bain communal courtyards, the residents have an immediate access to tools and knowledge, and a share of peoples' interests and expertise, such as dog care, childrearing, or health concerns. It is a relaxed space where the residents all learn to live with one another, a remedy to a sense of isolation or loneliness in an increasingly individualistic society. The residents know their neighbors; they plan and work together, share potluck suppers, or hold barbecue parties in the courtyards. Having many friendly neighbors, they have less concern for self or home security.

---

[2]   Crafternoon is a word invented by the residents at Bain Apartments Co-operative, denoting afternoons when they get together with neighbors to do crafts—sewing, quilting, mask making, papier-mâché, puppet making, etc.

At Church-Isabella Residence Co-operative in downtown Toronto, the communal courtyard is where they hold spring and autumn parties, clean up after winter and prepare for the spring to come, read a book on a summer afternoon, and have barbecues and meals with their families, friends, and neighbors in the summer. The courtyard creates a possibility of spontaneous social interaction and builds and sustains the community.

At Cranberry Commons Cohousing in British Columbia, a resident noted that her community members would like to sit in the courtyard and talk with people, while others enjoy bringing their guitar and play music in the courtyard on summer days.

At WindSong Cohousing Community in British Columbia, a resident appreciated the opportunities offered by the communal courtyard for brief encounters with people who were not particularly friends or ordinarily sought to have a visit with; thereby the courtyard helped strengthen the community ties. She also liked the spontaneous interactions with neighbors and the informal social encounters combining meetings with tea drinking.

At Wolf Willow Cohousing in Saskatchewan, two residents observed that their community members love the natural way they use the courtyard. They would meet spontaneously in the courtyard at various times of day when the weather permitted: coffee in the morning, cocktails or planned barbecues in the early

5.5 Courtyard as social space at Bain Apartments Co-operative North Oaks courtyard, Toronto, Ontario, Canada
Source: Photo by Donia Zhang, 2013.

evening, or just when they were watering the plants. All these events made them happy to be part of the community.

In another co-operative housing in Toronto, however, there was little use of the communal courtyard at the time of the research (2013). Earlier on, the residents could sit around the picnic table, having picnics or wine in the evenings, and the members whose windows face the courtyard were relaxed about the noise. Some residents said they would like to return to those days and wished that the community uses the courtyard more often to keep it active by inviting all members to participate in social events, both casual and yard-work oriented, because the more they use the courtyard, the better it becomes. This would require frequent organized activities by the co-operative management.

Co-operative Property Management

The co-operative management principles of democratic control by all the members have been a contributing factor to residents' happiness, because they are able to participate as volunteers in running the co-operative, and work together to create and sustain a safe and healthy place to live. The co-operative membership is open to all who accept the responsibilities of living by the co-operative principles, each member has a vote, and all members have an equal say in managing the co-operative. They set bylaws and policies, make decisions and elect leaders who report to them.

The co-operative housing creates a layered community. The residents belong to a courtyard, to a laneway, to the co-operative as a whole, and to various informal groups. The property and the buildings are owned by a non-profit organization, which is made up of all the members who currently live there. They collectively operate the property and are heavily involved in the maintenance work. They like the fact that the courtyard has been a unifying force on multiple levels.

However, some issues were raised by the residents that they required better co-operative policies and occupancy bylaws. Although tolerance is a good quality for communal living, it is sometimes necessary to discipline bad behaviors. For example, prohibit teenagers making loud noise in the communal courtyard after 10 pm. On the other hand, the policies should also encourage residents to use the courtyard properly rather than restricting their activities such as barbecuing or gathering in it. Otherwise, they would feel intimidated to use the courtyard. Some residents complained about smokers smoking too close to the ground-floor windows facing the courtyard, while others lamented about teenage girls going naked in the mini pool in the beginning of summer. There were also occasions when female members felt uncomfortable walking by some males in the courtyard who were making inappropriate comments about them. Additionally, there is an issue of too many dogs urinating in the courtyard that damages the grass.

The residents wished to establish well-stated rules for the communal courtyard, such as quiet times, the kind of toys that can be used, the type of furniture or decorations that can be kept, a budget for furniture and decorations, and responsibility for cleaning the courtyard. Dog owners should pick up dog feces, or no dogs allowed in the courtyard. To reduce noise, some residents suggested purchasing riding toys with rubber wheels, and putting a limit on the use of courtyard as daycare or children's playground as they can go to a nearby park to do so. Moreover, children should learn to respect their neighbors by not yelling.

Differences in Lifestyles

Sharing a communal courtyard has always been a challenge because people have different lifestyles. It is also related to intra-class differences in life. Learning to share a common space involves learning to accept noisier families, or families with diverse values that may not be in the everyday social sphere. This creates the opportunity to learn to set healthy boundaries, as well as open our minds to all kinds of differences.

Unwanted noise from neighbors has been an issue. Occasionally people get drunk in the courtyard late at night and make too much noise, disrupting and disrespecting other courtyard members. There is also sound transmission through the floors and walls that can be challenging if neighbors are loud. Sometimes a neighbor plays loud music (although that can happen in any high-density housing); other times parents let their children rule the courtyard, yelling and crying loudly. These are the unhappy things in the communal courtyards that residents at co-operative housing or cohousing complained about.

Lack of Private Back Yards

There was a criticism about the lack of privacy or personal space in the communal courtyards, as the residents said they had to be dressed for public in order to use the courtyard. Some residents regarded the communal courtyard as their private space and occasionally gathered a group of people outside their window for barbecue, but not everyone felt welcome to join.

Although many residents expressed they would like to raise their children in a communal courtyard because of the benefits of having private home within a shared outdoor space, some of them still wanted to increase their privacy by having an individual outdoor space, such as a small private back yard for every household, in addition to the communal courtyard. This improvement needs a creative solution to making people aware of the meaning of personal boundaries.

While others complained about some neighbors who did not understand boundaries would come over and talk their head off while they were reading a book. They suggested that higher and more robust fences within the city bylaws are needed to maximum privacy. Still others disapproved walking into the courtyard and having someone approach to them about volunteering for something or work that they would not want to do. Some participants felt obligated to participate in communal activities such as fall cleanup, shoveling snow, or courtyard meetings, when it was inconvenient for them to do so, or when they were having more of an indoor day.

Lack of Volunteerism and Neighbor Conflicts

Some things that have contributed to residents' unhappiness at co-operative housing are not related to the courtyard, but to the co-operative management. The co-operative members found that it has been difficult to get residents to attend committee meetings, and the same people volunteered for committees over and over again, while others would not volunteer at all. Some conflicts arose from people who had lived there many years and did not think things were done properly, they complained at meetings instead of actually getting involved. Not enough community resources had been put into conflict resolution and there was often not enough buy-in by the parties in conflict to resolve their issues. This reflects the wider cultural norms of Western society that emphasizes individualism and consumerism as primary values that undermine any adherence to co-operative values of sharing voluntarily and democratic control. The courtyards foster, but do not create, community; and they cannot prevent breakdowns in civility.

Improvements are difficult in a cultural climate where co-operative principles are not always valued. They are often paid lip service to, without enough financial support to provide adequate training to either staff or members. At best, people are often given the co-operative principles on paper or online, and then are told to follow them without any ongoing training on what they really mean because this is considered the responsibility of volunteers to implement, which can be faulty given the ups and downs of available volunteer time. It is therefore important to have good leadership among the residents, such as a good courtyard representative and many volunteer helpers. Every resident should pull together and put in volunteer effort to make their co-operative a better place.

MARRIAGE/WEDDING CEREMONIES/ANNIVERSARIES

Of the four ethnic Chinese weddings that the author attended in Toronto in 20 years (1995–2015), two took their vows in a marriage chamber of a town hall directed by a clerk, and the other two took their vows in a restaurant garden. In all cases, the wedding reception was held in a Chinese restaurant.

If a communal courtyard were available, it could be a convenient and inexpensive place to hold a marriage ceremony. For example, at Bain Apartments Co-operative in east Toronto, a resident revealed that a wedding took place at the Cedar Courtyard in 2012. At the Courtyard Housing Co-operative in midtown Toronto, the property manager mentioned that a wedding reception was held in the communal courtyard in 1993. At Church-Isabella Residence Co-operative, some of the members also chose to hold their weddings in the communal courtyard. It is anticipated that the communal courtyard could also assist neighbors to find love, as a resident at Bain Apartments Co-operative frankly said that she wished a handsome old man could move into the unit beneath her, and that they would fall madly in love and move into a two-bedroom unit above.

More than half of the surveyed ethnic Chinese were in their first marriage (54 percent; n = 171), over one third never married (36 percent), and only a few remarried (5 percent) or living common law (4 percent), whereas divorced or separated (1 percent), or widowed (0.6 percent) are rare. This finding reveals a highly successful marriage rate among ethnic Chinese in North America. Of those reported being married, intra-ethnic marriages are the most common (54 percent; n = 167), inter-racial marriages are much less (8 percent), and inter-ethnic marriages are unusual (4 percent).

These outcomes confirm the 2001 Census of Canada that Canadians of Chinese origin are more likely than other Canadians to be married. In 2001, 56 percent of ethnic Chinese aged 15 and over were married, compared with 50 percent of all Canadian adults. In contrast, people of Chinese origin are less likely to live in a common-law relationship. In 2001, only two percent of adults of Chinese origin were living common-law, compared with 10 percent of all Canadian adults (Lindsay, 2001, p. 13).

Previous research findings further reveal that married couples are happier than singles.[3] Other studies then find that married couples without children are happier than singles, single parents, or couples with children.[4] Therefore, children may not be a source of a couple's happiness, perhaps due to the laborious efforts in bringing them up, which is especially difficult for a couple without other family members' help, unlike in the past when extended family members lived together who could offer support in time of need to look after the children (Nias, 2001a). Theuns et al.'s (2010) findings show that relationship with a partner is weighted the most important, followed by relationships with friends and parents, respectively.

Although wedding anniversary celebration is a Western tradition, 44 percent (n = 169) of the surveyed ethnic Chinese respondents, and 18 of 25 (72 percent) ethnic Chinese interviewees, celebrated their wedding anniversaries. Twelve of 25 (48 percent) celebrated their wedding anniversaries with a restaurant meal, preceded by opening presents at home, or party in house occasionally.

Six of 25 (24 percent) Chinese interviewees celebrated their wedding anniversaries at home by cooking delicious food or eating a cake. Some only celebrated their major (5th, 10th, 15th, 20th, and 25th) wedding anniversaries. One participant revealed that they celebrated their 50th Gold Wedding Anniversary by making a picture frame for display at home. Another respondent said on their wedding anniversaries, her husband would give her $100 as a gift because money is more practical than souvenirs. Three participants had their wedding anniversary celebrations in a public place, or in boat cruise, or travel to regional scenic spots.

Regarding their mental health status, the majority of the Chinese participants reported as being "very healthy" (46 percent; n = 174) and "healthy" (43 percent), and "somewhat healthy" (11 percent) counts much less. Concerning their physical health status, more than half of them felt "healthy" (51 percent; n = 172) and "very healthy" (34 percent), and the "somewhat healthy" (14 percent) group is much less, only a few reported as being "unhealthy" (1 percent). Thus the ethnic Chinese participants perceived themselves having slightly better mental health

---

3   Bergsma, Poot, and Liefbroer, 2008; Frey and Stutzer, 2000; Nias, 2001a; Pew Research Center, 2006.

4   Frey and Stutzer, 2000; Nias, 2001a, p. 199.

than physical health. Most of the survey respondents are "happy" (46 percent; n = 176) or "very happy" (38 percent) about their homes, only a minority of them chose "somewhat happy" (15 percent) or "unhappy" (2 percent).

The Pearson Correlation shows a high, positive correlation between respondents' mental health status and their happiness about their homes (r = 0.582; n = 174; $p < 0.000$). Moreover, the Pearson Correlation shows a moderate, positive correlation between residents' physical health status and their happiness about their homes (r = 0.415; n = 172; $p < 0.000$).

Regarding the relationship between one's mental health and their happiness about his/her home, an interview respondent made a sensible comment:

> Sometimes, to improve physical health, one must first acquire a strong, healthy mental state. A person could have the biggest, most beautiful dream house, but if the person/owner does not feel a connection or attachment to it, a house contributes little to one's health.

RELATIONS AMONG FAMILY MEMBERS

The average surveyed Chinese household size in North America is 3.04 persons (n = 192), which is slightly lower than the finding of 3.2 persons by the US Census Bureau (2008) in the three states of California, New York, and Texas. This result implies a decline in ethnic Chinese household size in North America. Nevertheless, 3.04 persons per Chinese household is still higher than the average American household size of 2.58 persons in the 2010 Census (US Census Bureau, 2012), and also higher than the average Canadian household size of 2.5 persons in the 2011 Census (Statistics Canada, 2013). This outcome indicates that ethnic Chinese are still more family-oriented than the average North Americans.

Of the surveyed ethnic Chinese, one generation (50 percent; n = 173) and two generations (40 percent) of family members living in the same household are the most common, three generations is uncommon (9 percent). This result demonstrates that nuclear family structure is prevailing among them.

The 2001 Census of Canada shows that seniors of Chinese origin are more likely than other seniors to live with members of their extended family. In 2001, 16 percent of seniors of Chinese origin lived with the family of a son or daughter, while only five percent of all Canadian seniors did so, and 24 percent of Canadians of Chinese origin had children living at home, compared with 16 percent of the total Canadian population (Lindsay, 2001, p. 13). The 2002 Ethnic Diversity Survey reveals that 98 percent of Chinese immigrants' children lived with both parents until the age of 15 (Statistics Canada, 2008). The lack of English proficiency for many Chinese seniors in North America could be one reason for them to live with their children, and cultural tradition may certainly be another.

The surveyed ethnic Chinese or their ancestors mainly came from mainland China (78 percent; n = 162), some from Hong Kong (14 percent) or Taiwan (7 percent), while others (5 percent) from various parts of the world, including Southeast Asia, Middle East, Europe, and South America. Mandarin Chinese is reported as the most commonly spoken language at home (71 percent; n = 163), followed by English (50 percent), Cantonese (18 percent), other Chinese dialects (7 percent), French (1 percent), or Spanish/Portuguese/Italian (1 percent). The quality of interaction with their spouses/partners is generally "very good" (43 percent; n = 173) or "good" (23 percent), only a few said "OK" (9 percent) or "bad" (2 percent).

Regarding the quality of interaction with their children, "not applicable" (42 percent; n = 166) is the most common answer, indicating childless families or individuals are predominant among this sample group. This result may have affected their choice of courtyard housing. Nearly one third (32 percent) had "very good" and close to one-fifth (19 percent) had "good" interactions with their children. Only a minority of them said the interaction was "OK" (7 percent).

Pertaining to the quality of interaction with their parents or parents-in-law, an ambient relationship is revealed when adding "very good" (29 percent; n = 169) and "good" (28 percent) together which counts for more than half (57 percent), only a minority said "OK" (15 percent) or "bad" (2 percent).

The interview result confirms that 21 of 37 (57 percent) ethnic Chinese had "good," "very good," or "excellent" interaction with their family members. Some have lived with their parents by choice because of their mutual interdependence. They are happy to live in the same house because they can take care of one another, meanwhile, have their personal space. For instance, a Chinese resident described:

> I invited my parents for a short stay and I live with them now. It is nice to have someone to talk to and walk together in after-work hours, and reassuring to know that they are helping me taking care of the household while I am at work.

Kitchen is reported as the most often used family meeting area, and dining table and family room are also major interaction spots. Breakfast and dinner times are when family members have the most interaction. For those who do not live in the same house, they would visit each other regularly.

Six of 37 (16 percent) interviewees said they live by themselves or with their roommates, who see each other every day and often cook Chinese food together. No matter who is in need, they always give a hand. Five of 37 (14 percent) interviewees said their interaction with their family members is OK. They sometimes argue but care about one another.

Four of 37 (11 percent) interviewees mentioned that their family members live in China, but they maintain a good relationship and interaction by using Internet technology, such as webcam, instant messenger (QQ, Skype, Yahoo, MSN, WeChat, etc.), email, or telephone, to chat or correspond regularly. A retired Chinese resident in Florida said she used webcam almost every day to stay in touch with her family and friends in China.

Montgomery (2013, p. 54) argued that social isolation may be the greatest peril of city life. The more connected people are with family and community, the less likely they are to experience mental and physical health problems such as depression, colds, heart attacks, strokes, and cancer. Simple friendships with other people in a neighborhood are one of the best ways for stress reduction during economic downturns. This study argues that a courtyard, if made available in one's immediate home environment, would facilitate social interaction and reduce mental illness.

SUMMARY AND CONCLUSION

This chapter presented and analyzed the empirical findings on the matters that have contributed to social cohesion among ethnic Chinese in their homes in North America.

The results show that ethnic Chinese in North America have strong house-purchasing power due to their higher-than-average educational levels and professional profiles. They generally get along well with their neighbors, but mainly on a superficial level. In-depth communications would require more time and efforts on the parts of the neighbors, as well as a fenceless common space, such as a courtyard, to promote social interaction, and to attain social "oneness."

The interviews with non-Chinese residents living in co-operative housing in Toronto and cohousing across Canada reveal that the things that make them happy about the communal courtyards include: courtyards as children's playgrounds, courtyards as landscaped gardens, courtyards as social spaces, and co-operative property management. The things that make them unhappy include: differences in lifestyles, lack of private back yards, lack of volunteerism, and neighbor conflicts. Thus, privacy and community is like the *Yin* and *Yang* that require a healthy balance. And, of course, different people require a different balance. No matter how well they are designed, courtyards cannot satisfy everyone. Nevertheless, the social interactions generated from the communal courtyards may outweigh the downside of it.

The survey findings show that the majority of the ethnic Chinese participants in North America have had their first marriage, although slightly more than one third has remained single. It reveals a highly successful marriage rate among them and they tend to have good family relations as well. For those living away from their parents, they normally use the Internet technology to stay in touch with their family in China.

In Chapter 6 that follows, the cultural aspect of the ethnic Chinese in North America will be explored, to see if they still maintain their traditional cultural values at home.

6

Happiness as Knowing the Dao:
Time and Cultural Activities in the Homes

Human follows the earth.
Earth follows the universe.
The universe follows the Dao.
The Dao follows only itself.

Laozi, c.571–471 BCE, *Dao De Jing*, Verse 25

This chapter explores the cultural aspect of ethnic Chinese residents in North America. It seeks to know whether they still hold traditional Chinese philosophy as their beliefs. Moreover, it investigates whether and to what extent Western culture has influenced their lifestyles. As such, the chapter consists of four sections: philosophy and religion, daily activities, cultural festivities, and birthday celebrations.

PHILOSOPHY AND RELIGION

More than half of the surveyed ethnic Chinese participants in North America have a philosophy or religion (51 percent; n = 171), and the interview results confirm that 20 of 37 (54 percent) of them believed in a philosophy or religion. A number of the survey respondents have faith in *Feng Shui* (13 percent), or Buddhism (13 percent), or Catholicism (11 percent), or Protestantism (11 percent). Another small number of them identified themselves as Daoists (6 percent), or Confucians (6 percent), or Christians (6 percent), while less were interested in *Yi Jing* (4 percent). In addition, Atheism, Agnosticism, Positivism, and New Thought were mentioned by five participants, but no one cited Islam. These findings closely resemble that of the 2001 Census of Canada that, 44 percent of Canadians of Chinese origin had a religious affiliation, among them 14 percent were Buddhist, another 14 percent Catholic, and nine percent Protestant (Lindsay, 2001, p. 12).

This outcome indicates that, although 28 percent of the ethnic Chinese participants have converted to Christianity (when adding together the Christians,

Catholics, and Protestants), and 11 of 37 (30 percent) interviewees believed in Christianity, a significant 42 percent of the survey respondents still held traditional Chinese philosophy (when adding together the participants who believed in *Yi Jing*, *Feng Shui*, Daoism, Confucianism, and Buddhism). Therefore, it could be said that more ethnic Chinese in North America have maintained traditional Chinese faiths than those who have adopted Western ones.

For the interviewees who are influenced by Buddhism, their belief is sometimes reflected in their home decorations by placing a Buddha statue and/or a *Guanyin*[1] statue in their homes. Some informants favored Daoist philosophy and have made their home decorations simple and balanced. Other participants believed in *Feng Shui* and did not place the back of their desks or chairs towards the room doors, which would mean "bad luck." Another partaker believed in Communism but did not reflect this belief in his home decoration. One interviewee was fond of Permaculture,[2] and another had a blend of simple beliefs in Nature (e.g. plants, sunlight, views of four seasons) as an important theme in almost all her rooms, although technology (e.g. computers, television, radio) has also been an integral part of it.

For those participants believing in Christianity, their home decorations include placing a statue of Jesus Christ, the Son of God, a cross, a statue of St Mary, or related images in their homes. Their activities involved having monthly bible study meetings in English and Mandarin Chinese languages. This finding reveals Western cultural infiltration into ethnic Chinese population in North America.

Nonetheless, some said they believed in science or their own personal philosophy, and that their interior was decorated with plants and fish bowl, or traditional Chinese literature and calligraphy that are colorful, and have positive and motivational aspirations. Others hang their children's drawings, timetable, word-learning cards, and the like, in their homes.

Although this research was unable to generate a correlation study between happiness and religion, the survey conducted by the Pew Research Center (2006, p. 6) found that American people who attended religious services weekly or more were happier (43 percent very happy) than those who attended monthly or less (31 percent), or seldom or never (26 percent). Sternberg (2009, p. 214) observed that faith can be very profound and powerful to help trigger the internal healing pathways of the brain and body. A research by Ryff and Singer (2008) further found that personal growth, self-realization, and the fulfilment of one's true and best potential based on his/her talent and disposition has led to what Aristotle termed "eudaimonic" happiness, which requires virtuous actions rather than mere abstract ideas. This Western concept coincides with the Chinese Daoist notion of self-cultivation.

DAILY ACTIVITIES

Eating food is reported as the most common activity that makes the ethnic Chinese respondents happy at home (72 percent; n = 168), followed by listening to music

---

[1]   Meaning "Observing the Sounds (or Cries) of the World."
[2]   Permaculture advocates ecological design and natural farming that develops sustainable architecture and self-maintained agricultural systems modeled from natural ecosystems. It is an older way of sustaining a society, to keep a balance.

(67 percent), reading books/ebooks/newspapers/magazines (62 percent), watching television, or DVDs, or movies (57 percent), playing computer games/browsing the Internet (56 percent), drinking tea (48 percent), exercising/maintaining health/ natural healing (43 percent), listening to the radio (27 percent), gardening (26 percent), singing (25 percent), playing musical instruments (20 percent), holding parties (19 percent), drinking wine (19 percent), looking after children/elderly/family members (18 percent), doing painting (16 percent), playing table games (*weiqi*, *majiang*, cards, etc.) (14 percent), dancing (14 percent), repairing house (11 percent), composing essays/poetry (7 percent), practicing calligraphy (6 percent), sunbathing (5 percent), and making models (3 percent). In addition, two participants mentioned cooking and sleeping that make them happy, while several others indicated talking to family members in China via webcam and engaging in daily social interaction with people make them happy (Table 6.1).

Table 6.1   Respondents' daily activities at home to promote happiness

Happy activity	Percentage (n = 168)
1. Eating food	72%
2. Listening to music	67%
3. Reading books/eBooks/newspapers/magazines	62%
4. Watching television/DVDs/movies	57%
5. Playing computer games/browsing the Internet	56%
6. Drinking tea	48%
7. Exercising/maintaining health/natural healing	43%
8. Listening to the radio	27%
9. Gardening	26%
10. Singing	25%
11. Playing musical instruments	20%
12. Holding parties	19%
12. Drinking wine	19%
13. Looking after children/elderly/family members	18%
14. Doing painting	16%
15. Playing table games (weiqi, majiang, cards, etc.)	14%
15. Dancing	14%
16. Repairing house	11%
17. Composing essays/poetry	7%
18. Practicing calligraphy	6%
19. Sunbathing	5%
20. Making models	3%
21. Cooking	2 respondents
22. Sleeping	2 respondents
23. Talking to family members	2 respondents
24. Social interaction with people	2 respondents

Note: My survey results; several activities received the same number of responses and therefore have the same order number.

Just as Confucius who advocated learning music for happiness, this research finding shows that 67 percent (n = 168) of the survey respondents enjoyed listening to music, though only 20 percent of them playing musical instruments. It also echoes Sternberg's (2009, p. 63) observations that people have always used music to alter moods. The ancient Greeks, in their temples to the god of healing, Asclepius, used music to help heal the sick. Plato and Aristotle both wrote about music's healing power. Nevertheless, only recently have scientists developed technologies that could be used to understand how emotion and music are connected, and to ascertain that music can affect moods.

Although modern technologies have generated devices for people's recreations, it is satisfying to find that traditional health activities such as drinking tea, exercising/natural healing, and gardening, can still make people happy.

The US Census Bureau (2000a) also found that Asian-American men in the age group of 25–54 spent on average 50 percent more time on the Internet than all other men in the same age groups, and 9 percent more time than average reading newspapers. They spent less time than average watching television, 18 percent less time than average reading magazines, and a significant 55 percent less time than average listening to the radio. Internet and ethnic newspapers were clearly the preferred medium of communication when targeting Asian-Americans.

Ipsos Reid (2007) conducted 1,200 telephone interviews with first-generation Chinese-Canadians who were 18 years of age or older, and found that 92 percent of them watch television, 72 percent read newspapers/magazines, and 59 percent listen to the radio.

However, Montgomery (2013, pp. 154–5) argued that television—the great window to the world—has been a disaster for happiness because the more people watch it, the fewer friendships they are likely to have, the less trusting they become, and the less happy they are likely to be. The computer, Internet, iPad, or mobile devices, have mixed results. They can help people to interact and connect, but they cannot substitute face-to-face interactions, as a growing body of evidence reveals that online relationships are not as rich, honest, or supportive as having real person, since people are more likely to lie to each other when texting than when standing beside each other. When we stand by someone, we use all our senses: eyes, ears, and noses to receive subtle signals about who they are, what they like, and what they want. But we cannot do so with technical devices. This is a complex issue. It points to the need to design our living environments that have communal spaces, such as courtyards, to increase face-to-face social interactions.

My interviews with ethnic Chinese participants in North America reveal that their most common daily activity at home in an ordinary day is exercising (27 percent; n = 37), mostly in their basement during the winter and back yard during the summer. The variety of their daily exercises include practicing *taiji*, jogging, skipping a rope, walking after dinner, running on a treadmill at home or running in their neighborhoods (except for in bad weather), swimming in their community centers, or doing small apparatus exercise in their homes. Others also participate in their community health activities. For example, a participant described:

> *I go for the line dance class with a group of 8–10 senior people in the Community Center, twice a week and two hours each time.*

The author has also observed that during the warm seasons between 8–10 am every morning, a group of seniors do exercise together in a community park in Richmond Hill, Ontario, Canada. This practice is common in China nowadays (see Zhang, 2013) but uncommon in Canada. It is worth mentioning that this is predominantly a Chinese community and the group members mainly consist of ethnic Chinese people.

6.1   During the warm seasons, a group of seniors do exercise every morning in a community park, Richmond Hill, Ontario, Canada
Source: Photo by Donia Zhang, 2013.

Their second most common daily activity is browsing the Internet (22 percent; n = 37) in their study room, living room, family room, or bedroom. Their other daily activities in the order of occurrence include watching television (16 percent) in the living room or family room; reading (16 percent) (with iPad) in the living room, study room, kitchen, or family room; cooking (14 percent) in the kitchen and eating (14 percent) in the dinette or dining/living room; working (11 percent) in the home office or the study room; studying (11 percent) in the living room or bedroom. Nevertheless, some participants hardly stayed at home to do any activities, but always performed at their workplaces. For instance, a student revealed his dedication to the medical profession:

> [I] study, take exams, check the patients' rooms, write their medical records, and treat the patients; or do experiments with animals day and night, mostly in the hospital's labs. My home space is hardly used.

The interviewees' other daily activities include interacting with family members (parents, spouse, and children) (11 percent; n = 37) in the living room or children's bedroom; resting (11 percent) in the living room or study room during the day; sleeping (11 percent) in the bedroom; cleaning the house (8 percent); gardening (5 percent) (nurturing flowers, pruning, growing vegetables and fruit trees, such as mango, litchi, Chinese flowering quince) in the back yard during the summer; playing (computer) games (5 percent) in the living room or bedroom; playing piano (3 percent) in the living room; listening to the radio (3 percent); and doing charity work (3 percent; Table 6.2).

Table 6.2   Respondents' daily activities at home on an ordinary day

Daily activity (n = 37)	Space
1. Exercising	Basement (winter) and back yard (summer)
2. Browsing the Internet	Study room, living room, family room, bedroom
3. Watching television	Living room, family room
3. Reading (with iPad)	Study room, kitchen, family room, living room
4. Cooking	Kitchen
4. Eating	Dinette, dining room, living room
5. Working	Home office, study room
5. Studying	Living room, bedroom
5. Interacting with family members	Living room, children's bedroom
5. Resting	Living room, study room
5. Sleeping	Bedroom
6. Cleaning the house	All rooms
7. Gardening	Back yard (perhaps also front yard)
7. Playing (computer) games	Living room, bedroom
8. Playing piano	Living room
9. Listening to the radio	Any room

Note: My interview results; several activities received the same number of responses and therefore have the same order number.

The respondents conducted their favorite activities at home mostly after work between 8 pm–12 midnight (65 percent; n = 169), followed by 4 pm–8 pm (23 percent), 8 am–12 noon (13 percent), 12 noon–4 pm (10 percent), 12 midnight–4 am (6 percent), and 4 am–8 am (4 percent). This finding implies that they are mostly regular full-time employees.

Their favorite activities were mostly conducted at home on weekends of Saturdays (47 percent; n = 167) and Sundays (41 percent), with much less on Fridays (32 percent). Thursdays (24 percent), Wednesdays (22 percent), Tuesdays (22 percent), and Mondays (22 percent) have almost the same degree of occurrence. These findings imply that most of them work during the week days, and the results are consistent with that found in China (see Zhang, 2013).

Regarding the seasons that the informants conducted their favorite activities at home, the four seasons shared proximate responses: summer (41 percent; n = 164), spring (38 percent), autumn (38 percent), and winter (35 percent). This finding implies that these activities were carried out mainly indoors without being affected by external weather conditions. The average length of time the respondents spent on their favorite activities at home is 2.8 hours (n = 137) each time.

Pertaining to the frequency of their favorite activities at home, most of the participants selected "at least 1–3 times weekly" (60 percent; n = 163). Only a small number of them reported "at least 1–3 times monthly" (10 percent), or "at least 1–3 times quarterly" (4 percent), or "at least 1–3 times annually" (1 percent). This finding indicates that they generally enjoyed their favorite activities at home.

The public places that the respondents conducted their favorite activities are community/city park/garden (36 percent; n = 153), public library (29 percent), shopping mall (28 percent), local café/restaurant (24 percent), health center/gym (22 percent), cinema/theater (22 percent), bookstore (20 percent), community center (19 percent), office/studio (18 percent), museum/art gallery (18 percent), schoolyard (12 percent), street/lane (11 percent), and farmers market (9 percent). Moreover, several participants mentioned their house-yard, summer home, friend's home, school, church, vacation place, or beach (Table 6.3).

Table 6.3   Public places where respondents conduct their favorite activities

Public place	Percentage (n = 153)
1. Community/city park/garden	36%
2. Public library	29%
3. Shopping mall	28%
4. Local café/restaurant	24%
5. Health center/gym	22%
5. Cinema/theater	22%
6. Bookstore	20%
7. Community center	19%
8. Office/studio	18%
8. Museum/art gallery	18%
9. Schoolyard	12%
10. Street/lane	11%
11. Farmers market	9%
12. Others	
House-yard, summer home, friend's home, school, church, vacation place, beach	

Note: My survey results; several places received the same number of responses and therefore have the same order number.

6.2　A group of women dancing at lunchtime at College Park, Toronto, Ontario, Canada
Source: Photo by Donia Zhang, 2013.

6.3　Children playing at Withrow Park, Toronto, Ontario, Canada
Source: Photo by Donia Zhang, 2013.

6.4   People talking at Little Norway Park, Toronto, Ontario, Canada
Source: Photo by Donia Zhang, 2013.

6.5   View of autumn leaves at Heath Street Corner Park, Toronto, Ontario, Canada
Source: Photo by Donia Zhang, 2013.

CULTURAL FESTIVITIES

The Spring Festival (Lunar New Year or Chinese New Year) is the most celebrated (74 percent; n = 165) cultural festival by the surveyed ethnic Chinese in North America, followed by the Mid-Autumn Festival (Moon Festival) (49 percent), Lantern Festival (Spring Spirit Festival) (29 percent), Dragon Boat Festival (Double Fifth Festival) (19 percent), Thanksgiving to the Stove God (10 percent), and Winter Solstice Festival (8 percent).

While other festivals are less celebrated, such as the Qing Ming Festival (Clear Brightness Day) (6 percent), the Night of Sevens (Chinese Valentine's Day) (5 percent), Laba Festival (Congee Festival) (4 percent), Autumn Spirit Festival (4 percent), Blue Dragon Festival (Dragon Raising its Head) (3 percent), Mid-Summer Spirit Festival (2 percent), Double Ninth Festival (1 percent), Shangsi Festival (Spring Purification Festival) (1 percent), and Bathing and Basking Festival (1 percent; Table 6.4).

Table 6.4   Cultural festivals celebrated by ethnic Chinese in North America

Cultural festivals	Date	Percentage (n = 165)
1. Spring Festival (Lunar New Year, or Chinese New Year)	1st day of the 1st lunar month	74%
2. Mid-Autumn Festival (Moon Festival)	15th day of the 8th lunar month	49%
3. Lantern Festival (Spring Spirit Festival)	15th day of the 1st lunar month	29%
4. Dragon Boat Festival (Double Fifth Festival)	5th day of the 5th lunar month	19%
5. Thanksgiving to the Stove God	23rd day of the 12th lunar month	10%
6. Winter Solstice Festival	December 21–22	8%
7. Qing Ming Festival (Clear Brightness Day)	April 5, or April 4 on a leap year	6%
8. Night of Sevens (Chinese Valentine's Day)	7th day of the 7th lunar month	5%
9. Laba Festival (Congee Festival)	8th day of the 12th lunar month	4%
9. Autumn Spirit Festival	15th day of the 10th lunar month	4%
10. Blue Dragon Festival (Dragon Raising its Head)	2nd day of the 2nd lunar month	3%
11. Mid-Summer Spirit Festival	15th day of the 7th lunar month	2%
12. Double Ninth Festival	9th day of the 9th lunar month	1%
12. Shangsi Festival (Spring Purification Festival)	3rd day of the 3rd lunar month	1%
12. Bathing and Basking Festival	6th day of the 6th lunar month	1%

Note: My survey results; several festivities received the same number of responses and therefore have the same order number.

In addition, Christmas and North American Thanksgiving celebrations were also mentioned by several participants.

The interview results more or less confirm those of the survey that 32 of 37 (86 percent) interviewees celebrated the Spring Festival. Their celebrations typically included decorating their homes with traditional Chinese literary and calligraphy works, and pasting paper-cuts on the doors and windows. Some also gave red pocket money to their children on the New Year's Eve or the New Year's Day.

On the New Year's Eve, some residents would cook and make traditional Chinese food at home, and have a family reunion dinner that would usually contain a dish of fish (representing abundant savings annually), dumplings and/or *tangyuan*.[3] Others would order special dishes from a supermarket or restaurant that may include shark's fin, sea cucumber, abalone, barbecue pork, or radish cake. They also did various activities in their basement, living room, family room, or dining room. Still others invited their relatives and friends over for dinner. For example, a respondent revealed:

> We usually invite close friends, the living room is for men to talk about politics, the dining room is for the ladies to chat, and the family room is for the children and teens to play video games.

Some participants celebrated Chinese New Year with family and friends with a restaurant meal. For overseas Chinese students, they would normally hold a New Year's party in someone's dormitory, cook traditional Chinese food, have dinner together, play card games, and sing karaoke. Some then celebrated it together with other Chinese students at university or in a park setting. For Chinese Christians, they would often gather with other Chinese Christian fellows for a New Year feast in a restaurant, or make and eat dumplings with fellow friends at church. Sometimes they were invited to a theatre to watch Chinese festival live shows organized by the Chinese community. Every year, there are always ethnic Chinese in North America who will return to China to celebrate the Spring Festival with their family members.

The interview finding confirms the survey result that 19 of 37 (51 percent) interviewees celebrated the Mid-Autumn Festival. Their celebrations often include buying and eating moon cakes with family members, cooking traditional Chinese food for a family reunion dinner at home while watching television, with lanterns hanging in the kitchen and different fruits in the family room. Some respondents would place a table and chairs in their back yard while watching the full moon (if it is a clear night), eating moon cakes, savoring barbecue pork, starfruit (Carambola), and Pomelo (shaddock). For some overseas Chinese students whose family members were not in North America, they would normally celebrate it with their local community, or gather for a feast with other Chinese Christian fellows at church, or invite friends or be invited by friends to dine in their dormitory.

There is a close percentage between the survey (19 percent; n = 165) and the interviews that 6 of 37 (16 percent) interviewees celebrated the Dragon Boat

---

[3]   Stuffed small dumpling ball made of glutinous rice flour served in soup, popular in southern China.

Festival (Double Fifth Festival); they would cook traditional Chinese food, eat *zongzi*[4] and barbecue pork.

Although 8 percent (n = 165) of the survey respondents celebrated Winter Solstice Festival, only one of 37 (3 percent) interviewees celebrated it by eating chicken, duck, fish, and the like. It is noted that although southern Chinese people often say that "Winter Solstice is as big as the Spring Festival," it is in fact not celebrated as much as the Spring Festival.

Contrary to the survey finding that Lantern Festival is the third most commonly celebrated festival (29 percent; n = 165) by the ethnic Chinese in North America, only one of 37 (3 percent) interviewees mentioned it, perhaps because the festival has traditionally been considered as part of the Chinese New Year celebrations.

Four of 37 (11 percent) interviewees celebrated *all* Chinese festivals. Their celebrations normally include marking the dates on the calendar, reading about their legends, sending greetings to family and friends, and having a feast of traditional Chinese food, most often at home, sometimes in a friend's house, or at a church, or in a restaurant. For the overseas Chinese students, they usually invite other Chinese students and scholars with their families to parties, typically with 20–30 people in such a gathering.

The interior spaces that the participants normally use to conduct Chinese cultural festivities are the living room (51 percent; n = 162), dining room (38 percent), kitchen (33 percent), and family room (30 percent). When the weather permits, outdoor spaces they use include: back yard/garden (9 percent), community center (6 percent), community/city park/garden (4 percent), front yard/garden (3 percent), and schoolyard (3 percent).

Because courtyard houses/housing is uncommon in North America, only four percent of the survey participants lived in it, only one percent cited courtyard for their cultural festivities. However, my interviews with 20 non-Chinese informants in co-operative housing in Toronto and cohousing across Canada reveal that the communal courtyards are central spaces for conducting cultural festivities. A case in point is the Bain Apartments Co-operative in east Toronto that celebrated its centenary (100 years) on September 13 and 14, 2013, with live performances and activities in the communal courtyards.

BIRTHDAY CELEBRATIONS

The majority of the survey respondents (66 percent; n = 162) celebrated their birthdays, and 28 of 37 (76 percent) interviewees did so. One in five (20 percent) *sometimes* celebrated their birthdays. Their celebrations normally include receiving and opening gifts or money from family members, eating a birthday cake, cooking and having traditional Chinese food at home or in a friend's place, occasionally holding a birthday party at home, or having a restaurant meal. Some of them would have a day or two to a place not visited before, or travel to a different city or country. For some Chinese Christians, they sometimes celebrate their birthdays with other fellows at church.

---

[4]   A pyramid-shaped dumpling made of glutinous rice wrapped in bamboo or reed leaves.

6.6   Centennial celebrations at
Bain Apartments Co-operative North Maples courtyard, Toronto, Ontario, Canada
Source: Photo by Donia Zhang, 2013.

6.7   Centennial celebrations by the children at
Bain Apartments Co-operative North Maples courtyard, Toronto, Ontario, Canada
Source: Photo by Donia Zhang, 2013.

SUMMARY AND CONCLUSION

This chapter examined the cultural dimension of the ethnic Chinese residents in North America by unfolding their philosophical and religious beliefs and behaviors, revealing their daily activities at home, and recounting their Chinese cultural festivities and birthday celebrations.

The findings reveal that although a significant number (28 percent) of the participants have converted to Christianity, more of them (42 percent) still hold traditional Chinese philosophical beliefs such as Daoism, Confucianism, Buddhism, and *Feng Shui*. However, it is unsurprising to find that the extent of survival of traditional Chinese philosophy among the ethnic Chinese in North America is not as much as in contemporary China (see Zhang, 2013). This outcome denotes Western cultural infiltration is happening to the ethnic Chinese in North America.

The results also show that some basic human behaviors, such as eating food and listening to music, are still the participants' primary daily activities at home that make them happy. This finding complies with Confucian advocate of learning music for happiness (*Analects*, book 16, chapter 5). Moreover, modern technologies such as computers, televisions, ebooks/iPads, webcams, and the like, have occupied much of the residents' lives.

Some important Chinese cultural festivals, such as the Spring Festival, Mid-Autumn Festival, Lantern Festival, and Dragon Boat Festival, are commonly celebrated by the ethnic Chinese in North America. However, the Qing Ming Festival and Winter Solstice Festival that are widely celebrated in China are not celebrated as much in North America. This phenomenon may be due to the sample population who might be mostly from northern China because the Winter Solstice Festival is chiefly celebrated by contemporary southern Chinese people.

The study also reveals that birthdays are commonly celebrated by the informants, and that their celebrations normally involve having a special meal at home or in a restaurant with family and/or friends. For overseas Chinese students and Chinese Christians, they often celebrate it with other Chinese students and/or Christian fellows at dormitory, church, or restaurant.

In Chapter 7 that follows, a set of courtyard housing design principles based on the empirical findings will be presented.

7

Four Keystones of Courtyard Housing Design

The wise find pleasure in water;
the virtuous find pleasure in hills.

The wise are active;
the virtuous are tranquil.

The wise are joyful;
the virtuous are long-lived.

Confucius, 551–479 BCE, *Analects*, book 6, chapter 21

This chapter highlights the findings and suggests four keystones for courtyard housing design to promote health and happiness in accordance with traditional Chinese philosophy. The four keystones are: Health as Balancing *Yin Yang*: form and environmental quality; Health as Gathering *Qi*: space and construction quality; Happiness as Attaining Oneness: matters of social cohesion; and Happiness as Knowing the Dao: time and cultural activities.

These four keystones are set in the four pillars of sustainable development framework, which are environmental, economic, social, and cultural sustainability; in conjunction with the four themes of form, space, matter, and time (which have been elaborated in my previous work, Zhang, 2013), to establish a context of analysis for contemporary urban planning and architectural design. The ultimate goal is to include the human dimension in the planning and design processes, which is currently missing.

7.1   Four keystones of courtyard housing design to promote health and happiness in accordance with traditional Chinese philosophy
Source: Conception and drawing by Donia Zhang, 2013.

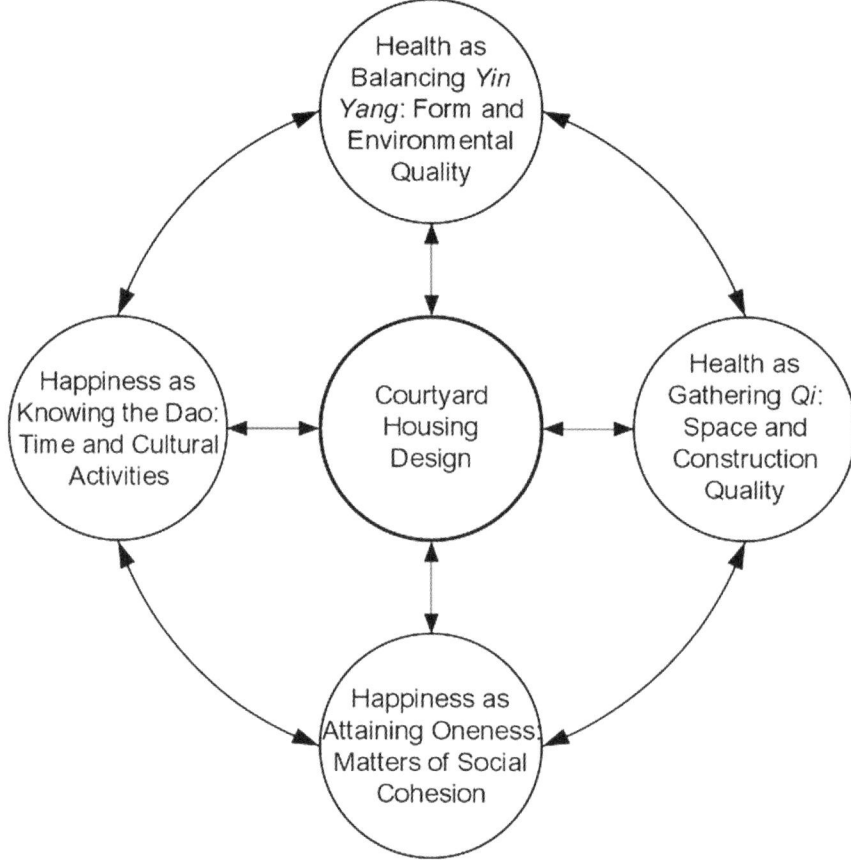

The specific meaning in each domain of Figure 7.1 is as follows:

1.   Health as Balancing *Yin Yang*: the form of courtyard housing that promotes health should have *Yin Yang* balance, and its environmental quality should be conducive to public health;
2.   Health as Gathering *Qi*: the space of courtyard housing that promotes health should help gather *qi* (cosmic energy), and its construction quality should be enduring and sustainable;
3.   Happiness as Attaining Oneness: the matters that facilitate social cohesion should help achieve oneness or unity that will ultimately lead to happiness;
4.   Happiness as Knowing the Dao: the time and cultural activities conducted in courtyard housing should follow the cyclic movements of time and the four seasons, and by doing so, humans can obtain happiness.

These four keystones also fit into Veenhoven's framework of *Four Qualities of Life* (2000) as shown in Table 7.1.

Table 7.1   Matrix of measurement for courtyard housing to promote health and happiness

	Outer quality	*Inner quality*
Chances	Health as Balancing *Yin Yang*: form and environmental quality	Happiness as Attaining Oneness: matters of social cohesion
Results	Health as Gathering *Qi*: space and construction quality	Happiness as Knowing the Dao: time and cultural activities

Note: Tabulation showing how the study fits into Veenhoven's *Four Qualities of Life* (2000).

Table 7.1 denotes that form and space belong to the outer quality of the physical environment, and matter and time fall within the inner quality of humans. Moreover, the environmental quality (chance) will affect the construction quality (result), and the degrees of social cohesion (chance) will influence the cultural activities (result) to be conducted in courtyard housing. Thus, these four keystones interact with one another and are interrelated with one another. They should be considered as inseparable whole rather than as independent parts when it comes to courtyard housing design.

HEALTH AS BALANCING *YIN YANG*: FORM AND ENVIRONMENTAL QUALITY

Yin Yang balance and harmony is fundamental in traditional Chinese philosophy as well as in traditional Chinese medicine. This pair of polar opposite helps to diagnose illnesses in order to obtain the health of human mind and body. In Chinese courtyard house (and garden) design, *Yin Yang* has also played an important role as elaborated in Chapter 2. The empirical findings show that in housing design in North America, the *Yin Yang* concept is also applicable. This section summarizes the results on the form and environmental quality of the housing investigated.

Location

The survey results show that neighborhood safety, proximity to an educational institution, convenience to shopping and other service facilities, and a clean natural environment are ethnic Chinese residents' primary concerns when choosing a place to live in North America. These findings comply with those of Sternberg (2009), US Census Bureau (2000a), UNESCO (2012), and WHO (2012), but contradict to that of Howell (2014). Moreover, walking-friendly neighborhood has received much attention because walking is a health-promoting activity that can help prevent many potential illnesses. This finding is congruent with the arguments of Björk et al. (2008) and Sternberg (2009).

Exterior Form

Single-detached houses, semi-detached houses, row/town houses, walk-up apartments, and tower blocks are common residential building forms in North America. Existing literature shows that courtyard housing, although rare here, appear in various parts of California, with some scattered in Portland (Oregon), New Orleans (Louisiana), Chicago (Illinois), New York City, and perhaps also other American cities. The empirical findings reveal that 30 percent of housing co-operatives in Toronto, Ontario, Canada have communal courtyards, and that courtyard is a common feature in the newly emerged cohousing across Canada. Moreover, the "China City of America" project that is being built in the Sullivan County, NY has incorporated Chinese-style courtyard houses in the design.

Although 60 percent of the surveyed ethnic Chinese in North America preferred single-detached houses, a significant 21 percent of them favored courtyard houses/housing for more social interaction to promote social health of the occupants. Lee (2002)'s survey also showed that Chinese residents in Vancouver desired courtyard housing.

Nevertheless, it is observed that housing form preference reflects people's living requirements at different stages of their lives. For example, for those families with young children and senior members, a courtyard is often preferred as a recreational space for children's play and retirees' socialization. Whereas for students and working individuals, a courtyard may not matter to them as much since they will spend most of their waking hours in schools or at workplaces. Therefore, a variety of housing forms will satisfy different demands.

Exterior Walls

To promote a healthy environment, the survey respondents favored natural building materials such as brick, stone, and wood for their exterior walls over concrete or prefabricated panel. This result shows their environmental consciousness.

A significant number (43 percent) of the interviewed ethnic Chinese preferred their house exterior walls in a traditional Chinese architectural style, to reflect their cultural background and identity, to honor their cultural roots, and to pass their architectural tradition down to their future generations.

Nevertheless, an equal number (43 percent) of the interviewed ethnic Chinese did not favor their house exterior in traditional Chinese architectural style, as they felt that they should "do in Rome as the Romans do." Living in North America, they would like to blend into the multicultural communities here. Some also expressed financial restrictions or implications of building a Chinese-style home in terms of its initial costs and resale values. While several others cared more about the material durability and interior layout of their houses rather than the exterior style.

Gate Orientation

Regarding their ideal home's main gate orientation, the surveyed ethnic Chinese favored south more than north, and east more than west. This finding is consistent with *Feng Shui* theory, likely due to the sunlight quality. Nevertheless, a significant number of them did not mind about their gate orientation, indicating that it did not matter to them.

Window Orientation

South-facing window orientation for all the rooms is the most preferred by the surveyed ethnic Chinese in North America, which complies with *Feng Shui* theory, and which confirms the finding of Hughes (2013). Some survey participants would also like north and east orientations for their kitchen windows, and east-facing kitchen is also congruent with *Feng Shui*. Nevertheless, more than half of them were unsure or did not know, indicating that window orientation did not matter to them.

Eberhard (2009) observed that although many architectural design professionals and people in the general public would like to have large windows to allow natural light into the rooms and to provide views to the outside, caution should be taken about the discomfort glare caused by too much natural light from windows falling on not well-lit work surfaces (p. 83). Sunshade is often necessary to reduce the amount of glare, particularly for west-facing windows in the summer.

Regarding the window cross-ventilation orientation, the surveyed ethnic Chinese preferred south–north more than other orientations; it is again in compliance with *Feng Shui* theory. However, nearly half of them had no preference, suggesting that window cross-ventilation orientation did not matter to them.

Yards and Gardens

Although the surveyed ethnic Chinese very much appreciated their front yards and back yards, 70 percent of the interviewed ethnic Chinese preferred a communal courtyard in housing design because a central courtyard can provide safety for children's play, social interaction among neighbors, and cultural activities at group gatherings. These factors will promote mental and physical health of the occupants. Thus a courtyard has been an important feature in 30 percent of co-operative housing in Toronto and most cohousing across Canada. Nonetheless, some residents expressed reservation about a communal courtyard because of the unwanted noise generated from neighbors, while others favored a private courtyard. This research also indicates that balcony is highly welcomed in housing design, particularly for apartment buildings.

Other researchers have found that residents whose apartments located near plots of green performed better on attention tests and coped better with major life problems than those whose units were identical in design but located near barren areas (Sternberg, 2009, p. 279). It implies that to promote health, an environment should include eco-friendly features such as gardens, views of nature, balconies, artwork, calming colors, soothing music, sounds of nature, as well as construction materials that improve indoor air quality by reducing noxious gas, renewable energy systems, recycled water for irrigation, and spaces where family members can gather for mutual support (Sternberg, 2009, pp. 166, 237).

Roofs

To promote physical health, the surveyed ethnic Chinese preferred pitched roofs much more than flat ones because pitched roofs can provide more protection from the sun, rain, and snow, better preserve heat in the winter; and the volume ceilings facilitate indoor air circulation to make the interior cooler in the summer. Thus it is more suitable for North American climate. The respondents argued that aesthetically, pitched roofs look better as they give the house a sense of three dimensions.

Nonetheless, those favored flat roofs contended that they can offer roof terraces/gardens. As long as it is well-insulated, a roof terrace/garden can offer an immediate outdoor space for relaxation and recreation, especially in the summer. It can also be created as a green space where one can grew plants and vegetables to enhance the natural environment.

To promote environmental health, the surveyed ethnic Chinese considered clay tile as the best roof material, this result in fact reflects Chinese building tradition. Other natural materials such as cedar and slate were also preferred more than synthetic material such as concrete, suggesting their environmental consciousness.

HEALTH AS GATHERING *QI*: SPACE AND CONSTRUCTION QUALITY

Qi, which can be translated as "cosmic breath," "life force," or "matter-energy," is the core concept in traditional Chinese philosophy. Chinese philosophers and medical practitioners consider that every living being in the universe is due to the force of *qi*. When the *qi* gathers there is life, when it disperses, there is death (Chapter 2). As such, the spatial design and construction of a house/housing should help gather *qi* to promote health and life. This section summarizes the results on the space and construction quality of the housing investigated.

Interior Space

This research finds that ethnic Chinese in North America desired an average interior space of 195 sqm (2,093 sqf) for a family of 3–4 persons. This number is lower than the existing average American single-detached house of 230 sqm (2,470 sqf, excluding basement), but higher than the existing average Canadian single-detached house of 186 sqm (2,000 sqf, excluding basement). Although some respondents preferred bigger houses, others contended that the interior space should be proportional to the number of household members living inside (congruent with *Feng Shui* theory) so that the space will facilitate family members' communication, and that they do not have to clean extra, unused rooms. They estimated that on average, 50–60 sqm for a person is about right, and that each room should be at least 10–15 sqm for air circulation and people's movements. This space will help gather *qi*.

Interior Colors

It is generally observed that interior colors also affect occupants' happiness. In an earlier, unpublished study by the author on color connotations associated with orientation and emotion, the survey respondents' top color choice for happiness is yellow, for grief is grey, and for love is red.

Scholars such as Eberhard (2009), Sternberg (2009), and Zeki (1999) have all examined how human brains respond to certain colors that affect their perceptions and moods. They argued that these responses are hard-wired in the genes, and that color choices have neuroscientific basis. Nevertheless, different people have different reactions to colors; people who share similar personality traits often share parallel color choices.

The research also finds that the respondents' top color choice for east is yellow, for south is red or green, for west is orange, and for north is blue. Moreover, it suggested that views of greeneries make people happier than barren landscapes, and that the sun is the most important factor for their association of color and orientation.

Floor Levels

To promote physical health, the ethnic Chinese in North America predominantly preferred the ground/first floor as their main activity space, followed by the second floor and third floor, although a minority of them would like the fourth floor or above. Rooftop and basement were less favored. This finding is consistent with *Feng Shui* theory and reflects my previous study results in China (see Zhang, 2013). Open plan for the first floor is very much desired by the respondents for more natural light, air flow, open view, and people movement.

Furniture Styles and Materials

The interior furniture styles of the surveyed ethnic Chinese in North America were varied, with "mixed style" being the most common. They seemed to prefer natural materials, such as wood and bamboo, for their interior furniture, although bamboo is a less common furniture material in North America at the time of the survey (2013). Synthetic material was their common furniture material but was least favored. This finding reveals their environmental health consciousness.

Facility Provision

The research finds that conventional facilities such as running water and electricity are still crucial to have, an Internet cable/digital subscriber line is now more important than a telephone line or television cable. The surveyed ethnic Chinese thought that green plants are more conducive to their physical health than gas, and that solar panels are desirable. These findings reveal that although technology has made significant changes to people's lives, incorporating nature into home design will surely benefit occupants' health in enduring ways.

Construction Quality

Generally, the construction quality of ethnic Chinese housing in North America is found to be good or very good, as there was no complaint about it from the survey or interviews. This finding makes a stark contrast to that in the renewed and new courtyard housing in Beijing (see Zhang, 2013).

Construction quality has been regarded as of paramount importance in the entire building process because it is against which the final product is judged despite its good design intentions. Good quality construction helps extend the lifespan of buildings and is conducive to economic sustainability, which may ultimately contribute to environmental health and sustainability.

Maintenance and Management

The surveyed ethnic Chinese found that building maintenance work should be conducted at least once every five years, and that the quality of maintenance carried out by their property managements was generally good, OK, or very good. Well-maintained buildings contribute to residents' perceptions of healthy homes.

Car Park Spaces

Most of the survey participants preferred two car park spaces at home, and this finding reflects a common design for single-family homes in North America. It is generally observed that less car dependency will encourage more walking, which may contribute to better physical health of the residents.

HAPPINESS AS ATTAINING ONENESS: MATTERS OF SOCIAL COHESION

In traditional Chinese philosophy, universal love and oneness are lofty goals to be valued. The universal love advocated by Mozi (c. 470–391 BCE) demands that we regard other people as ourselves, and others' parents and children as our own. This principle helps to achieve social harmony and happiness (Chapter 2). This section summarizes the findings on the matters of social cohesion of ethnic Chinese residents in North America.

Education, Occupation, and House-Purchasing Power

The surveyed ethnic Chinese in North America were highly educated, with 26 percent having a doctorate or professional degree, 56 percent having a master's degree, and 88 percent having a bachelor's degree. Their high educational profiles may have contributed to their high occupational profiles, as most of them were professionals employed full-time. These findings comply with those of the US Census Bureau (2000a) and the 2001 Census of Canada (Lindsay, 2001).

Most of the surveyed ethnic Chinese in North America owned their homes, and their homeownership rate is significantly higher than the national average, a finding that is consistent with those of Dooley (2003) and Cruz-Viesca and Chiu (2008). This result is likely due to the fact that most Chinese who came to North America in recent decades were the "best and brightest" from Chinese universities who stayed after their graduation from North American universities. This sample population does not represent the average level of the entire Chinese nation.

Social Relations with Neighbors

The survey finds that generally, social relations between ethnic Chinese and their North American neighbors are good or very good. However, the interview results reveal a significant 41 percent of the ethnic Chinese participants having *no* interaction or *very little* interaction with their neighbors. For those living in detached and row/town houses, social interactions mostly occurred at their front yards/gardens, with much less at their back yards/gardens. Some of them observed that their back yard fences hinder their contact with neighbors, and that if there is a communal courtyard, it will help with their neighborly communication; as Montgomery (2013) and Sternberg (2009) argued that strong and positive social relations are the basis of happiness and health.

My interviews with non-Chinese living in co-operative housing in Toronto and cohousing across Canada reveal that the things that make them happy about the communal courtyards include: courtyards as children's playgrounds, courtyards as landscaped gardens, courtyards as social spaces, and co-operative property management. Nevertheless, there are also things that make them unhappy about the communal courtyards that include differences in residents' lifestyles, lack of private back yards, lack of volunteerism, and neighbor conflicts.

The survey shows that other social interaction spaces for ethnic Chinese in North America include: front porch, garage, apartment buildings' foyer/lobby/hallway, meeting/common room, laundry room, elevator, corridor, patio, gym, swimming pool, pedestrian walkway, community/city park/garden, community center, street/lane, schoolyard, public library, health center, grocery/food store, local café/restaurant, shopping mall, farmers market, balcony/deck, and roof terrace/garden.

Marriage/Wedding Ceremonies/Anniversaries

Ethnic Chinese marriage ceremonies in North America are typically held in a town hall or a restaurant garden, and the wedding receptions often occur in a Chinese restaurant. A communal courtyard, if available, could be a good place for marriage ceremonies to take place as in the cases of three housing co-operatives in Toronto.

More than half of the surveyed ethnic Chinese participants are in their first marriage, and the finding confirms that of the 2001 Census of Canada (Lindsay, 2001). This study shows that intra-ethnic marriages are the most common, and inter-racial marriages are rare.

Research done by others indicated that married couples are happier than singles, single parents, or couples with children, and that relationship with a partner is weighted the most important. Although wedding anniversary celebration is a

Western tradition, about half of the ethnic Chinese informants celebrated their wedding anniversaries.

The majority of the surveyed ethnic Chinese reported as having very good or good mental and physical health; and their mental and physical health correlate with their happiness about their homes.

Relations among Family Members

The surveyed ethnic Chinese household size is 3.04 persons, and most of them are first-generation Chinese having lived in North America for an average of 16 years. One generation or two generations living in the same household is the norm, three generations living together is rare. Mandarin Chinese is the most commonly spoken language at home, followed by English and Cantonese.

The quality of interaction with their family members is generally good or very good, although there is a significant number (42 percent) of childless families or individuals. Some working people purposely chose to live with their parents for mutual dependence as they can take care of one another. Their homes are normally big enough for them to have good family interaction; meantime, their homes allow them to have personal space.

For those whose parents live in China or elsewhere outside North America, they regularly communicate with one another using webcam, instant messaging, email, or other modern technologies. Montgomery (2013) maintained that good relationships with family and friends may be the best remedy for mental and physical health.

HAPPINESS AS KNOWING THE DAO: TIME AND CULTURAL ACTIVITIES

Daoists and Confucians both revere the Dao because they believe that it is the natural law that humans must obey, otherwise adverseness or calamities will act on humans. In everyday life, knowing the Dao is to conduct activities in harmony with the cyclic movements of the universe to obtain personal happiness (Chapter 2). This section summarizes the findings on the time and cultural activities of ethnic Chinese residents in North America.

Philosophy and Religion

More than half of the surveyed ethnic Chinese in North America have a philosophy or religion, and this finding is close to that of the 2001 Census of Canada (Lindsay, 2001). Their beliefs include *Feng Shui*, *Yi Jing*, Daoism, Confucianism, Buddhism, Christianity, Catholicism, and Protestantism, and these ideologies are somewhat reflected in their home decorations.

Overall, more of them have maintained traditional Chinese faiths than those who have adopted Western ones. Some of them also mentioned Atheism, Agnosticism, Positivism, and New Thought, but no one cited Islam.

Studies by others (Pew Research Center, 2006; Ryff and Singer, 2008; Sternberg, 2009) show that having a faith or partaking in religious activities correlate with healing, health, and happiness.

Daily Activities

The top 10 daily activities that make the surveyed ethnic Chinese happy include: eating food, listening to music, reading books/ebooks/newspapers/magazines, watching television/DVDs/movies, playing computer games/browsing the Internet, drinking tea, exercising/maintaining health/natural healing, listening to the radio, gardening, and singing.

This result complies with Confucian advocate of learning music to bring people happiness, as well as ancient Greek philosophers Plato and Aristotle's contention that music has healing power. Modern technologies have also discovered the connection between emotion and music (Sternberg, 2009). Although modern technologies have generated devices for people's recreations, it is gratifying to find that traditional health activities such as drinking tea, exercising/natural healing, and gardening, can still make people happy.

The top 10 daily activities that make the interviewed ethnic Chinese happy include: exercising, browsing the Internet, watching television, reading, cooking and eating, working, studying, interacting with family members (parents, spouse, and children), resting, and sleeping. Therefore, exercising is both a healthy and happy activity.

The respondents conduct their favorite activities at home mostly after work between 8 pm–12 midnight, mostly on weekends of Saturdays and Sundays and in all four seasons. The average length of time they spend on their favorite activities at home is 2.8 hours.

If not at home, the public places that the respondents conduct their favorite activities are community/city park/garden, public library, shopping mall, local café/restaurant, health center/gym, cinema/theater, bookstore, community center, office/studio, museum/art gallery, schoolyard, street/lane, farmers market, school, church, vacation place, or beach. It is interesting to note that Chinese residents in China also cited community/city park/garden as the most common place outside their homes for conducting cultural activities (see Zhang, 2013).

Cultural Festivities

The Spring Festival (Lunar New Year or Chinese New Year) is the most celebrated cultural festival by the surveyed ethnic Chinese in North America, followed by the Mid-Autumn Festival (Moon Festival), Lantern Festival (Spring Spirit Festival), Dragon Boat Festival (Double Fifth Festival), Thanksgiving to the Stove God, and the Winter Solstice Festival. Some participants also celebrate Christmas and North American Thanksgivings.

The spaces where their celebrations typically occur include their homes, restaurants, dormitories, universities, schools, or churches. When the weather permits, they also celebrate in their back yards/gardens, community centers, community/city parks/gardens, front yards/gardens, and schoolyards.

Because courtyard is uncommon in North America, only a few ethnic Chinese mentioned they celebrate the cultural festivals in the courtyard. Nevertheless, the non-Chinese residents in co-operative housing in Toronto and cohousing across Canada have reported using their communal courtyards to perform festivities.

Birthday Celebrations

The majority of the surveyed and interviewed ethnic Chinese celebrate their birthdays at home, or in a restaurant, or traveling to a different city or country. Some Chinese Christians also celebrate with other fellow friends at church.

SUMMARY AND CONCLUSION

This chapter highlighted the key findings from the research and proposed a theoretical and practical framework of four keystones of courtyard housing design for health and happiness. This set of principle can be used as design indicators based on traditional Chinese philosophy, which may have implications for China and elsewhere in the world where courtyard house/housing has been a traditional housing form. It may also have implications for multicultural countries and communities such as North America, Australia, and parts of Europe, where they are contemplating to create courtyard houses/housing for their citizens' social and cultural health and happiness. The indicators are summarized in Table 7.2.

Table 7.2   Four keystones of courtyard housing design for health and happiness

Material/dwelling culture (archi-culture, tangible)		Immaterial/spiritual culture (socio-culture, intangible)	
Health as Balancing Yin Yang: form and environmental quality	Health as Gathering Qi: space and construction quality	Happiness as Attaining Oneness: matters of social cohesion	Happiness as Knowing the Dao: time and cultural activities
Location Exterior form Exterior walls Gate orientation Window orientation Yards and gardens Roofs	Interior space Interior colors Floor levels Furniture styles and materials Facility provision Construction quality Maintenance and management Car park spaces	Education, occupation, and house-purchasing power Social relations with neighbors Marriage/wedding ceremonies / anniversaries Relations among family members	Philosophy and religion Daily activities Cultural festivities Birthday celebrations

Note: My creation based on this and my previous research in China (see Zhang, 2013). Most of the indicators are applicable to housing and neighborhood design in general, while some of them are unique to courtyard housing design.

In the final Chapter 8 that follows, the key contributions of the study will be encapsulated, and two schemes of courtyard garden houses based on the findings will be proposed, to promote residents' social and cultural health and happiness.

8

Conclusion: Courtyard Housing for Health and Happiness

A smile in the morning is like the sunshine,
A smile in the afternoon makes the sun shy away,
A smile in the evening is like the moonlight,
A smile at night when you kiss for good night.

Donia Zhang, 2002, Smile

In Christian belief, the paradise "Garden of Eden" has two trees: the tree of knowledge, and the tree of life. In Chinese *Feng Shui* theory, a courtyard should have at least two trees to guard against misfortune. This concluding chapter takes these metaphors and is organized in three sections: contribution to the tree of knowledge, contribution to the tree of life, and creation of courtyard garden houses.

CONTRIBUTION TO THE TREE OF KNOWLEDGE

This study is a thorough investigation of ethnic Chinese perceptions of health and happiness in housing in North America. Most of the empirical findings are a contribution to new knowledge. It used a combined/mixed method of an online survey (quantitative) with follow-up interviews (qualitative) to explore the topic in breadth (survey) and depth (interview). The results show that although 60 percent (n = 314) of the surveyed ethnic Chinese preferred single-detached houses for privacy, 21 percent (n = 314) of them and 11 percent (n = 37) of the interviewed ethnic Chinese favored courtyard houses/housing. Moreover, 70 percent (n = 37) of the interviewed ethnic Chinese desired a communal courtyard in their immediate residential environment for better social interaction and neighborly communication. Thus, private back yards/gardens (*yin*) and communal courtyards (*yang*) could be a pair of indispensable and complementary spaces in housing designs in the future. However, it should also be remembered that 30 percent (n = 37) of the interviewed ethnic Chinese did not want a communal courtyard, mainly for privacy concerns.

The findings may have implications for other ethnic groups in North America, whose traditional housing form is courtyard houses/housing, including but not limited to East Asian, Indian/South Asian, Persian/Iranian, Iraqi, and Spanish/Hispanic communities. The outcomes may as well have social significance for multicultural planning policies and multicultural design guidelines, which is Architectural Multiculturalism, and real estate development in North America.

CONTRIBUTION TO THE TREE OF LIFE

Health and happiness are fundamental to the survival of humankind. Housing, if carefully designed, can help promote health and happiness. Happiness and harmony are the same human desire, as according to Plato, happiness is the harmony of the soul. The Chinese have historically favored harmony on four levels: harmony with heaven, harmony with earth, harmony with humans, and harmony with self (see Zhang, 2013). These four harmonies mean that humans need to be in touch with nature in order to be healthy and happy. Also, we cannot talk about health without considering the social factor because people cannot obtain mental health without interacting with others.

My previous research in China shows that a courtyard helps maintaining physical health or natural healing, and facilitates social interaction and cultural activities (Zhang, 2013). This study confirms this claim and adds to it that a courtyard is conducive to mental health and happiness.

Eberhard (2009) thus described the philosophical meanings of a Chinese courtyard as such: "The courtyard of a house is like a well. Looking up, one sees and senses the *yang* of the sky; looking down, one sees and senses the *yin* of the Earth. Both forces meet and merge in the courtyard" (p. 108, italics are mine), suggesting that the courtyard provides communication between human and nature, and that the idea originated from Chinese search for harmony in the living environment.

Because there are now many ethnic Chinese in North America and that, because many ethnic Chinese still adhere, albeit in various degrees, to certain ideas in classical Chinese culture, there is a substantial real and potential demand for courtyard housing. However, due to historical circumstances, courtyard housing is not a wide-spread housing form in North America, and to popularize it would require much effort on the parts of urban planners, architects, researchers, and residents.

In urban planning, it would require zoning changes to legitimize courtyard housing designs in North American cities and towns. In architectural design, I have proposed two schemes that accommodate traditional Chinese thinking to a North American setting, as presented in the following section.

CREATION OF COURTYARD GARDEN HOUSES

These two designs emerged from the evidence gathered in my survey and interviews. They are single-detached houses with front and back yards/gardens and a communal courtyard, because the research finds that most ethnic Chinese in North America preferred single-detached houses for privacy and a communal courtyard for social interaction and cultural activities.

Exterior Form

The proposed eight (Scheme A) and four (Scheme B) units of single-detached courtyard garden houses clustered as a compound combine a courtyard as in traditional Chinese architectural culture, with front and back yards/gardens as in Western residential tradition, suggesting a new suburban planning system. The communal courtyard offers a platform for social interaction and neighborly communication to take place.

The exact dimensions of the grid may vary according to different site conditions and marketers' demands. Nevertheless, the minimum courtyard dimension should be 25 m (see Zhang, 2009/2010/2011, 2013). This design actually saves land because the American average lot size for an average single-family home of 230 sqm (2,470 sqf) is 22 m × 36 m (75 ft × 120 ft). It would require a land area of 6,336 sqm (88 m × 72 m) to build eight houses as such. Scheme A in fact occupies 6,084 sqm (78 m × 78 m) of land for eight single-detached houses of 240 sqm each, which is lower than the existing American average. Whereas Scheme B only takes up a land area of 2,640 sqm (66 m × 40 m) for four single-detached houses of 240 sqm each.

The designs of the courtyard garden houses have a clear demarcation of semi-public and private outdoor spaces because my past and present research findings show that communal courtyards/gardens are conducive to social interaction and private yards/gardens to self-cultivation. Moreover, small, enclosed compounds without automobiles promote better social interaction and cultural activities than large-scale housing estates.

8.1 Proposed North American courtyard garden house system for Scheme A based on the "Nine Squares" system
Source: Design and drawing by Donia Zhang, 2012–2014.

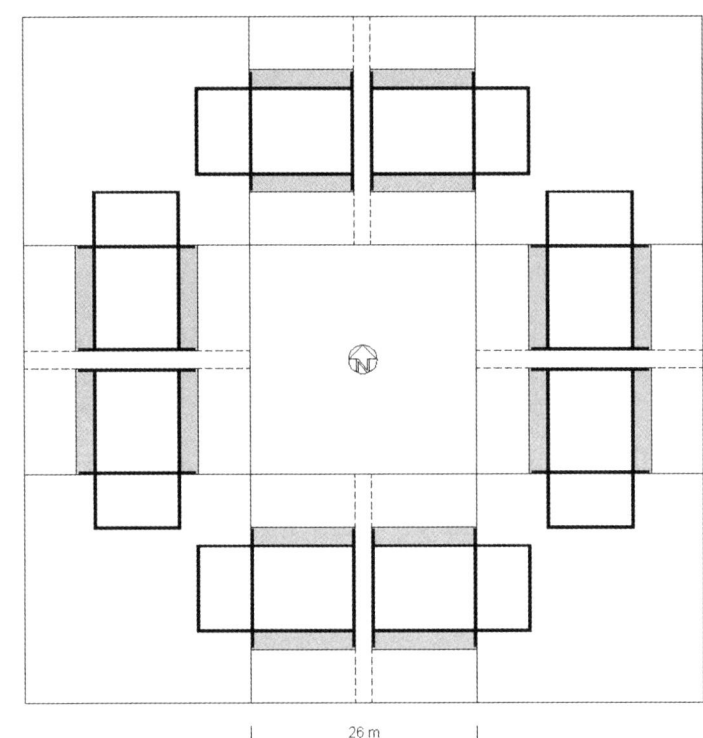

26 m

8.2 Proposed North American courtyard garden house system for Scheme B based on the "Six Squares" system
Source: Design and drawing by Donia Zhang, 2012–2014.

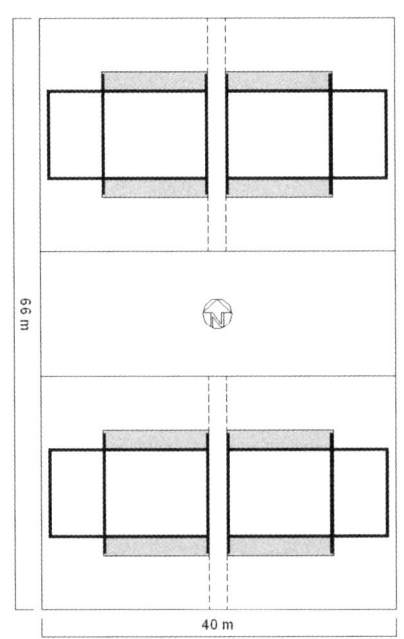

66 m

40 m

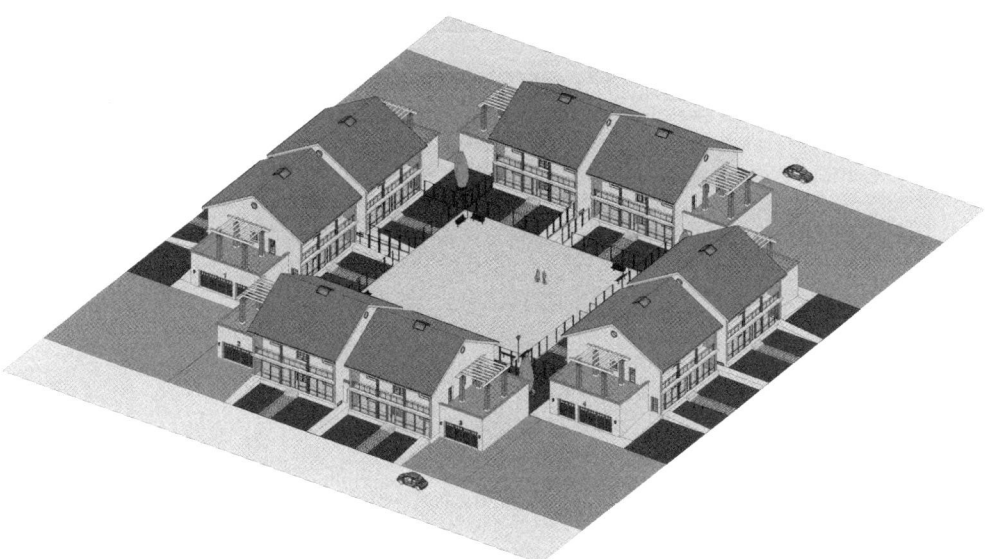

8.3   Scheme A of the proposed courtyard garden house compound housing eight nuclear families
Source: Design and model by Donia Zhang, 2012–2014.

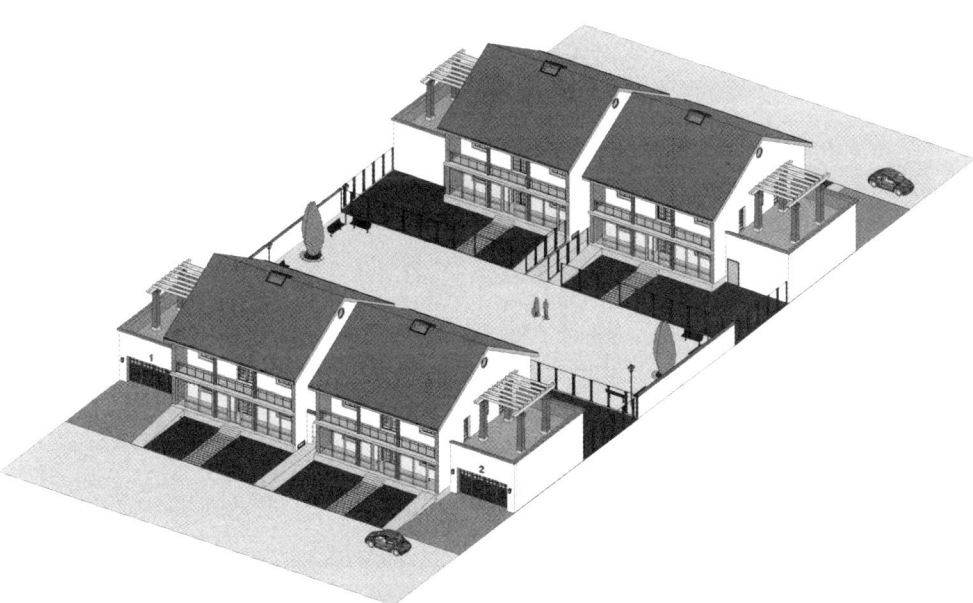

8.4   Scheme B of the proposed courtyard garden house compound housing four nuclear families
Source: Design and model by Donia Zhang, 2012–2014.

Gate and Access

Each housing unit has verandas, balconies, and barrier-free accesses. The main gate of each house is at the center of the front façade, with a second gate in the middle of the back façade. The courtyard can be accessed from the passage between two houses, with a lockable iron gate for safety.

8.5   Scheme A of the proposed courtyard garden house compound site plan
Source: Design and drawing by Donia Zhang, 2012–2014.

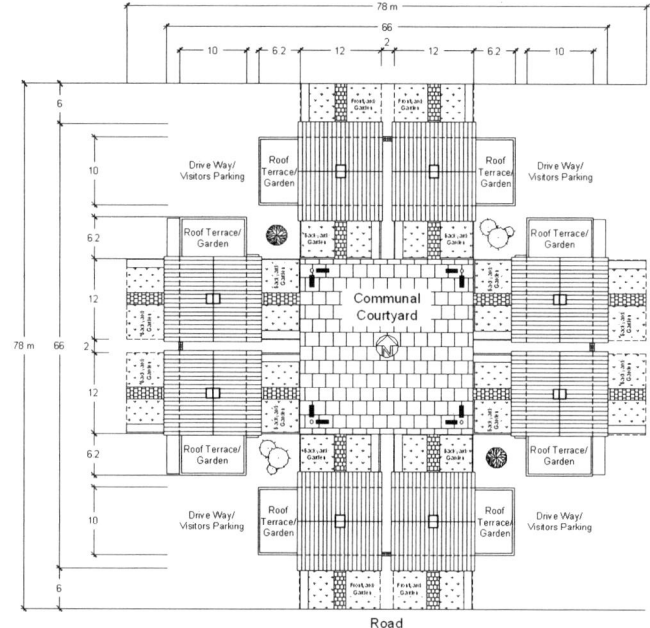

8.6   The pattern of Scheme A of the proposed courtyard garden house compound
Source: Design and drawing by Donia Zhang, 2012–2014.

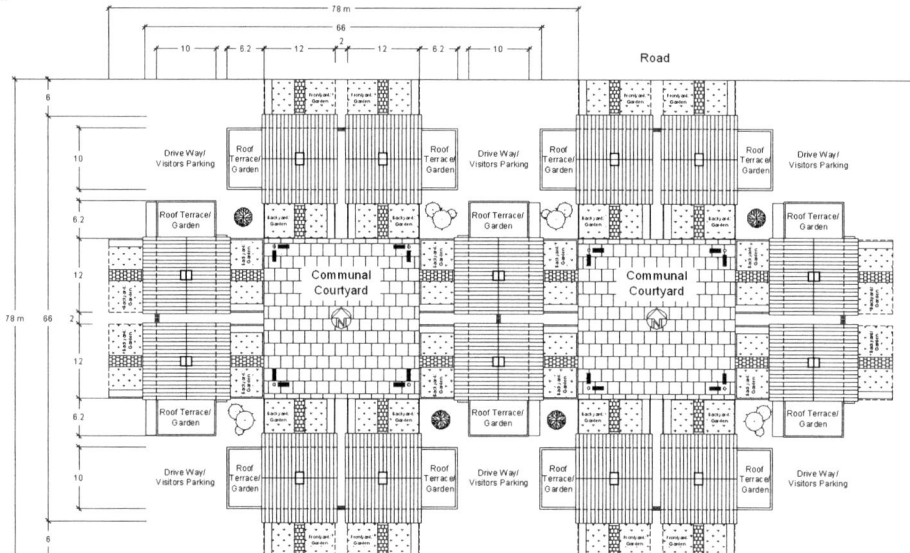

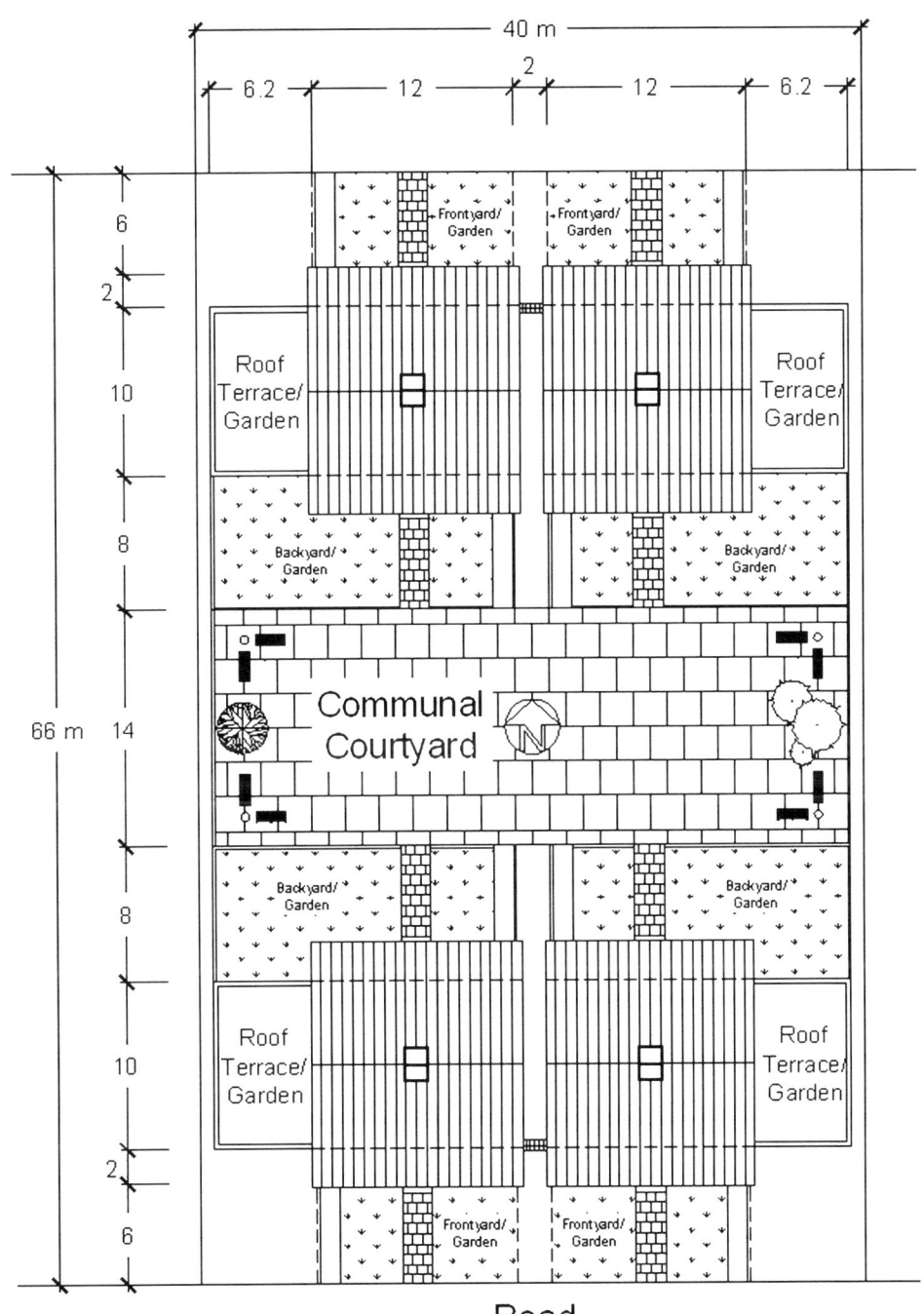

8.7   Scheme B of the proposed courtyard garden house compound site plan
Source: Design and drawing by Donia Zhang, 2012–2014.

Windows

Because residents preferred window orientations for better sunlight, natural ventilation, and views of nature, each housing unit is designed with a skylight and windows facing all four directions. Different window patterns add variety to an urban scene as well as for house identity.

8.8   Scheme A courtyard garden house elevations with three sets of different window patterns
Source: Design and drawing by Donia Zhang, 2012–2014.

8.9   Scheme B courtyard garden house elevations with three sets of different window patterns
Source: Design and drawing by Donia Zhang, 2012–2014.

Yards and Gardens

Since communal courtyards/gardens facilitate social interaction and private yards/gardens foster self-cultivation, providing both in the immediate surroundings of each house is best. The garden designs may follow the principles exhibited in classical Chinese gardens for a holistic approach to the human body-mind-spirit connection. Rainwater cisterns can be placed in the communal courtyard to collect rainwater to be purified and used by the residents. This eco-friendly design can reduce running water consumption and costs.

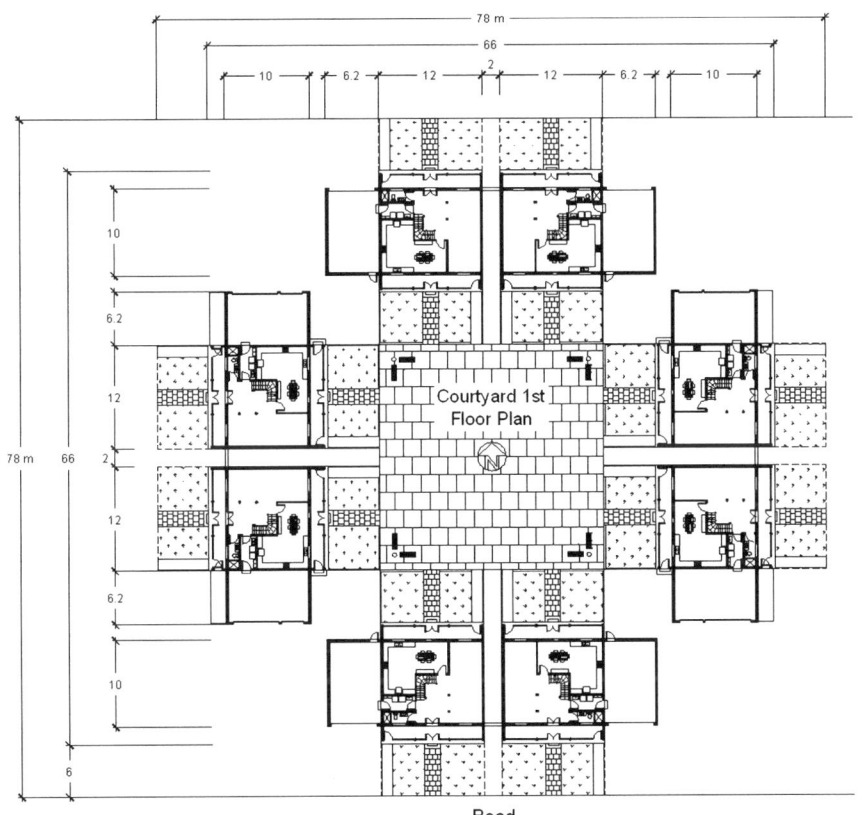

8.10   Scheme A courtyard garden house compound ground/first-floor plan
Source: Design and drawing by Donia Zhang, 2012–2014.

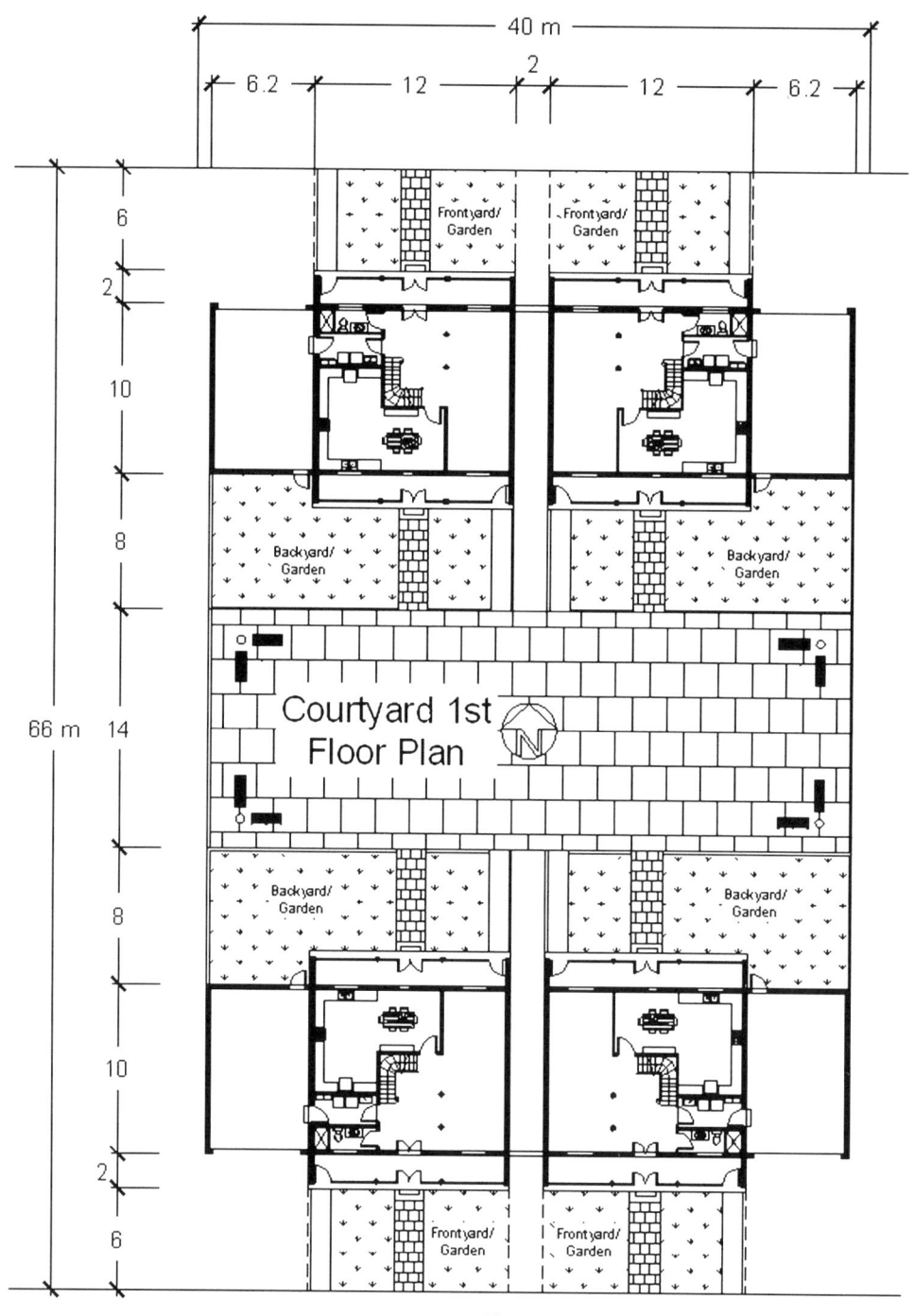

8.11 Scheme B courtyard garden house compound ground/first-floor plan
Source: Design and drawing by Donia Zhang, 2012–2014.

Roofs

As residents preferred pitched roofs more than flat ones for better thermal performance as well as aesthetic reasons, pitched roofs at a slope of 30 degrees are designed for both schemes. A skylight is also designed for each housing unit for admitting an even amount of daylight. Eaves are designed at 2.3 m deep to shelter the balconies (2 m deep) and prevent rainwater from slanting in. Solar panels can be placed on the roofs to generate electricity and reduce energy consumption.

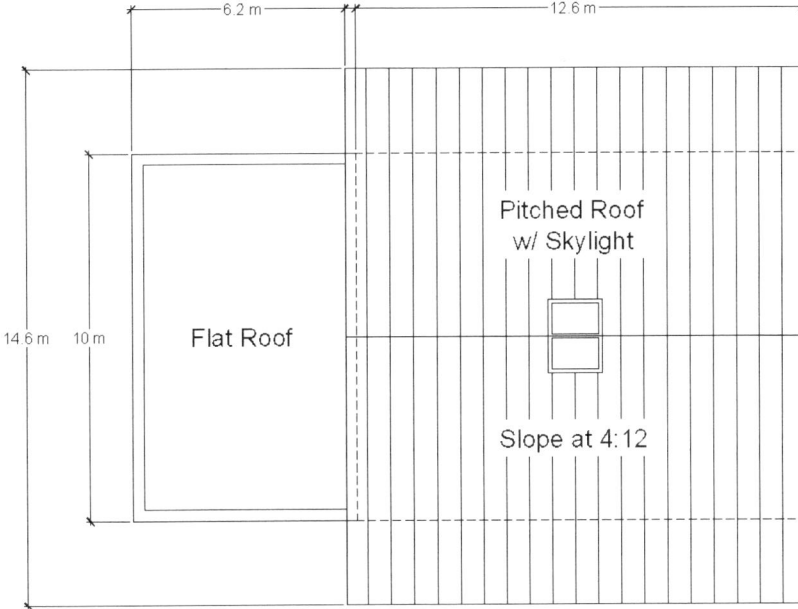

8.12   Courtyard garden house roof plan
Source: Design and drawing by Donia Zhang, 2012–2014.

Interior Space

In both schemes, each housing unit is rectangular in plan, with a width of 12 m, depth of 10 m, and a total internal floor area of 240 sqm (excluding basement and garage) for a 3–4-person household.

8.13   Proposed courtyard garden house semi-basement plan
Source: Design and drawing by Donia Zhang, 2012–2014.

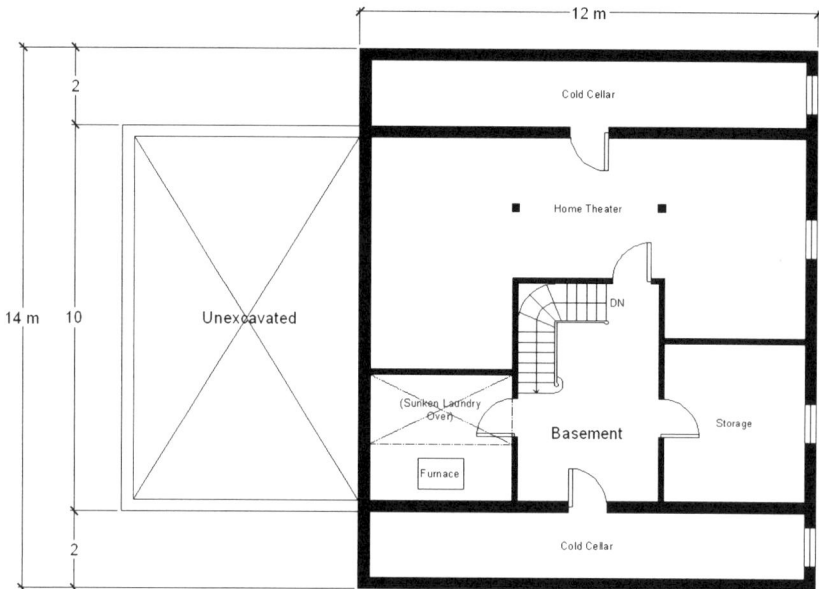

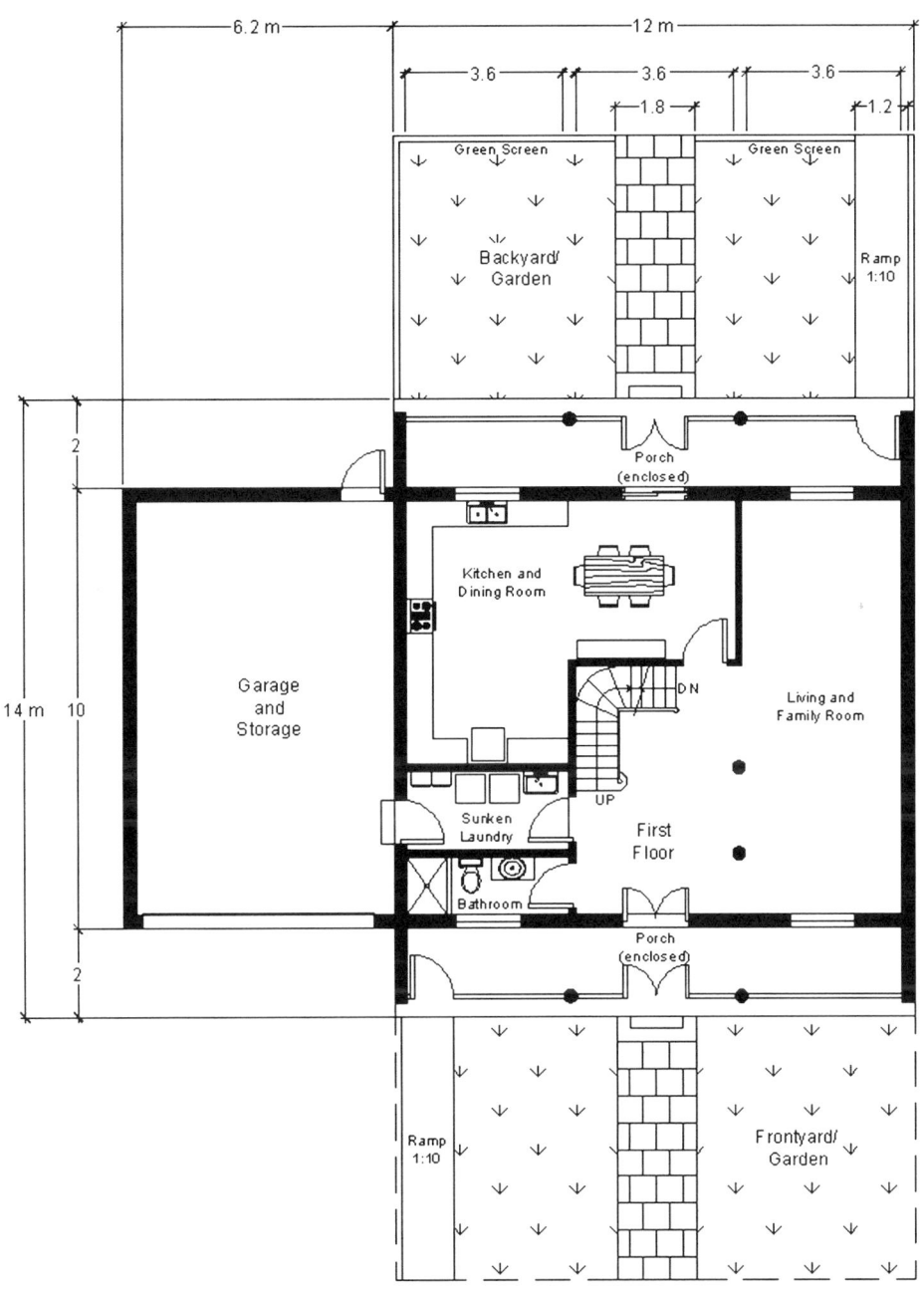

8.14 Scheme A of the proposed courtyard garden house ground/first-floor plan
Source: Design and drawing by Donia Zhang, 2012–2014.

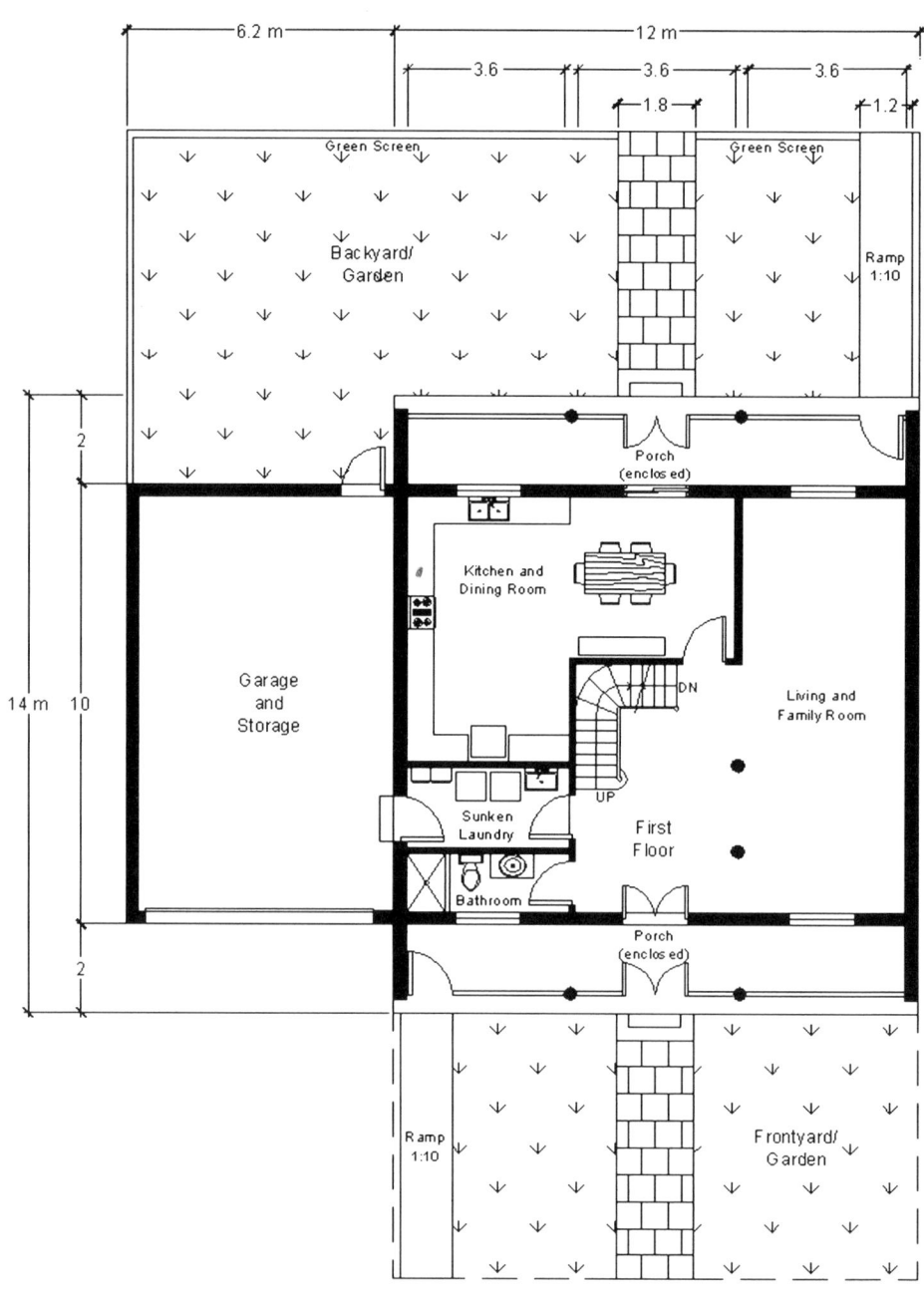

8.15   Scheme B of the proposed courtyard garden house ground/first-floor plan
Source: Design and drawing by Donia Zhang, 2012–2014.

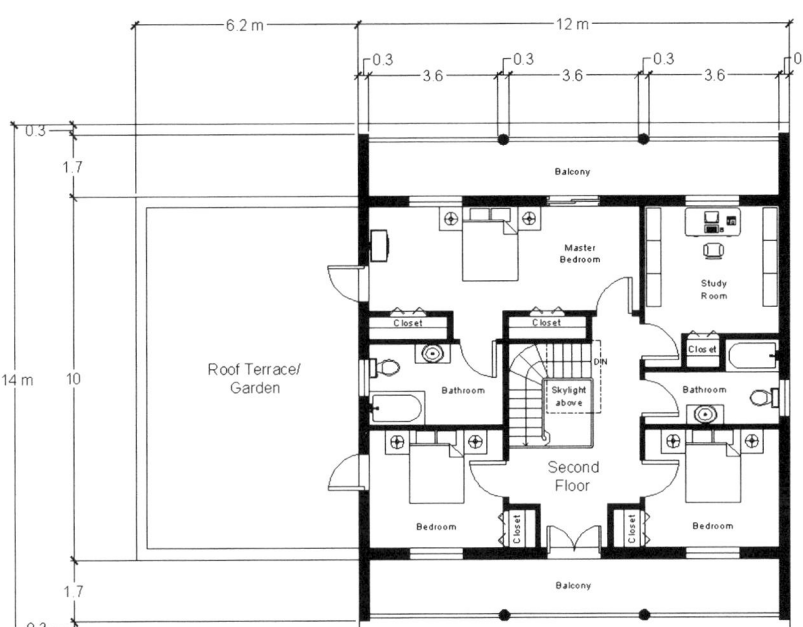

8.16   Proposed courtyard garden house second-floor plan
Source: Design and drawing by Donia Zhang, 2012–2014.

Floor Levels

My past and present research has shown that Chinese residents predominantly preferred housing of 1–3 storeys. Hence, the proposed courtyard garden houses are designed with 2.5 storeys plus a semi-basement.

Facility Provision

Besides the basic modern facilities such as running water, electricity, gas, heating system, air-conditioning, television and Internet cables, telephone lines, and so on, each housing unit is also designed with a storage space inside the garage for storing gardening tools and recycling and garbage bins. A lamp post for night-time users and a drainage hole for draining rainwater should be installed in the communal courtyard.

Car Park Spaces

For different household requirements and site design considerations, each of the south- and north-facing units has a two-car garage, and each of the east- and west-facing units has a three-car garage. These arrangements ensure the courtyards and gardens are safe places for children's play, and the elderly to conduct social and cultural activities.

Density and Plot Ratio

Assuming 3–5 persons in each household, Scheme A has a density of 39–66 persons per hectare, or 16–27 persons per acre, and plot ratio of 1:1.06 (Table 8.1); whereas Scheme B has a density of 45–76 persons per hectare, or 18–31 persons per acre, and plot ratio of 1:0.95 (Table 8.2). However, the less quantifiable, social and cultural implications of the designs cannot be easily estimated.

Table 8.1   Scheme A courtyard garden house density and plot ratio

Courtyard garden house Scheme A	
Built floor areas "A":	
A0 = 1,907 sqm (garages, roof terraces, porches, balconies, stairs, and ramps)	
A1 = 10×12×8 = 960 sqm (1st floor)	
A2 = 10×12×8 = 960 sqm (2nd floor)	
A = A0 + A1 + A2 = 3,827 sqm (total)	
Number of households: 8	
Number of persons: 24–40 (3–5 persons per household)	
Site area = X × Y = 66×66–190×4 = 3,596 sqm	
Plot area = 78×78 = 6,084 sqm = 0.6084 hectare = 1.5 acre	
Density =	Number of persons in block
	Plot area
Density = 39–66 persons/hectare = 16–27 persons/acre	
Plot ratio =	Site area
	Built floor area
Plot ratio = 1:1.06	

Note: 1 hectare = 2.47105 acre = 10,000 sqm; or 1 acre = 0.404685 hectare = 4,046.8 sqm; basement does not count.

Table 8.2   Scheme B courtyard garden house density and plot ratio

Courtyard garden house Scheme B	
Built floor areas "A":	
A0 = 953 sqm (garages, roof terraces, porches, balconies, stairs, and ramps)	
A1 = 10×12×4 = 480 sqm (1st floor)	
A2 = 10×12×4 = 480 sqm (2nd floor)	
A = A0 + A1 + A2 = 1,913 sqm (total)	
Number of households: 4	
Number of persons: 12–20 (3–5 persons per household)	
Site area = X × Y = 54×38.4–12.4×4 = 2,024 sqm	
Plot area = 66×40 = 2,640 sqm = 0.264 hectare = 0.65 acre	
Density =	Number of persons in block
	Plot area
Density = 45–76 persons/hectare = 18–31 persons/acre	
Plot ratio =	Site area
	Built floor area
Plot ratio = 1:0.95	

Note: 1 hectare = 2.47105 acre = 10,000 sqm; or 1 acre = 0.404685 hectare = 4,046.8 sqm; basement does not count.

Table 8.3   Summary of the proposed new courtyard garden houses

Design element	Scheme A	Scheme B	Reasons
1. Exterior form	Using the "Nine Squares" system; 78 m × 78 m standardized compound for 8 households	Using the "Six Squares" system; 66 m × 40 m standardized compound for 4 households	Cultural tradition and standardization
2. Gate and access	House gates at the center of each unit; verandas, balconies, and barrier-free access; courtyard gate between two houses	House gates at the center of each unit; verandas, balconies, and barrier-free access; courtyard gate between two houses	Cultural tradition, nature connection, and care for the disadvantaged groups
3. Windows	A skylight with windows facing 4 cardinal directions	A skylight with windows facing 4 cardinal directions	Sunlight, natural ventilation, and views of nature
4. Yards and gardens	26 m × 26 m courtyard with 8 private gardens	14 m × 40 m courtyard with 4 private gardens	Social interaction and self-cultivation
5. Roofs	Grey-tiled pitched roofs at a slope of 4:12	Black-tiled pitched roofs at a slope of 4:12	Cultural tradition and thermal comfort
6. Interior space	240 sqm	240 sqm	Spacious for a 2–5 person household
7. Floor levels	2.5 storeys plus a semi-basement	2.5 storeys plus a semi-basement	Residents' preference
8. Facility provision	Basic modern facilities	Basic modern facilities	Conveniences
9. Car park spaces	2–3-car garages with storage space; visitor parking on the driveways	2–3-car garages with storage space; visitor parking on the driveways	Abundance even for visitors
10. Density; plot ratio	39–66 persons/ha; 1:1.06	45–76 persons/ha; 1:0.95	Spatial comfort

Discussion

The density of a neighborhood affects health. Sternberg (2009) argued that denser social support networks make people healthier. Nevertheless, too many residents in an area may be overcrowded and infectious disease may flourish; too few, people may experience isolation and depression. Just enough will have a secure network of social ties to help people through good and bad times (Montgomery, 2013, p. 126; Sternberg, 2009, p. 291).

A study conducted by the Regional Plan Association on the optimum density for energy efficiency in the New York City suggested that per-capita energy consumption decreased up to a density of 39 persons per acre, or 13 house units per acre (Lyle, 1994, p. 130). Based on this assumption, Scheme B is more energy-efficient than Scheme A, which may reduce the energy costs of the houses, and which may make the residents happy. Nevertheless, Scheme A has a larger and more authentic courtyard space for social and cultural activities, but the optimum density for social and cultural network connection cannot be easily estimated.

Multiple courtyard garden house compounds can be built side by side in the residential lane structures in North American suburbs. This kind of communal living is important, philosophically and practically. Housing should be designed and built to help people live in harmony with the environment and other humans to sustain their health and happiness.

These two schemes are merely a suggestion—different interpretations of the guiding principles established in this section may result in different designs which may bring variety and diversity to a city and which may have implications for other places in the world. The ultimate goal of the proposal is for the betterment of human habitat pattern to enhance community development.

Appendix: Survey Questionnaire

PART I. ENVIRONMENTAL, ARCHITECTURAL, SPATIAL, AND CONSTRUCTIONAL ASPECTS

Location

1. Which country in North America do you live?
   - ☐ i.   USA
   - ☐ ii.   Canada

2. Which city do you live closest to?
   - ☐ i.   New York City
   - ☐ ii.   Los Angeles
   - ☐ iii.   San Francisco
   - ☐ iv.   Vancouver
   - ☐ v.   Toronto
   - ☐ vi.   Other (please specify)

3. Why did you choose to live in your neighborhood? Please select all that apply.
   - ☐ i.   Sunny area
   - ☐ ii.   Clean air, land, and water
   - ☐ iii.   Short walking/driving distance to a park/garden/green space
   - ☐ iv.   Short walking/driving distance to a good school/college/university
   - ☐ v.   Short walking/driving distance to workplace
   - ☐ vi.   Short walking/driving distance to a hospital
   - ☐ vii. Short walking/driving distance to family/friends
   - ☐ viii. Safe neighborhood
   - ☐ ix.   Walkable neighborhood
   - ☐ x.   Chinese community

☐   xi.   Community services
☐   xii.   Short walking/driving distance to shops/grocery/food stores
☐   xiii.   Short walking/driving distance to a farmers market
☐   xiv.   Short walking distance to public transit
☐   xv.   Aesthetics
☐   xvi.   All of the above
☐   xvii.   None of the above
☐   xviii.   Other (please specify)

Exterior Form

4.   Please indicate your building type.

	(1) Single-detached house	(2) Semi-detached house	(3) Row house	(4) Courtyard house/ housing	(5) Apartment in a building that has fewer than 5 storeys	(6) Apartment in a building that has 5 or more storeys
(a) Which type of house/ housing do you currently live?	☐	☐	☐	☐	☐	☐
(b) Which type of house/ housing may ideally promote physical health?	☐	☐	☐	☐	☐	☐

Exterior Walls

5. Please indicate your exterior walls.

	(1) Brick	(2) Concrete	(3) Stone	(4) Wood	(5) Prefabricated panel	(6) Unsure/I don't know
(a) What is the material of your house/housing exterior walls? Please select all that apply	☐	☐	☐	☐	☐	☐
(b) What material of exterior walls may ideally promote healthy environment? Please select all that apply	☐	☐	☐	☐	☐	☐

Gate Orientation

6. Please tell me about your home's front gate.

	(1) East	(2) Southeast	(3) South	(4) Southwest	(5) West	(6) Northwest	(7) North	(8) Northeast	(9) Unsure/I don't know
(a) What is the orientation of your home's front gate (or front entrance in the case of an apartment building)?	☐	☐	☐	☐	☐	☐	☐	☐	☐
(b) What orientation of your home's front gate (or front entrance in the case of an apartment building) may ideally promote physical health?	☐	☐	☐	☐	☐	☐	☐	☐	☐

Window Orientation

7. Which window orientation of your rooms may ideally promote physical health?

	(1) East	(2) Southeast	(3) South	(4) Southwest	(5) West	(6) Northwest	(7) North	(8) Northeast	(9) Sky	(10) Unsure/I don't know
(a) Living room	☐	☐	☐	☐	☐	☐	☐	☐	☐	☐
(b) Family room	☐	☐	☐	☐	☐	☐	☐	☐	☐	☐
(c) Study room	☐	☐	☐	☐	☐	☐	☐	☐	☐	☐
(d) Kitchen	☐	☐	☐	☐	☐	☐	☐	☐	☐	☐
(e) Dining room	☐	☐	☐	☐	☐	☐	☐	☐	☐	☐
(f) Bedroom	☐	☐	☐	☐	☐	☐	☐	☐	☐	☐
(g) Bathroom	☐	☐	☐	☐	☐	☐	☐	☐	☐	☐

8. Which window cross-ventilation orientation of your home may ideally promote physical health?

☐ i.   South–North
☐ ii.   East–West
☐ iii.   Northeast–Southwest
☐ iv.   Northwest–Southeast
☐ v.   Unsure/I don't know

Yards and Gardens

9. Please tell me about your home's outdoor spaces.

	(1) Front yard/ garden	(2) Back yard/ garden	(3) Courtyard/ garden	(4) Balcony/ deck	(5) Patio	(6) Roof terrace/ garden
(a) Does your home have the following outdoor spaces? Please select all that apply	☐	☐	☐	☐	☐	☐
(b) Which outdoor spaces around your home may ideally promote physical health? Please select all that apply	☐	☐	☐	☐	☐	☐

10. Do you grow food, vegetables, or fruits in the outdoor spaces around your home?

☐   i.   Yes
☐   ii.   No
☐   iii.   Not applicable

Roofs

11. Please tell me about your roof.

	(1) Pitched	(2) Flat	(3) Semi-pitched and semi-flat	(4) Not applicable	(5) Unsure/I don't know
(a) What roof shape does your house/ housing have?	☐	☐	☐	☐	☐
(b) What roof shape may ideally promote physical health? Please select all that apply	☐	☐	☐	☐	☐

12. Please tell me about your roof material.

	(1) Clay tiles	(2) Slate	(3) Concrete	(4) Metal/ copper	(5) Thatch	(6) Cedar	(7) Asphalt shingles	(8) Vinyl	(9) Unsure/I don't know
(a) What roof material do you have for your house/housing?	☐	☐	☐	☐	☐	☐	☐	☐	☐
(b) What roof material may ideally promote healthy environment? Please select all that apply	☐	☐	☐	☐	☐	☐	☐	☐	☐

Interior Space

13. How many family members live in your household? _____ persons
14. What is your home interior floor area? _____ sqm
15. What is your ideal size of home interior space that may promote physical health? ____sqm
16. What is your ideal room size that may promote physical health (in square meters)?

   ☐   i.   Living room _____sqm
   ☐   ii.   Family room _____sqm
   ☐   iii.   Study room _____sqm
   ☐   iv.   Kitchen _____sqm
   ☐   v.   Dining room _____sqm
   ☐   vi.   Bedroom _____sqm
   ☐   vii.   Bathroom _____sqm

Floor Level

17. Which floor level may ideally promote physical health? Please select all that apply.

   ☐   i.   Basement
   ☐   ii.   First floor
   ☐   iii.   Second floor
   ☐   iv.   Third floor
   ☐   v.   Rooftop
   ☐   vi.   Unsure/I don't know
   ☐   vii.   Not applicable
   ☐   viii.   Other (please specify)

Furniture Style and Material

18. What interior furniture style do you have at home? Please select all that apply.

   ☐   i.   Classical Chinese style
   ☐   ii.   Classical Western style
   ☐   iii.   Modern Chinese style
   ☐   iv.   Modern Western style
   ☐   v.   Mixed style
   ☐   vi.   No discernible style
   ☐   vii.   Other (please specify)

19. Please indicate your interior furniture material.

	(1) Wood	(2) Bamboo	(3) Cane	(4) Untreated cotton	(5) Synthetic material (plywood, etc.)	(6) Metal	(7) Glass
(a) What material is your home interior furniture made of? Please select all that apply	☐	☐	☐	☐	☐	☐	☐
(b) Which material for furniture may ideally promote physical health? Please select all that apply	☐	☐	☐	☐	☐	☐	☐

Facility Provision

20. What facilities in your home may ideally promote physical health? Please select all that apply.
- ☐ i.   Clean running water
- ☐ ii.   Electricity
- ☐ iii.   Gas
- ☐ iv.   Telephone line
- ☐ v.   Television cable
- ☐ vi.   Internet cable/digital subscriber line
- ☐ vii.   Heating system
- ☐ viii.   Air conditioner
- ☐ ix.   Air humidifier
- ☐ x.   Smoke detectors
- ☐ xi.   Carbon monoxide detectors
- ☐ xii.   Heat recovery ventilators (HRVs)
- ☐ xiii.   Energy recovery ventilators (ERVs)
- ☐ xiv.   Water purification system
- ☐ xv.   Solar panel
- ☐ xvi.   Whirlpool bathtub/Jacuzzi
- ☐ xvii.   Swimming pool

☐   xviii.   Green plants
☐   xix.   All of the above
☐   xx.   Other (please specify)

Construction Quality

21. How is the quality of construction of your house/housing unit?
☐   i.   Very good
☐   ii.   Good
☐   iii.   OK
☐   iv.   Bad
☐   v.   Very bad

Maintenance and Management

22. How healthy is your house/housing unit?
☐   i.   Very healthy
☐   ii.   Healthy
☐   iii.   Somewhat healthy
☐   iv.   Unhealthy
☐   v.   Very unhealthy

23. How often do you renovate your home interior? Once every
_____ years;

24. How often does the property management renovate your building? Once every ____ years;

25. How often to renovate a home may ideally promote physical health? Once every ___ years

26. How is the quality of maintenance work done by your property management?
☐   i.   Very good
☐   ii.   Good
☐   iii.   OK
☐   iv.   Bad
☐   v.   Very bad
☐   vi.   Not applicable

Car Park Space

27. How many car park spaces for your household may ideally promote physical health?
   - ☐ i.   None
   - ☐ ii.   One
   - ☐ iii. Two
   - ☐ iv.   Three
   - ☐ v.   Four
   - ☐ vi.   Unsure/I don't know
   - ☐ vii. Other (please specify)

PART II. ECONOMIC, SOCIAL, CULTURAL, AND BEHAVIORAL ASPECTS

Education, Occupation, and House-Purchasing Power

28. What is your educational level?
   - ☐ i.   High school graduate
   - ☐ ii.   Some college
   - ☐ iii. Associate's degree
   - ☐ iv.   Bachelor's degree
   - ☐ v.   Master's degree
   - ☐ vi.   Doctorate or professional degree
   - ☐ vii. Other (please specify)

29. What is your occupation?
   - ☐ i.   Legislators, senior officials, and managers
   - ☐ ii.   Professionals
   - ☐ iii.   Technicians and associate professionals
   - ☐ iv.   Clerks
   - ☐ v.   Service workers and shop and market sales workers
   - ☐ vi.   Skilled agricultural and fishery workers
   - ☐ vii.   Craft and related trades workers
   - ☐ viii. Plant and machine operators and assemblers
   - ☐ ix.   Elementary occupations
   - ☐ x.   Armed forces
   - ☐ xi.   Student

30. What is your employment status?
   - ☐ i.   Full-time employed
   - ☐ ii.   Part-time employed
   - ☐ iii. Self-employed
   - ☐ iv.   Unemployed
   - ☐ v.   Retired

31. What is your annual income level?
- ☐   i.   No income
- ☐   ii.   Below $30,000
- ☐   iii.   Between $30,000–$50,000
- ☐   iv.   Between $50,000–$100,000
- ☐   v.   Above $100,000

32. Do you own or rent your house/housing unit?
- ☐   i.   Own it
- ☐   ii.   Rent it
- ☐   iii.   Other (please specify)

Social Relations with Neighbors

33. How is the quality of interaction between you and your neighbors?
- ☐   i.   Very good
- ☐   ii.   Good
- ☐   iii.   OK
- ☐   iv.   Bad
- ☐   v.   Very bad
- ☐   vi.   No interaction

34. Which spaces help your relationship with neighbors? Please select all that apply.
- ☐   i.   Community/city park/garden
- ☐   ii.   Community center
- ☐   iii.   Health center/gym
- ☐   iv.   Schoolyard
- ☐   v.   Farmers market
- ☐   vi.   Shopping mall
- ☐   vii.   Local café/restaurant
- ☐   viii.   Grocery/food store
- ☐   ix.   Public library
- ☐   x.   Street/lane
- ☐   xi.   Front yard/garden
- ☐   xii.   Back yard/garden
- ☐   xiii.   Courtyard/garden
- ☐   xiv.   Balcony/deck
- ☐   xv.   Roof terrace/garden
- ☐   xvi.   All of the above
- ☐   xvii.   None of the above
- ☐   xviii.   Other (please specify)

Marriage/Wedding Anniversaries

35. What is your marital status?
- ☐ i. Never married
- ☐ ii. Living common law
- ☐ iii. First marriage
- ☐ iv. Divorced or separated
- ☐ v. Remarried
- ☐ vi. Widowed

36. If you are married, is your spouse of Chinese origin?
- ☐ i. Yes, it is an intra-ethnic marriage
- ☐ ii. No, it is an inter-ethnic marriage
- ☐ iii. No, it is an inter-racial marriage
- ☐ iv. Not applicable

37. Do you celebrate your wedding anniversaries?
- ☐ i. Yes
- ☐ ii. No
- ☐ iii. Not applicable

Relations among Family Members

38. How many generations of family members live in your household?
- ☐ i. One generation
- ☐ ii. Two generations
- ☐ iii. Three generations
- ☐ iv. Four generations
- ☐ v. Other (please specify)

39. Please tell me about the quality of interaction with your family members.

	(1) Very good	(2) Good	(3) OK	(4) Bad	(5) Very bad	(6) Not applicable
(a) How is the quality of interaction between you and your spouse/partner?	☐	☐	☐	☐	☐	☐
(b) How is the quality of interaction between you and your child(ren)?	☐	☐	☐	☐	☐	☐
(c) How is the quality of interaction between you and your parent(s) or parent(s)-in-law?	☐	☐	☐	☐	☐	☐

Philosophy and Religion

40. Do you have any of the following faiths? Please select all that apply.
☐   i.   *Yi Jing*
☐   ii.   *Feng Shui*
☐   iii.   Confucianism
☐   iv.   Daoism
☐   v.   Buddhism
☐   vi.   Catholic
☐   vii.   Protestant
☐   viii.   Islam
☐   ix.   No faith
☐   x.   Other (please specify)

41. How happy are you with your home?
☐   i.   Very happy
☐   ii.   Happy
☐   iii.   Somewhat happy
☐   iv.   Unhappy
☐   v.   Very unhappy

42. Please tell me about your health.

	(1) Very healthy	(2) Healthy	(3) Somewhat healthy	(4) Unhealthy	(5) Very unhealthy
(a) What is your mental health status?	☐	☐	☐	☐	☐
(b) What is your physical health status?	☐	☐	☐	☐	☐

Daily Activities

43. Which daily activity(ies) at home make(s) you happy? Please select all that apply.

☐ i.   Watching TV/DVDs/movies
☐ ii.   Playing computer games/browsing the Internet
☐ iii.   Reading books/ebooks/newspapers/magazines
☐ iv.   Listening to the radio
☐ v.   Listening to music
☐ vi.   Eating food
☐ vii.   Drinking tea
☐ viii.   Drinking wine
☐ ix.   Sunbathing
☐ x.   Gardening
☐ xi.   Exercising/maintaining health/natural healing
☐ xii.   Dancing
☐ xiii.   Singing
☐ xiv.   Playing musical instruments
☐ xv.   Holding parties
☐ xvi.   Playing table games (*weiqi*, *majiang*, cards, etc.)
☐ xvii.   Doing painting
☐ xviii.   Practising calligraphy
☐ xix.   Composing essays/poetry
☐ xx.   Making models
☐ xxi.   Repairing house
☐ xxii.   Looking after children/elderly/family members
☐ xxiii.   All of the above
☐ xxiv.   None of the above
☐ xxv.   Other (please specify)

44. What time(s) do you conduct your favorite activity at home? Please select all that apply.

☐ i.   4 am–8 am
☐ ii.   8 am–12 noon

☐   iii.   12 noon–4 pm
☐   iv.   4 pm–8 pm
☐   v.   8 pm–12 midnight
☐   vi.   12 midnight–4 am
☐   vii.   Irregular

45. What day(s) do you conduct your favorite activity at home? Please select all that apply.
☐   i.   Monday
☐   ii.   Tuesday
☐   iii.   Wednesday
☐   iv.   Thursday
☐   v.   Friday
☐   vi.   Saturday
☐   vii.   Sunday
☐   viii.   Irregular

46. What season(s) do you conduct your favorite activity at home? Please select all that apply.
☐   i.   Spring
☐   ii.   Summer
☐   iii.   Autumn
☐   iv.   Winter
☐   v.   Irregular

47. How long do you normally spend on your favorite activity at home each time? ___ hours

48. How often do you normally spend on your favorite activity at home?
☐   i.   At least 1–3 times weekly
☐   ii.   At least 1–3 times monthly
☐   iii.   At least 1–3 times quarterly
☐   iv.   At least 1–3 times annually
☐   v.   Irregular

49. Where do you conduct your favorite activity if not at home? Please select all that apply.
☐   i.   Community/city park/garden
☐   ii.   Community center
☐   iii.   Health center/gym
☐   iv.   Schoolyard
☐   v.   Farmers market
☐   vi.   Shopping mall
☐   vii.   Local café/restaurant
☐   viii.   Public library

☐   ix.   Bookstore
☐   x.   Museum/art gallery
☐   xi.   Cinema/theater
☐   xii.   Street/lane
☐   xiii.   Office/studio
☐   xiv.   Other (please specify)

Chinese Cultural Festivities

50. Which Chinese cultural festivities make you happy? Please select all that apply.
☐   i.   Spring Festival (Lunar New Year, 1st day of the 1st lunar month)
☐   ii.   Lantern Festival (Spring Spirit Festival, 15th day of the 1st lunar month)
☐   iii.   Blue Dragon Festival (Dragon Raising its Head, 2nd day of the 2nd lunar month)
☐   iv.   Shangsi Festival (Spring Purification Festival, 3rd day of the 3rd lunar month)
☐   v.   Qing Ming (Clear Brightness Festival, April 5, April 4 on a leap year)
☐   vi.   Dragon Boat Festival (5th day of the 5th lunar month)
☐   vii.   Bathing and Basking Festival (6th day of the 6th lunar month)
☐   viii.   Night of Sevens (Chinese Valentine's Day, 7th day of the 7th lunar month)
☐   ix.   Mid-Summer Spirit Festival (15th day of the 7th lunar month)
☐   x.   Mid-Autumn Festival (or Moon Festival, 15th day of the 8th lunar month)
☐   xi.   Double Ninth Festival (9th day of the 9th lunar month)
☐   xii.   Autumn Spirit Festival (15th day of the 10th lunar month)
☐   xiii.   Winter Solstice Festival (December 21–22)
☐   xiv.   Laba Festival (Congee Festival, 8th day of the 12th lunar month)
☐   xv.   Thanksgiving to the Stove God (23rd day of the 12th lunar month)
☐   xvi.   All of the above
☐   xvii.   None of the above
☐   xviii.   Other (please specify)

51. Which spaces do you use to conduct Chinese cultural festivities? Please select all that apply.
☐   i.   Living room
☐   ii.   Family room
☐   iii.   Study room
☐   iv.   Kitchen
☐   v.   Dining room
☐   vi.   Loft space

- ☐ vii. Sunspace
- ☐ viii. Front yard/garden
- ☐ ix. Back yard/garden
- ☐ x. Courtyard/garden
- ☐ xi. Balcony/deck
- ☐ xii. Roof terrace/garden
- ☐ xiii. Community/city park/garden
- ☐ xiv. Community center
- ☐ xv. Schoolyard
- ☐ xvi. Street/lane
- ☐ xvii. All of the above
- ☐ xviii. None of the above
- ☐ xix. Other (please specify)

Birthday Celebrations

52. Do you celebrate birthdays?
- ☐ i. Yes
- ☐ ii. No
- ☐ iii. Sometimes

53. Welcome to add comments on the housing in which you live that have not been asked in the questionnaire.

Participant Information

54. What is your age? _____ (you must be 16 years or older)

55. What is your gender?
- ☐ i. Male
- ☐ ii. Female
- ☐ iii. Third gender/intersex

56. Which generation of Chinese are you in North America?
- ☐ i. First generation
- ☐ ii. Second generation
- ☐ iii. Third generation
- ☐ iv. Other (please specify)

57. What language(s) do you speak at home? Please select all that apply.
☐   i.   Mandarin
☐   ii.   Cantonese
☐   iii.   Other Chinese dialect
☐   iv.   English
☐   v.   French
☐   vi.   Other (please specify)

58. Which country/region did you or your ancestors come from? Please select all that apply.
☐   i.   Mainland China
☐   ii.   Taiwan
☐   iii.   Hong Kong
☐   iv.   Other (please specify)

59. Have you lived in a traditional Chinese courtyard house in your country of origin?
☐   i.   Yes
☐   ii.   No

60. How long have you lived in North America? _____ years

61. Would you like to participate in a follow-up email or telephone interview?
☐   i.   Yes
☐   ii.   No

62. Would you like to receive the results of the study?
☐   i.   Yes
☐   ii.   No

63. If yes, please leave your email and/or telephone number.
    a.   Email: _____
    b.   Phone: _____
    c.   Name (optional): _____
    d.   Address (optional): _____
         _____

Thank you for your participation in the study. Your input is vital to the success of the project.

COLOR CONNOTATIONS ASSOCIATED WITH ORIENTATION AND EMOTION

Q1. The box below represents four orientations: north, east, south, and west. Please fill in each quarter of the box with a color of your choice, and briefly state reasons why you choose that particular color for that quarter of box.

1. East
2. South
3. West
4. North

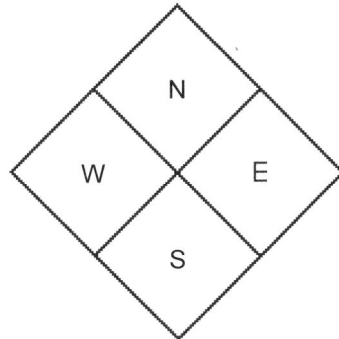

Q2. Please state the color you think most appropriate for the expression of the below-mentioned emotion, and give reasons wherever possible:
5. Happiness:
6. Grief:
7. Love:
8. Hate:

Q3. Do you think there is a correlation between emotion and north–south/east–west orientation? Please circle the answer below and, if yes, please briefly state which emotion correlates to which orientation and why.   Yes / No
9. Why?

Thank You!

INTERVIEW QUESTIONNAIRE FOR ETHNIC CHINESE RESIDENTS

Q1. What housing form may promote physical and mental health, and why?

Q2. Will you be happier if your house exterior is in a traditional Chinese architectural style, and why?

Q3. Do you like the idea of having a communal courtyard near your home, and why? Do you like to have balconies?

Q4. What roof shape may promote physical health, and why? Do you like to have a roof terrace/garden?

Q5. How large is your home interior space that may promote physical health, and why? Do you prefer an open plan for your first floor?

Q6. Which floor level may promote physical health, and why?

Q7. How is the quality of interaction between you and your neighbors? Which space(s) help your relationship with neighbors? Please explain.

Q8. How is the quality of interaction between you and your family members (spouse/partner, children, and parent(s) or parent(s)-in-law)? Please explain.

Q9. Do you believe in any philosophy or religion? If yes, is this belief reflected in your home decoration?

Q10. What is your major activity at home in an ordinary day? Which space do you use for this activity?

Q11. What traditional Chinese cultural festivals do you celebrate? Where and how do you celebrate them?

Q12. Where and how do you celebrate birthdays and wedding anniversaries, if applicable?

INTERVIEW QUESTIONNAIRE FOR NON-CHINESE RESIDENTS

Q1. What are the things that make you *happy* about the life in the communal courtyard?

Q2. What are the things that make you *unhappy* about the life in the communal courtyard?

Q3. What can be done to improve your living experience in the communal courtyard?

INTERVIEW QUESTIONNAIRE FOR PLANNERS

Q1. Are there any planning regulations for building courtyard housing in North America?

Q2. What are the planning regulations?

Q3. What can planners do to better facilitate Chinese residential cultural tradition in North America?

Bibliography

Abada, T., Hou, F., and Ram, B. (2008). *Group differences in educational attainment among the children of immigrants*. Research Paper, University of Western Ontario, and Statistics Canada Business and Labour Market Analysis Division. Retrieved July 7, 2012 from: http://www.statcan.gc.ca/pub/11f0019m/11f0019m2008308-eng.pdf.

Achugbue, E. (2005). Multiculturalism and planning: Lessons from Vancouver. Master's in City Planning thesis, Massachusetts Institute of Technology, USA.

Adair, J. (2003). *Canadian builders add luxury features, energy efficiency*. Retrieved July 13, 2013 from: http://realtytimes.com/rtpages/20030313_cabuilders.htm.

Agrawal, S. (2012). *The practice of multicultural planning in American and Canadian cities*. Association of European Schools of Planning, 26th Annual Congress, July 11–15, 2012, Ankara, Turkey. Retrieved July 18, 2013 from: http://www.arber.com.tr/aesop2012.org/abstractsebook/Abstract/Abstract315.pdf.

Agyeman, J. (2011). *Grow Canada? Multiculturalism, environmental policy and planning*. Retrieved July 15, 2013 from: http://julianagyeman.com/2011/03/multiculturalism-environmental-policy-and-planning.

Ahmed, S., Castaneda, C., Fortier, A.-M., et al. (eds) (2003). *Uprooting/regroundings: Questions of home and migration*. Oxford and New York: Berg.

Arends, B. (2014). *It's official: America is now no. 2*. Retrieved December 28, 2014 from: http://www.marketwatch.com/story/its-official-america-is-now-no-2-2014-12-04.

Argyle, M. (2001). Personality and happiness: Who are the happy people? In S. McCready (ed.), *The discovery of happiness*. Naperville, IL: Sourcebooks, pp. 172–83.

Aristotle (1926). *The "art" of rhetoric* (translated by J.H. Freese). Cambridge, MA: Loeb Classical Library, Harvard University Press.

—— (1999). *Nicomachean ethics* (translated by T. Irwin, 2nd edn). Indianapolis, IN: Hackett.

Ashton, J., Grey, P., and Barnard, K. (1986). Healthy cities: WHO's new public health initiative. *Health promotion international*, 1(3), pp. 319–24.

Aterman, P. (1993). Housing policy and immigration: The case of the Chinese in Montreal. Master's Thesis in Urban Planning, School of Urban Planning, Faculty of Graduate Studies and Research, McGill University, Canada.

Austin, A. (2013). *100 Bain Avenue, Toronto, Canada's Garden City 1913–2013: The early years*. Toronto, ON: Alvyn Austin.

Awofeso, N. (2003). The healthy cities approach: Reflections on a framework for improving global health. *Bulletin of the World Health Organization*. Retrieved August 12, 2012 from: http://www.scielosp.org/scielo.php?pid=S0042-96862003000300013&script=sci_arttext.

Baird, D. (2002). *A thousand paths to happiness*. Hallmark: Gift Books.

Baker-Laporte, P., Elliott, E., and Banta, J. (2008). *Prescriptions for a healthy house: A practical guide for architects, builders and homeowners* (3rd edn). Gabriola Island, BC: New Society Publishers.

Bartlett, T. (2014). *A tape-measure for well-being*. Retrieved May 16, 2014 from: http://chronicle.com/blogs/percolator/a-tape-measure-for-well-being/34283.

Bashir, S.A. (2002). Home is where the harm is: Inadequate housing as a public health crisis. *American journal of public health*, 92(5), pp. 733–8.

Becker, R.O. and Selden, G. (1998). *The body electric: Electromagnetism and the foundation of life*. New York, NY: William Morrow Paperbacks, an imprint of HarperCollins.

Bentham, J. (1789). *Introduction to the principles of morals and legislation*. London: Payne.

Bergsma, A. and Ardelt, M. (2012). Self-reported wisdom and happiness: An empirical investigation. *Journal of happiness studies*, 13, pp. 481–99.

Bergsma, A., Poot, G., and Liefbroer, A.C. (2008). Happiness in the garden of Epicurus. *Journal of happiness studies*, 9, pp. 397–423.

Berman, A. (2001). *Your naturally healthy home: Stylish, safe, simple*. Emmaus, PA: Rodale Press.

Beynon, D. (2009). Architecture, multiculturalism and cultural sustainability in Australian cities. *International journal of environmental, cultural, economic and social sustainability*, 5(2), pp. 45–58.

Biswas-Diener, R., Kashdan, T.B., and King, L.A. (2009). Two traditions of happiness research, not two distinct types of happiness. *Journal of positive psychology*, 4(3), pp. 208–11.

Björk, J., Albin, M., Grahn, P., et al. (2008). Recreational values of the natural environment in relation to neighbourhood satisfaction, physical activity, obesity and wellbeing. *Journal of epidemiology and community health*, 62(e2).

Blaser, W. (1995). *Courtyard house in China: Tradition and present* (2nd enlarged edn). Basel/Boston/Berlin: Birkhäuser Verlag.

Blunt, A. and Dowling, R. (2006). *Home*. New York, NY: Routledge.

BMJ (2008). *How should health be defined?* Retrieved August 11, 2012 from: http://www.bmj.com/content/337/bmj.a2900.full.

Boonekamp, G.M.M., Colomer, C., Tomás, A., et al. (1999). Healthy cities evaluation: The co-ordinators perspective. *Health promotion international*, 14(2), pp. 103–10.

Boothroyd, P. and Eberle, M. (1990). *Healthy communities: What they are, how they're made*. Vancouver, BC: Center for Human Settlements, University of British Columbia.

Borjas, G.J. (2002). *Homeownership in the immigrant population*. NBER Working Paper 8945, National Bureau of Economic Research, Cambridge, MA.

Bower, J. (2000). *The healthy house: How to buy one, how to build one, how to cure a sick one* (4th edn). Boise, ID: Healthy House Institute.

Broffman, W. (2008). *Romancing the courtyard*. Retrieved March 28, 2013 from: http://www.multihousingpro.com/article.php?AID=313.

Bryson, B. (1996). *Made in America: An informal history of the English language in the United States*. New York, NY: HarperCollins/William Morrow Paperbacks.

California Association of Realtors (2011). *2011 annual housing market survey*. California, CA: California Association of Realtors.

Callahan, D. (1973). The WHO definition of "health." *The Hastings Center studies*, 1(3), pp. 77–87.

Canada Mortgage and Housing Corporation (1994/2009). *Healthy housing: Practical tips for your home*. Retrieved July 10, 2012 from: http://www.cmhc-schl.gc.ca/odpub/pdf/60916E.pdf.

—— (1996). *Chinese elderly: Social integration in Metro Toronto Housing Company Ltd.* Ottawa, ON: CMHC.

—— (1996–2012). *What does the term "healthy house" mean?* Retrieved July 10, 2012 from: https://www.cmhc-schl.gc.ca/en/co/maho/yohoyohe/heho/hehoto/hehoto_003.cfm#1.

—— (2013). *Canadian housing observer*. Ottawa, ON: CMHC.

Canada Post (2013). *Chinatown gates: Souvenir sheet*. Retrieved May 30, 2013 from: http://www.canadapost.ca/shop/stamp-collecting/details-april-june-2013/p-403892145.jsf?execution=e1s1.

Canadian Cohousing Network (2004). *About us*. Retrieved August 26, 2013 from: http://www.cohousing.ca/aboutus.htm.

Canadian Home Builders' Association (2013). *Pulse survey*. Ottawa, ON: CHBA.

Canadian Tuberculosis Committee (2007). Housing conditions that serve as risk factors for tuberculosis infection and disease. *Canadian communicable disease report*, 33.

Carver, H. (1948). *Houses for Canadians: A study of housing problems in the Toronto area*. Toronto, ON: University of Toronto Press.

Case Adams Naturopath (2012). *Electromagnetic health: Making sense of the research and practical solutions for electromagnetic fields (EMF) and radio frequencies (RF)*. Wilmington, DE: Logical Books.

Chang, I. (2003). *The Chinese in America: A narrative history*. New York, NY: Viking Press.

Chang, S.C.Y. (1997). *Child care needs of Chinese immigrant families in B.C.: A case study*. Centre for Human Settlements, School of Community and Regional Planning, University of British Columbia, Vancouver, Canada.

Chen, S. (2002). *Being Chinese, becoming Chinese American*. Champaign, IL: University of Illinois Press.

Chen, W. (2006). *The impact of Internet use on transnational entrepreneurship: The case of Chinese immigrants to Canada*. Retrieved July 7, 2012 from: http://homes.chass.utoronto.ca/~wellman/undergrad05/chen.pdf.

China City of America (2014). *China City of America becoming reality in Catskills*. Retrieved September 30, 2014 from: http://www.chinacityofamerica.com.

China City of America Introductory Meeting, Town of Thompson, NY (2013, May 15). Retrieved June 15, 2013 from: http://www.youtube.com/watch?v=Mw6gr6FAH5M.

China City of America Presentation, Mamakating, NY (2013, May 23). Retrieved June 15, 2013 from: http://www.youtube.com/watch?v=7_ZvP97KxgE.

Chiras, D.D. (2000). *The natural house: A complete guide to healthy, energy-efficient, environmental homes*. White River Junction, VT: Chelsea Green.

Chu, K. and Schmit, J. (2012, April 3). U.S. home market pulls in more Chinese buyers. *USA Today*. Retrieved July 23, 2012 from: http://www.usatoday.com/money/economy/housing/story/2012-04-03/us-homes-lure-chinese-buyers/53977638/1Doing.

City of Portland (2008). *Courtyard housing: A catalogue of designs and design principles* (Portland Courtyard Housing Design Competition). Portland, OR: Strategy Custom Publishing.

City of Toronto Healthy City Office (1991). *The liveable metropolis*. Toronto, ON: Metropolitan Toronto Planning Department.

Committee of 100 (2006). *Committee of 100 announces results of landmark national survey on American attitudes towards Chinese Americans and Asian Americans*. Retrieved July 7, 2012 from: http://www.committee100.org/media/media_eng/042501.html.

Conference Board of Canada (2010). *Building from the ground up: Enhancing affordable housing in Canada*. Ottawa, ON: The Conference Board of Canada. Retrieved August 24, 2012 from: http://www.conferenceboard.ca/documents.aspx?did=3530.

Confucius (551–479 BCE). *Confucian analects, the great learning, and the doctrine of the mean* (translated and annotated by J. Legge, 1893/1971). New York, NY: Dover Publications.

Cooper, M. (2001). *Housing affordability: A children's issue* (Canadian Policy Research Networks Discussion Paper No. F11). Ottawa, ON: Canadian Policy Research Networks.

Cooper, M. and Rodman, M. (1992). *New neighbours: A case study of cooperative housing in Toronto*. Toronto, ON: University of Toronto Press.

Cott, N. (2009). *Health and the environment: Global warming and health*. New York, NY: AlphaHouse.

Coyne, C.J. and Boettke, P.J. (n.d.). *Economics and happiness research: Insights from Austrian and public choice economics*. Retrieved September 6, 2012 from: http://www.ccoyne.com/happiness_and_economics.pdf.

Cravit, C.R. (2006–2009). *Happiness and your health*. Fifty-Plus.Net International Inc. Retrieved August 18, 2012 from: http://www.50plus.com/Health/BrowseAllArticles/index.cfm?documentID=15200.

Creative City Network of Canada (2004). *Quality of place, quality of life*. Special Edition 1. Vancouver, BC: Creative City Network of Canada.

—— (2005). *Nurturing culture and creativity to build community*. Special Edition 2. Vancouver, BC: Creative City Network of Canada.

—— (2006). *Culture: The forth pillar of sustainability*. Special Edition 3. Vancouver, BC: Creative City Network of Canada.

—— (2007). *Models of sustainability incorporating culture*. Special Edition 4. Vancouver, BC: Creative City Network of Canada.

Cruz-Viesca, M.D. and Chiu, B. (2008). *Following the path to Asian American homeownership*. Asian Real Estate Association of America (AREAA) via American Community Survey, pp. 9–11. Retrieved July 8, 2012 from: http://areaa.org/resources/AREAA_Demographic_Report.pdf.

DeVoretz, D.J. (2009). *Immigrant circulation and citizenship: Hotel Canada?* Retrieved July 7, 2012 from: http://www.asiapacific.ca/sites/default/files/filefield/PP_09_4_DD_HotelCanada.pdf.

Dooley, T. (2003). *Industry watch: Chinese lead immigrant groups in homeownership*. National Association of Realtors. Retrieved July 8, 2012 from: http://realtormag.realtor.org/news-and-commentary/feature/article/2003/01/industry-watch-chinese-lead-immigrant-groups-homeownersh.

Doran, C.F. (2001). *Why Canadian unity matters and why Americans care: Democratic pluralism at risk*. Toronto, ON: University of Toronto Press.

Duhl, L. (2005). Healthy cities and the built environment. *Built environment*, 31(4), pp. 356–61.

Dunn, J.R. (2002). *The population health approach to housing: A framework for research*. Ottawa, ON: Canada Mortgage and Housing Corporation. Retrieved August 27, 2012 from: ftp://ftp.cmhc-schl.gc.ca/chic-ccdh/Research_Reports-Rapports_de_recherche/eng_bilingual/Population%20health%20approach%20to%20housing.pdf.

Durrett, C. (2009). *Senior cohousing handbook: A community approach to independent living* (2nd edn). Gabriola Island, BC: New Society Publishers.

Easterlin, R. (2003). Explaining happiness. *Proceedings of the National Academy of Sciences*, 100(19), pp. 11176–83.

Eberhard, J.P. (2007). *Architecture and the brain: A new knowledge base from neuroscience*. Atlanta, GA: Greenway Communications.

Eberhard, J.P. (2009). *Brain landscape: The coexistence of neuroscience and architecture*. Oxford: Oxford University Press.

Ekblad, S., Chen, C-H., Huang, Y.-Q., et al. (1992). Effects of dwelling types and facilities on crowding, stress, life satisfaction and health of households in western Beijing. *Ekistics*, 354/355, pp. 195–205.

Ekblad, S. and Werne, F. (1990). Housing and health in Beijing: Implications of high-rise housing on children and the aged. *Journal of sociology and social welfare*, 17(1), pp. 51–77.

Enterprise Foundation (2002). *Rivermont House Carrfour Supportive Housing, Miami, Florida*. Retrieved July 5, 2005 from: http://www.enterprisefoundation.org/resources/erd/resource.asp?id=1584&c=7&a=view&f=browse.

Fincher, R. (2003). Planning for cities of diversity, difference and encounter. *Australian Planner*, 40(1), pp. 55–8.

Foroohar, R. (2007). *The joy of economics*. Retrieved August 9, 2012 from: http://www.thedailybeast.com/newsweek/2007/04/04/the-joy-of-economics.html.

Fortier, A.-M. (2001). "Coming home": Queer migrations and multiple evocations of home. *European journal of cultural studies*, 4, pp. 405–24.

Frey, B.S. and Stutzer, A. (2000). Happiness prospers in democracy. *Journal of happiness studies*, 1, pp. 79–102.

Gadd, J. (2004, July 30). Toronto's enigmatic architect. *Globe and Mail*. Updated March 18, 2009. Retrieved August 17, 2013 from: http://www.theglobeandmail.com/life/home-and-garden/real-estate/torontos-enigmatic-architect/article4090015/.

Gage, F.H. (2009). Foreword: From the perspective of a neuroscientist. In J.P. Eberhard, *Brain landscape: The coexistence of neuroscience and architecture*. New York, NY: Oxford University Press, pp. xii–xiv.

Good News Toronto (2012). Toronto architect envisions community-based village. Retrieved August 27, 2013 from: http://www.goodnewstoronto.ca/2012/04/toronto-architect-envisions-community-based-village/.

Goonewardena, K., Rankin, K.N., and Weinstock, S. (2004). Diversity and planning education: A Canadian perspective. *Canadian journal of urban research*, 13(1), Supplement, pp. 1–26.

Gorman, R. (2014). *China overtakes the US as world's largest economy*. Retrieved December 28, 2014 from: http://www.aol.com/article/2014/12/04/china-overtakes-the-us-as-worlds-largest-economy/21003035/.

Government of Canada (2007). *From mosaic to harmony: Multicultural Canada in the 21st century*. Ottawa, ON: Policy Research Initiative. Retrieved August 31, 2012 from: http://www.horizons.gc.ca/doclib/SP_div_Mosaic_%20e.pdf.

—— (2009). *Understanding Canada's "3M" (multicultural, multi-linguistic and multi-religious) reality in the 21st century*. Ottawa, ON: Policy Research Initiative. Retrieved July 5, 2012 from: http://www.horizons.gc.ca/doclib/2009-0015-eng.pdf.

Grad, F.P. (2002). Public health classics: The preamble of the constitution of the World Health Organization. *Bulletin of the World Health Organization*, 80(12). Retrieved August 11, 2012 from: http://www.who.int/bulletin/archives/80%2812%29981.pdf.

Graham, C. (2005). *The economics of happiness*. Economic Studies Program, The Brookings Institution, Washington DC. Retrieved August 9, 2012 from: http://www.brookings.edu/views/papers/graham/2005graham_dict.pdf.

Green Calgary (2013). *Co-housing: Creating community in Calgary*. Retrieved October 28, 2013 from: http://www.greencalgary.org/resources/co-housing-creating-community-in-calgary.

Greenberg, R. (2004). P.S. 1's winning design for a courtyard to help New Yorkers celebrate the summer. *Architectural record*, 192(7).

Hall, E.T. (1976). *Beyond culture*. New York, NY: Anchor Books.

Hamilton, J. (1860/2009). *The happy home: Affectionately inscribed to the working people*. Bibliolabs.com: BiblioLife.

Hancock, T. (1993). The evolution, impact, and significance of the healthy cities/communities movement. *Journal of public health policy*, 14(1), pp. 5–18.

—— (1997). Healthy cities and communities: Past, present, and future. *National civic review*, 86(1), pp. 11–21.

Hardy Stevenson and Associates Limited (2005). *Planning in a multicultural environment*. Retrieved September 3, 2013 from: http://www.hardystevenson.com/research/message_board.php?ID=4.

Hargreaves, A. and Webster, R. (2000). *Social sustainability and local distinctiveness: Arguments for the positive evaluation of place-centered awareness*. Paper presented at the ENHR 2000 Conference, June 26–30, 2000, Gavle.

Harland, M. (1896/2011). *The secret of a happy home*. New York, NY: The Christian Herald Association, Louis Klopsch, Proprietor, Bible House.

Hawkes, J. (2001). *The fourth pillar of sustainability: Culture's essential role in public planning*. Australia: Common Ground.

Hawthorne, C. (2005, September 15). Courts with a new spark: L.A.'s architectural heritage. *Los Angeles Times (Home)*. Retrieved August 27, 2013 from: http://articles.latimes.com/2005/sep/15/home/hm-courtyard15.

Hayward, K., Pannozzo, L., and Colman, R. (2005). Draft: Developing indicators for the educated populace domain of the Canadian Index of Wellbeing. Interim Report. Halifax: GPI Atlantic.

Healthy House (2007). *Healthy house: Creating healthier indoor environments*. Melbourne, Victoria, Australia. Retrieved July 10, 2012 from: http://www.healthyhouse.com/.

Healthy House Institute (2006–2012). *Healthy house institute for a healthier home: The resource for a better, safer indoor environment*. Retrieved July 10, 2012 from: http://www.healthyhouseinstitute.com/.

Healthy-House.co.uk (n.d.). *The healthy house: Electromagnetic and radiation protection*. Retrieved July 10, 2012 from: http://www.healthy-house.co.uk/products/electromagnetic_and_radiation_protection.php.

Helliwell, J.F., Layard, R., and Sachs, J. (eds) (2012). *World happiness report*. New York, NY: Earth Institute, Columbia University. Retrieved July 10, 2012 from: http://www.earth.columbia.edu/sitefiles/file/Sachs%20Writing/2012/World%20Happiness%20Report.pdf.

Howell, J. (2014). *Chinese real estate buyers "not interested in the environment."* Retrieved May 22, 2014 from: http://www.opp-connect.com/22/05/2014/chinese-real-estate-buyers-not-interested-in-the-environment/.

Hsu, S.N.-J. (2002). A transformation of traditional Chinese residential architecture in Richmond, B.C. (Greater Vancouver). Master's of Architecture thesis, Dalhousie University, Halifax, Nova Scotia, Canada.

Huang, A. (2006). *The silent spikes: Chinese laborers and the construction of North American railroads*. Beijing: China Intercontinental Press.

Hughes, C.J. (2013, August 8). Chinese invest in Queens real estate. *The New York Times*. Retrieved August 11, 2013 from: http://www.nytimes.com/2013/08/11/realestate/chinese-invest-in-queens-real-estate.html?hp&_r=1&pagewanted=all&#h.

Hust, D. (2013). *Chinese "city."* Retrieved June 15, 2013 from: http://www.sc-democrat.com/news/2013May/17/news.htm.

Huta, V. and Ryan, R.M. (2010). Pursuing pleasure or virtue: The differential and overlapping well-being benefits of hedonic and eudaimonic motives. *Journal of happiness studies*, 11, pp. 735–62.

Hwang, S., Fuller-Thomson, E., Hulchanski, J.D., et al. (1999). *Housing and population health: A review of the literature*. Ottawa, ON: Canada Mortgage and Housing Corporation.

Ipsos Reid (2007). *Canadian Chinese media monitor: Greater Toronto Area*. Fairchild Television. Retrieved July 5, 2012 from: http://www.fairchildtv.com/english/ppt/ipsos_reid_2007_tor.pdf.

Ison, E. (2009). The introduction of health impact assessment in the WHO European healthy cities network. *Health promotion international*, 24(supplement 1), pp. i64–i71.

Jacobs, J.M. (2004). Too many houses for a home: Narrating the house in the Chinese diaspora. In Cairns, S. (ed.), *Drifting: Architecture and migrancy*. London and New York, NY: Routledge, pp. 164–83.

Jarmusch, A. (2004). Lofts at Laurel Court: West Hollywood, California. *Architectural record*, 192(11), pp. 204–7.

Jenkin, F. (1879/2010). *Healthy houses*. New York, NY: Harper & Brothers/Nabu Press.

Journey of Civilization (2013, May 13). *Lóu Yulie: Three-level health preservation*. 《文明之旅》楼宇烈: 三理养生. Retrieved May 29, 2013 from: http://news.cntv.cn/2013/05/13/VIDE1368458640353498.shtml.

Kasser, T. and Sheldon, K.M. (2002). What makes for a merry Christmas? *Journal of happiness studies*, 3, pp. 313–29.

Kayan, C. (2011). Neuro-architecture: Enriching healthcare environments for children. Master's thesis at Chalmers Architecture, Chalmers University of Technology, Sweden.

Keister, D. (2005). *Courtyards: Intimate outdoor spaces*. Layton, UT: Gibbs Smith Publisher.

Kellogg, C. (2006, February 1). Case for courtyards pix: How Moule and Polyzoides fought southern California. *Interior design*. Retrieved March 28, 2013 from: http://www.interiordesign.net/article/481093-The_Case_For_Courtyards_pix.php.

Kennedy, D.J. (1997). *Secret to a happy home*. New Kensington, PA: Whitaker House.

Kenny, A. (2001). Beyond a warm feeling: Two more elements of well-being. In S. McCready (ed.), *The discovery of happiness*. Naperville, IL: Sourcebooks, pp. 222–37.

Kenny, A. and Kenny, C. (2006). *Life, liberty, and the pursuit of utility: Happiness in philosophical and economic thought* (St. Andrews Studies in Philosophy and Public Affairs). Exeter, UK: Imprint Academic.

Kenzer, M. (1999). Healthy cities: A guide to the literature. *Environment and urbanization*, 11(1), pp. 201–20. Retrieved August 12, 2012 from: http://eau.sagepub.com/content/11/1/201.full.pdf.

Keswick, M. (2003). *Chinese garden: History, art and architecture*. Cambridge, MA: Harvard University Press.

Kickbush, I. (2003). The contribution of the World Health Organization to a new public health and health promotion. *American journal of public health*, 93(3), pp. 383–8.

—— (2007). The move towards a new public health. *Promotion and education*, 14(9), p. 9.

King, A.D. (1997). Excavating the multicultural suburb: Hidden histories of the bungalow. In Silverstone, R. (ed.), *Visions of suburbia*. London: Routledge, pp. 55–85.

Knapp, R.G. (2005a). *Chinese houses: The architectural heritage of a nation*. North Clarendon, VT: Tuttle Publishing.

—— (2005b). Siting and situating a dwelling: Fengshui, house-building rituals, and amulets. In R.G. Knapp and K.-Y. Lo (eds), *House home family: Living and being Chinese*. Honolulu: University of Hawai'i Press, pp. 99–137.

—— (2005c). In search of the elusive Chinese house. In R.G. Knapp and K.-Y. Lo (eds), *House home family: Living and being Chinese*. Honolulu: University of Hawai'i Press, pp. 37–71.

—— (2010). *Chinese houses of Southeast Asia: The eclectic architecture of sojourners and settlers* (photographs by A.C. Ong, foreword by G. Wang). Rutland, VT: Tuttle Publishing.

—— (2011). *Things Chinese: Antiques, crafts, collectibles* (photography by M. Freeman). Rutland, VT: Tuttle Publishing.

—— (2013). *The Peranakan Chinese home*. Rutland, VT: Tuttle Publishing.

Knapp, R.G. and Lo, K.-Y. (eds) (2005). *House home family: Living and being Chinese*. Honolulu: University of Hawai'i Press.

Kou, X. (2005). *A treasure dictionary for prosperous residences: A guide to residential Feng Shui* (《旺宅宝典: 住宅风水指南》, Chinese edition). Beijing: Culture and Art Press.

Krieger, J. and Higgins, D. (2002). Housing and health: Time again for public heath action. *American journal of public health*, 92(5), pp. 758–68.

Lai, D.C. (2010). *Chinese community leadership: Case study of Victoria in Canada*. Hackensack, NJ: World Scientific.

Land, P. (2006). Courtyard housing: An "afterthought." In B. Edwards, M. Sibley, M. Hakmi et al. (eds), *Courtyard housing: Past, present, and future*. New York, NY: Taylor and Francis.

Laozi (c. 571–471 BCE). *Tao te ching* (translated by S. Mitchell, 1988). New York, NY: HarperPerennial.

—— (c. 571–471 BCE). *Tao te ching: An illustrated journey* (translated by S. Mitchell, 1999). New York, NY: HarperCollins.

—— (c. 571–471 BCE). *Tao te ching* (translated by D. Lin, 2006). Woodstock, VT: Skylight Paths Publishing.

Lasner, M. (2012). *High life: Condo living in the suburban century*. New Haven, CT: Yale University Press.

Lau, K.-K. (1991). An interpretation of Confucian virtues and their relevance to China's modernization. In S. Krieger and R. Trauzettel (eds), *Confucianism and the modernization of China*. Mainz, Germany: Hase and Koehler Verlag, pp. 210–28.

Layard, R., Clark, A., and Senik, C. (2012). The causes of happiness and misery. In J.F. Helliwell, R. Layard, and J. Sachs (eds), *World happiness report*. New York, NY: Earth Institute, Columbia University, pp. 58–89.

Lee, J.C. (2002). Visioning diversity: Planning Vancouver's multicultural communities. Master's of Arts in Planning thesis, University of Waterloo, Canada.

de Leeuw, E. (1999). Healthy cities: Urban social entrepreneurship for health. *Health promotion international*, 14(3), pp. 261–70.

de Leeuw, E. (2009). Evidence for healthy cities: Reflections on practice, method and theory. *Health promotion international*, 24, Special Supplement on European Healthy Cities, pp. i19–i36.

Leigh, C. (2004, September 15). California dreaming: Architects aim to reconcile growth with LA's past. *Features*. Retrieved March 28, 2013 from: http://www.princeton.edu/~paw/archive_new/PAW04-05/01-0915/features2.html.

Levin, I. (2012). Chinese migrants in Melbourne and their house choices. *Australian geographer*, 43(3), pp. 303–20.

Ley, D. (1995). Between Europe and Asia: The case of the missing sequoias. *Ecumene: A journal of environment/culture/meaning*, 2, pp. 185–210.

—— (2003). Forgetting postmodernism? Recuperating a social history of local knowledge. *Progress in human geography*, 27(5), pp. 537–60.

Li, J. (2001). Expectations of Chinese immigrant parents for their children's education: The interplay of Chinese tradition and the Canadian context. *Canadian journal of education*, 26(4), pp. 477–94.

Li, P.S. (1999). *Chinese: Encyclopedia of Canada's peoples*. Toronto, ON: Multicultural History Society of Ontario.

Li, S. (2008). *Illustrative annotations of the Yellow Emperor's canon of residences: Understanding the way of Chinese living* (《图解黄帝宅经: 认识中国居住之道》, Chinese edition). Shaanxi, China: Shaanxi Normal University Press.

Li, W. (1998). Anatomy of a new ethnic settlement: The Chinese ethnoburb in Los Angeles. *Urban studies*, 35, pp. 479–501.

—— (2005). Beyond Chinatown, beyond enclave: Reconceptualizing contemporary Chinese settlements in the United States. *GeoJournal*, 64, pp. 31–40.

Liang, S.C. (1998). *Frozen music* (《凝动的音乐》, Chinese edition). Tianjin: Hundred Flowers Literature and Art Publishing House.

Lindsay, C. (2001). *Profiles of ethnic communities in Canada: The Chinese community in Canada*. Ottawa, ON: Social and Aboriginal Statistics Division, Statistics Canada.

Liu, H. (2005). Asian-American ideas (cultural migration). In M.C. Horowitz (ed.), *New dictionary of the history of ideas*. Detroit, MI: Charles Scribner's Sons, vol. 1, pp. 158–60.

Liu, X. (2002). The origins of Chinese architecture. In X. Fu, D. Guo, X. Liu et al., *Chinese architecture*. New Haven, CT: Yale University Press, pp. 11–31.

Logan, J.J. (2010). "There's no place like home": A snapshot of the settlement experiences of newcomer Tibetan women in Parkdale, Toronto. MA thesis, Department of Geography, York University, Canada.

Louie, V.S. (2004). *Compelled to excel: Immigration, education, and opportunity among Chinese Americans*. Palo Alto, CA: Stanford University Press.

Lu, L. (2001). Understanding happiness: A look into the Chinese folk psychology. *Journal of happiness studies*, 2, pp. 407–32.

Luó, Z.W. (2006). Foreword: Feng Shui theory and ancient Chinese architectural planning and construction. In Z.Z. Luò, *Feng Shui and modern residences* (《风水学与现代家居》, Chinese edition). Beijing: China City Press, pp. 1–19.

Luò, Z.Z. (2006). *Feng Shui and modern residences* (《风水学与现代家居》, Chinese edition). Beijing: China City Press.

Lupone, L. (1999). Feng Shui: Therapy for the new millennium. *Complementary health practice review*, 5(2), pp. 115–20.

Lyle, J.T. (1994). *Regenerative design for sustainable development*. Toronto, ON: John Wiley and Sons.

Ma, B. (1999). *The architecture of the quadrangle in Beijing* (《北京四合院建筑》, Chinese edition). China: Tianjin University Press.

Mar, L.R. (2010). *Brokering belonging: Chinese in Canada's exclusion era 1885–1945*. Don Mills, ON: Oxford University Press.

Masuda, J.R., Poland, B., and Baxter, J. (2010). Reaching for environmental health justice: Canadian experiences for a comprehensive research, policy and advocacy agenda in health promotion. *Health promotion international*, 25(4), pp. 453–63.

Mattern, K. (2013). *China city in Mamakating: $6 billion project part of a national effort?* Retrieved June 15, 2013 from: http://www.gunkjournal.com/2013/05/30/news/1305300.html.

Maxim, E. (2010). *Riding the waves: Diagnosing, treating and living with EMF sensitivity*. Elizabeth Maxim.

McCamant, K. and Durrett, C. (2011). *Creating cohousing: Building sustainable communities*. Gabriola Island, BC: New Society Publishers.

McCamant, K., Durrett, C., and Hertzman, E. (1988/1994). *Cohousing: A contemporary approach to housing ourselves* (2nd revised edn). New York, NY: Ten Speed Press.

McCready, S. (2001). *The discovery of happiness*. Naperville, IL: Sourcebooks.

McDonald, M. (2005, September). Courtyard housing. *Clem Labinet's period homes*. Active Interest Media, pp. 18–21.

Medianu, N. (2007). Diversity and urban citizenship in Canadian cities. Institute for the Humanities at Simon Fraser University. Retrieved July 5, 2012 from: http://www.humanities-online.ca/index.php/humanities/article/viewFile/18/22.

Mencius (372–289 BCE). *The works of Mencius* (translated and annotated by J. Legge, 1895/1970). New York, NY: Dover Publications.

Meng, C. (1981). *Chinese American understanding: A sixty-year search*. New York, NY: China Institute in America.

Michalos, A.C. (2007). Education, happiness and wellbeing (first draft for discussion). Institute for Social Research and Evaluation, University of Northern British Columbia, Prince George, BC, Canada.

Milroy, B.M. and Wallace, M. (2002). *Ethnoracial diversity and planning practices in the Greater Toronto Area: Final report*. Joint Centre of Excellence for Research on Immigration and Settlement—Toronto (CERIS) Working Paper No. 18.

—— (2004a). *Multicultural planning practices in the GTA*. Retrieved September 3, 2013 from: http://www.ceris.metropolis.net/Virtual%20Library/housing_neighbourhoods/milroy_wallace.html.

—— (2004b). *Ethnoracial diversity and planning practices in the Greater Toronto Area: Final report*. Joint Centre of Excellence for Research on Immigration and Settlement—Toronto (CERIS), 12. Policy Matters, November 2004.

Miscevic, D. and Kwong, P. (2000). *Chinese Americans: The immigrant experience*. Fairfield, CT: Hugh Lauter Levin Associates.

—— (2007). *Chinese America: The untold story of America's oldest new community*. New York, NY: New Press.

Mitchell, K. (2004). Conflicting landscapes of dwelling and democracy in Canada. In S. Cairns (ed.), *Drifting: Architecture and migrancy*. London and New York, NY: Routledge, pp. 142–63.

Moloughney, B. (2004). *Housing and population health: The state of current research knowledge*. Ottawa, ON: Canadian Institute of Health Information. Retrieved August 24, 2012 from: from https://secure.cihi.ca/free_products/HousingPopHealth_e.pdf.

Monbiot, G. (2014, October 15). The age of loneliness is killing us. *The Guardian*. Retrieved November 18, 2014 from: http://www.theguardian.com/commentisfree/2014/oct/14/age-of-loneliness-killing-us?CMP=ema_565.

Montgomery, C. (2013). *Happy city: Transforming our lives through urban design*. Toronto, ON: Doubleday Canada/Penguin Random House Canada.

Morley, R.L., Mickalide, A.D., and Mack, K.A. (eds) (2011). *Healthy and safe homes: Research, practice, and policy*. Washington DC: American Public Health Association.

Mozi (1929/1978). *The ethical and political works of Motse* (translated by W.P. Mei, who omits the Canons, Daqu, Xiaoqu, and the military chapters. English translation of the Canons is based on that in A.C. Graham's *Later Mohist logic, ethics, and science*). Hong Kong: Chinese University Press.

National Association of Realtors (2012). *Profile of international home buying activity 2012*. Retrieved July 26, 2012 from: http://www.realtor.org/reports/profile-of-international-home-buying-activity.

—— (2013). *2013 profile of international home buying activity: Purchases of U.S. real estate by international clients for the twelve month period ending March 2013*. Retrieved August 11, 2013 from: http://www.realtor.org/reports/profile-of-international-home-buying-activity.

National Center for Environmental Health (2008). *Healthy community design: Fact sheet series*. Division of Emergency and Environmental Health Services. Retrieved August 12, 2012 from: http://www.cdc.gov/healthyplaces/factsheets/Healthy_Community_Design_factsheet_Final.pdf.

Nayar, J. (2011). *The happy home project: A practical guide to adding style and substance to your home*. Maidenhead, Berkshire: Filipacchi Publishing.

New South Wales Government (n.d.). *Implementing the principles of multiculturalism locally: A planning framework for councils*. Community Relations Commission for a Multicultural NSW.

Newman, M. (2002, July 24). Courtyard housing revival. *Architecture week*, pp. D1.1–2. Retrieved July 21, 2013 from: http://www.mparchitects.com/site/press/courtyard-housing-revival.

Nias, D. (2001). Managing good and bad fortune: Opportunities for happiness. In S. McCready (ed.), *The discovery of happiness*. Naperville, IL: Sourcebooks, pp. 184–207.

O'Brien, C. (2008). Sustainable happiness: How happiness studies can contribute to a more sustainable future. *Canadian psychology*, 49(4), pp. 289–95.

O'Neill, M. and Simard, P. (2006). Choosing indicators to evaluate healthy cities projects: A political task? *Health promotion international*, 21(2), pp. 145–52. Retrieved August 12, 2012 from: http://heapro.oxfordjournals.org/content/21/2/145.full.

O'Neill, T. (2003, January 20). Community regained: The environmental-friendly "cohousing" movement takes root in B.C. *Report/Newsmagazine (national edition)*, 30(2), pp. 37–9.

Ouellet, F., Durand, D., and Forget, G. (1994). Preliminary results of an evaluation of three healthy cities initiatives in the Montreal area. *Health promotion international*, 9(3), pp. 153–9.

Paganelli, J. (2012). *Happy home: Twenty sewing and craft projects to pretty up your home*. San Francisco, CA: Chronicle Books.

Painter, G., Yang, L., and Yu, Z. (2002). Why are Chinese homeownership rates so high?: Assimilation, ethnic concentration, and nativity. Preliminary draft, Lusk Center for Real Estate, University of Southern California.

Pan, G. (2002). The Yuan and Ming dynasties. In X. Fu, D. Guo, X. Liu et al. , *Chinese architecture*. New Haven, CT: Yale University Press, pp. 199–259.

Peterson, C., Park, N., and Seligman, M.E.P. (2005). Orientations to happiness and life satisfaction: The full life versus the empty life. *Journal of happiness studies*, 6, pp. 25–41.

Pew Research Center (2006). *Are we happy yet?* Retrieved August 18, 2012 from: http://pewresearch.org/pubs/301/are-we-happy-yet.

Plato (1924). *Laches, Protagoras, Meno, Euthydemus* (translated by W.R.M. Lamb). Cambridge, MA: Loeb Classical Library, Harvard University Press.

Plümer, K.D., Kennedy, L., and Trojan, A. (2010). Evaluating the implementation of the WHO Healthy Cities Programme across Germany (1999–2002). *Health promotion international*, 25(3), pp. 342–54.

Poland, B.D. (1996a). Knowledge development and evaluation in, of and for healthy community initiatives. Part I: Guiding principles. *Health promotion international*, 11(3), pp. 237–47.

—— (1996b). Knowledge development and evaluation in, of and for healthy community initiatives. Part II: Potential content foci. *Health promotion international*, 11(4), pp. 341–9.

Polyzoides, S., Sherwood, R., and Tice, J. (1982/1992). *Courtyard housing in Los Angeles: A typological analysis*. New York, NY: Princeton Architectural Press.

Pon, G. (2005). Antiracism in the cosmopolis: Race, class, and gender in the lives of elite Chinese Canadian women. *Social justice*, 32(4), pp. 161–79.

Preston, V. and Lo, L. (2000). "Asian theme" malls in suburban Toronto: Land use conflicts in Richmond Hill. *Canadian geographer*, 44, pp. 182–90.

—— (2010). *Ethnic enclaves in multicultural cities: New retailing patterns and new planning dilemmas*. Retrieved July 18, 2013 from: http://www.metropolis.net/pdfs/fow_16aug10_e.pdf.

Qadeer, M.A. (1997). Pluralistic planning for multicultural cities: The Canadian practice. *Journal of the American Planning Association*, 63(4), pp. 481–94.

—— (2009). What is this thing called multicultural planning? *The bridge*, 2(9), pp. 10–13. Retrieved July 15, 2013 from: http://www.metropolis.net/pdfs/qadeer_extracted_plan_canada_e.pdf.

Qadeer, M.A. and Agrawal, S. (2010). *The city and integration of immigrants: Urban planning policies for multicultural cities*. Retrieved July 18, 2013 from: http://www.metropolis.net/mediacentre/brown_bag_24nov10_e.pptx.

Ranson, R. (1991). *Healthy housing: A practical guide*. London and New York, NY: Taylor & Francis.

Rapport, N. and Dawson, A. (eds) (1998). *Migrants of identity: Perceptions of home in a world of movement*. Oxford and New York, NY: Berg.

Reynolds, J.S. (2002). *Courtyards: Aesthetic, social, and thermal delight*. New York, NY: John Wiley and Sons.

Roy, P. (2007). *The triumph of citizenship: The Japanese and Chinese in Canada 1941–67*. Vancouver, BC: UBC Press.

Ryff, C.D. and Singer, B.H. (2008). Know thyself and become what you are: A eudaimonic approach to psychological well-being. *Journal of happiness studies*, 9, pp. 13–39.

Sabatini, F. (2011). *The relationship between happiness and health: Evidence from Italy*. Health, Economics and Data Group, University of York, UK.

Sandercock, L. (2000). When strangers become neighbours: Managing cities of difference. *Planning theory and practice*, 1(1), pp. 13–30.

Satow, J. (2015). The lure of the gold coast: Wealthy Chinese buyers head to New York's suburbs. *New York Times*, February 6, 2015. Retrieved February 8, 2015 from: http://mobile.nytimes.com/2015/02/08/realestate/wealthy-chinese-buyers-head-to-new-yorks-suburbs.html?referrer=&_r=0.

Scarre, G. (2001). The greatest happiness of the greatest number: Utilitarianism and enlightenment. In S. McCready (ed.), *The discovery of happiness*. Naperville, IL: Sourcebooks, pp. 152–71.

Schneider-Skalska, G. (2011). *Designing a healthy housing environment: Selected problems*. Saarbrücken: Lambert Academic Publishing.

ScottHanson, C. and ScottHanson, K. (2004). *Cohousing handbook: Building a place for community*. Gabriola Island, BC: New Society Publishers.

See, L. (1996). *On gold mountain: The one-hundred-year odyssey of my Chinese American family*. Hopkinton, MA: Vintage Books.

Seneca, L.A. (2012). *Treatises on providence, on tranquility of mind, on shortness of life, on happy life*. Charleston, SC: Nabu Press.

Smith, L. (2001). Heavenly bliss and earthly delight: Happiness in the Christian Middle Ages. In S. McCready (ed.), *The discovery of happiness*. Naperville, IL: Sourcebooks, pp. 116–35.

Somerville, T., Li, Q., and Teller, P. (2007). *Are renters being left behind?: Homeownership and wealth accumulation in Canadian cities*. Discussion paper presented at the Centre for Urban Economics and Real Estate. Retrieved July 5, 2012 from: http://cuer.sauder.ubc.ca/download/research/discussion/2007_feb_somerville.pdf.

Statistics Canada (2006). *Ethnic origins, 2006 counts, for Canada, provinces and territories—20%sampledata*. Retrieved July 5, 2012 from: http://www12.statcan.ca/census-recensement/2006/dp-pd/hlt/97-562/pages/page.cfm?Lang=E&Geo=PR&Code=01&Table=2&Data=Count&StartRec=1&Sort=3&Display=All&CSDFilter=5000.

—— (2008). *2002 ethnic diversity survey*. Ottawa, ON: Statistics Canada.

—— (2013). *Household size by province and territory (2011 census)*. Retrieved July 15, 2013 from: http://www.statcan.gc.ca/tables-tableaux/sum-som/l01/cst01/famil53a-eng.htm.

Sternberg, E.M. (2009). *Healing spaces: The science of place and well-being*. Cambridge, MA and London, England: The Belknap Press of Harvard University Press.

Sternberg, E.M. and Wilson, M.A. (2006). Neuroscience and architecture: Seeking common ground. *Cell 127*, pp. 239–42.

Taylor, M. (2010). The healthy cities movement (working paper for the Lancet Commission on Healthy Cities). MSc Urban Studies, Department of Geography, University College London. Retrieved July 10, 2012 from: http://www.ucl.ac.uk/healthy-cities/outputs/Working_Paper.

Theuns, P., Verresen, N., Mairesse, O., et al. (2010). An experimental approach to the joint effects of relations with partner, friends and parents on happiness. *Psicológica*, 31, pp. 629–45.

Thomas, M. (1997). Discordant dwellings: Australian houses and the Vietnamese diaspora. In I. Ang and M. Symonds (eds), *Home, displacement, belonging, communal/plural 5*. Research Centre in Intercommunal Studies, Sydney, pp. 95–114.

Tian, G. (1999). *Canadian-Chinese: Coping and adapting in North America*. Lewiston, NY: Edwin Mellen Press.

Tickner, N. (2008). *Major study of Chinese Americans debunks "Model Minority" myth*. University of Maryland. Retrieved July 7, 2012 from: http://newsdesk.umd.edu/sociss/release.cfm?ArticleID=1786.

Toronto Public Health (2011). *Healthy Toronto by design*. Retrieved August 22, 2012 from: http://www.toronto.ca/health/hphe/pdf/healthytoronto_oct04_11.pdf.

—— (2012). *The walkable city: Neighbourhood design and preferences, travel choices and health*. Retrieved August 24, 2012 from: http://www.toronto.ca/health/hphe/pdf/walkable_city.pdf.

Toronto Public Library (2013). *Chinatown, then and now*. Retrieved August 1, 2013 from: http://www.torontopubliclibrary.ca/ktr/one-book-chinatown.jsp.

Trulove, J.G. (2006). *New sustainable homes: Designs for healthy living*. New York, NY: Harper Design.

Tung, M. (2000). *Chinese Americans and their immigrant parents: Conflict, identity, and values*. New York, NY: Routledge.

Ulrich, R.S. (1984). View through a window may influence recovery from surgery. *Science 224*, pp. 420–21.

UNESCO (2012). *Facts and figures from the United Nations World Water Development Report 4: Managing water under uncertainty and risk.* Retrieved August 11, 2012 from: http://www. hydrology.nl/images/docs/ihp/WWDR4/WWDR4_Facts_Figures.pdf.

US Census Bureau (2000a). *Asian American comprehensive profile.* Améredia Incorporated.

—— (2000b). *Chinese American demographics.* Améredia Incorporated. Retrieved July 8, 2012 from: http://www.ameredia.com/resources/demographics/chinese.html.

—— (2006). *Highlights of annual 2006 characteristics of new housing.* Retrieved March 31, 2013 from: http://www.census.gov/const/www/highanncharac2006.html.

—— (2008). *American community survey, selected population profiles, S0201.* Retrieved December 22, 2014 from: http://factfinder2.census.gov/faces/tableservices/jsf/pages/ productview.xhtml?src=bkmk.

—— (2010a). *Race reporting for the Asian population by selected categories: 2010.* Retrieved July 6, 2012 from: http://factfinder2.census.gov/faces/tableservices/jsf/pages/ productview.xhtml?pid=DEC_10_SF1_QTP8&prodType=table.

—— (2010b). *Profile of general population and housing characteristics: 2010. Demographic profile data New York-Newark-Bridgeport, NY-NJ-CT-PA CSA.* Retrieved July 7, 2012 from: http://factfinder2.census.gov/faces/tableservices/jsf/pages/productview. xhtml?pid=DEC_10_DP_DPDP1.

—— (2010c). *Profile of general population and housing characteristics: 2010. Demographic profile data San Jose-San Francisco-Oakland, CA CSA.* Retrieved July 7, 2012 from: http:// factfinder2.census.gov/faces/tableservices/jsf/pages/productview.xhtml?pid=DEC_10_ DP_DPDP1.

—— (2012). *Households and families: 2010.* Retrieved July 15, 2013 from: http://www.census. gov/prod/cen2010/briefs/c2010br-14.pdf.

Veenhoven, R. (2000). Four qualities of life: Ordering concepts and measures of the good life. *Journal of happiness studies*, 1, pp. 1–39.

—— (2003). Hedonism and happiness. *Journal of happiness studies*, 4 (special issue on "Art of Living"), pp. 437–57.

—— (2008). Healthy happiness: Effects of happiness on physical health and the consequences for preventive health care. *Journal of happiness studies*, 9, pp. 449–69.

—— (2011). *World database of happiness: Example of a focused "findings archive."* Working Paper No. 169, German Data Forum (RatSWD), Federal Ministry of Education and Research.

Vickery, J. (2012). *Why is China building mega-cities in the U.S.?* Retrieved June 15, 2013 from: http://www.policymic.com/articles/8617/why-is-china-building-mega-cities-in-the-u-s.

Walljasper, J. (2013). *How to design our neighborhoods for happiness.* Retrieved October 28, 2013 from: http://www.yesmagazine.org/happiness/how-to-design-our-neighborhoods-for-happiness.

Wang, B. (1997). *Yellow emperor's canon of internal medicine* (《黄帝内经》, translated by L. Wu and Q. Wu). Beijing: China Science and Technology Press.

Wang, K. (2001). Dao, Confucianism, and Buddhism: Happiness in Chinese philosophy and religion. In S. McCready (ed.), *The discovery of happiness.* Naperville, IL: Sourcebooks, pp. 36–55.

Wargo, J. (2009). *Green intelligence: Creating environments that protect human health*. New Haven, CT: Yale University Press.

Waterman, A.S., Schwartz, S.J., and Conti, R. (2008). The implications of two conceptions of happiness (hedonic enjoyment and eudaimonia) for the understanding of intrinsic motivation. *Journal of happiness studies*, 9, pp. 41–79.

WHO Regional Office for Europe (2009). *Phase V (2009–2013) of the World Health Organization Healthy Cities Network: Goals and requirements*. Copenhagen: Regional Office for Europe.

Wigle, J. (1998). *Healthy cities/healthy communities* (ICURR literature summary no. 2). Retrieved July 10, 2012 from: http://www.muniscope.ca/_files/file.php?fileid=fileynZstnCalg&filename=file_ICURR_LITERATURE_SUMMARY_NO2_a.pdf.

Winward, R. (2012). *Happy home*. London: Merrell Publishers.

Wolff, T. (2003). The healthy communities movement: A time for transformation. *National civic review*, 92(2), pp. 95–111. Retrieved July 10, 2012 from: http://www.ncl.org/publications/ncr/92-2/Wolff92-2.pdf.

World Health Organization (1986, November 21). *The Ottawa Charter for health promotion*. First International Conference on Health Promotion, Ottawa. Retrieved August 11, 2012 from: http://www.who.int/healthpromotion/conferences/previous/ottawa/en/index.html.

—— (1994). *Healthy cities in action*. Copenhagen: World Health Organization.

—— (1998). *Health promotion glossary*. Retrieved August 12, 2012 from: http://www.who.int/healthpromotion/about/HPR%20Glossar%201998.pdf.

—— (2003). *Healthy cities around the world: An overview of the healthy cities movement in the six WHO regions*. Retrieved July 10, 2012 from: http://www.euro.who.int/__data/assets/pdf_file/0015/101526/healthycityworld.pdf.

—— (2006). *Constitution of the World Health Organization (45th ed. of Basic Documents)*. Retrieved August 11, 2012 from: http://www.who.int/governance/eb/who_constitution_en.pdf.

—— (2012). *The determinants of health*. Retrieved August 11, 2012 from: http://www.who.int/hia/evidence/doh/en/.

Worrall, B.L. (2006). *Finding memories, tracing routes: Chinese Canadian family stories*. Chinese Canadian Historical Society of British Columbia.

Wu, F.H. (2001). *Yellow: Race in America beyond black and white*. New York, NY: Basic Books.

Xie, J. (1991). *Housing search behaviour: A case study of Chinese new immigrants in metropolitan Toronto*. Master's thesis in Urban and Regional Planning, School of Urban and Regional Planning, Queen's University, Canada.

Yu, D. (1991). The concept of "great harmony" in the Book of Changes (Zhou Yi): Confucian philosophical theories on conflict and harmony. In S. Krieger and R. Trauzettel (eds), *Confucianism and the modernization of China*. Mainz: Hase and Koehler Verlag, pp. 51–62.

Zeisel, J. (2006). *Inquiry by design: Environment/behavior/neuroscience in architecture, interiors, landscape, and planning*. New York/London: W.W. Norton & Company.

Zhang, D. (2009/2010/2011). *Courtyard houses of Beijing: Past, present, and future*. Saarbrucken: VDM Verlag.

—— (2013). *Courtyard housing and cultural sustainability: Theory, practice, and product*. Farnham: Ashgate.

Zhang, G. and Veenhoven, R. (2008). Ancient Chinese philosophical advice: Can it help us find happiness today? *Journal of happiness studies*, 9, pp. 425–43.

Zheng, H. (2012). *China to build cities and economic zones in Michigan and Idaho*. Retrieved June 15, 2013 from: http://www.policymic.com/articles/8603/china-to-build-cities-and-economic-zones-in-michigan-and-idaho.

Zhuang, Z.C. (2008). *Ethnic retailing and the role of municipal planning: Four case studies in the Greater Toronto Area*. Doctor of Philosophy in Planning thesis, University of Waterloo, Canada.

Zhuangzi (c. 369–286 BCE). *The complete works of Chuang Tzu* (translated by B. Watson, 1968). New York, NY: Columbia University Press.

Zeki, S. (1999). *Inner vision: An exploration of art and the brain*. Oxford: Oxford University Press.

Zi, T. (2006). *Illustrative annotations of the Yellow Emperor's canon of internal medicine: Understanding the Chinese way of preserving health* (《图解黄帝内经: 认识中国式养生》, Chinese edition). Shaanxi, China: Shaanxi Normal University Press.

Zimmerman, M.E. (2003). Architectural ethics, multiculturalism, and globalization. *Professional ethics*, 11(4), pp. 1–14.

Index

Analects, 33, 35, 104, 105
Architectural Multiculturalism, 18–19, 120
architecture, 19, 22, 37, 40, 47, 66, 92
Aristotle, 2, 92, 94, 115
art, xv–xvi, 2, 34, 52, 97, 109, 115

Bain Apartments Co-operative, 11, 13, 52–3, 80–83, 86, 102–3
balcony, 51, 54, 56, 59, 78–9, 109, 113, 124, 129, 134–5
bathroom, 50, 62
bedroom, 50, 52, 62, 67, 82, 86, 95–6
birthday, 91, 102, 104, 116
Buddhism, 17, 67, 91–2, 104, 114
building material, 47, 108

California, 8–12, 16, 18, 44, 76, 88, 108
car park space, 61, 72–3, 112, 116, 133, 135
Catholic, 91–2, 114
China City of America, 18, 41, 108
Chinatown, xvi–xvii, 17
Chinese New Year, *see* Spring Festival
Christian, 6, 34, 37, 91–2, 101–2, 104, 114, 116, 119
Christmas, 101, 115
Church-Isabella Residence Co-operative, 13, 81–3, 86
cohousing, 13, 51, 78–9, 82–3, 85, 90, 102, 108–9, 113, 116
communal courtyard, 13, 20, 44, 51–2, 54, 59, 77–9, 82–6, 90, 102, 108–9, 113, 116, 119, 121, 127, 133
Confucius, Confucian, Confucianism, xv, 17, 21, 24, 33–5, 38, 91–2, 94, 104–5, 114–15

construction quality, 21, 60–61, 70–73, 105–7, 110, 112, 116
co-operative housing/housing co-operative, 11–14, 52, 54, 78–9, 82, 84–6, 90, 102, 108, 113, 116
courtyard garden house, 22, 117, 119, 121–36
courtyard house/housing, xvii, 7–11, 13, 18, 20–22, 24–5, 30–31, 33, 38, 41–4, 47, 49, 54–5, 59, 70, 78, 86, 89, 102, 104–8, 112, 116, 119–20
Courtyard Housing Co-operative, 13, 86
cultural activities, 7, 21, 59, 91, 105–7, 109, 114–16, 120–21, 133, 136
cultural festivities, 91, 102, 104, 115–16
culture, xv, 4, 8, 19, 36, 49, 52, 91, 116, 120–21

daily activities, 72, 91, 93–6, 104, 115–16
Dao, Daoist, Daoism, *Dao De Jing*, xv, 17, 21, 23, 24, 28, 32–39, 75, 91–2, 104–7, 114, 116
daylight, 129
deck, *see* balcony
delight, 6, 9, 33, 35, 65
density, 6, 39, 85, 133–6
dining room, 31, 50, 62, 96, 101–2
door, 5, 32–3, 51–2, 54, 82, 92, 101
Dragon Boat Festival (Double Fifth Festival), xv–xvi, 100, 104, 115

earth, 23, 25, 27, 29–32, 34, 68, 75, 91, 120
Eberhard, John Paul, 22, 61, 66, 109, 111, 120
education, xv, 3, 6, 17–18, 39, 75, 90, 107, 112, 116
electromagnetic field/radiation, 22, 27

exterior form, 25, 39, 41, 59, 108, 116, 121, 135
exterior walls, 39, 41, 47, 49, 59, 108, 116

facility provision, 61, 70–71, 73, 111, 116, 133, 135
Feng Shui, xv, 22, 24–5, 27–9, 31–3, 50, 59, 68, 91–2, 104, 109–11, 114, 119
floor levels, 61, 68–9, 73, 111, 116, 133, 135
foyer, see lobby
furniture styles and materials, 61, 69, 73, 111, 116

Garden City movement, 11
gate orientation, 39, 50, 59, 108–9, 116

happiness/happy, 1–6, 16, 19–23, 30, 33–8, 47, 49, 51, 63, 65, 67–8, 72–3, 75–7, 79, 84, 87–94, 104–7, 111–17, 119–20, 136
  definition of, 2
Happy City movement, 3–5
happy homes, 5–6
harmony, 2, 19, 23–4, 33–4, 38, 52, 107, 112, 114, 120, 136
health/healthy, 1, 3–7, 16, 19–25, 27, 29, 31, 37–40, 44, 46–7, 50–52, 57–63, 66, 68–73, 77–8, 82, 84–5, 87–90, 93–4, 97, 105–17, 119–20, 135–6
  definition of, 1
Healthy City/Community movement, 3–5
healthy housing, 5
holistic, 1–3, 35, 127

interior colors, 61, 63, 72–3, 111, 116
interior space, 32, 44, 58, 61–3, 72–3, 102, 110, 116, 130, 135
Internet, 70–71, 73, 89–90, 93–6, 111, 115, 133

joy, 5, 33, 35, 65, 105

kitchen, 31, 44, 50, 62, 65, 68–9, 89, 95–6, 101–2, 109

Laozi, 23, 28, 34–6, 75, 91
living room, 44, 50, 59, 62, 95–6, 101–2
lobby, 78, 113
location, 17, 31–2, 39–40, 107, 116
lunar new year, see Spring Festival

maintenance and management, 61, 71, 73, 112, 116
marriage, 6, 75, 86–7, 90, 113, 116
Mengzi (Mencius), 33, 35
Mid-Autumn Festival (Moon Festival), xv, 100–101, 104, 115
Montgomery, Charles, 4–5, 37, 43, 51–2, 62, 77–9, 89, 94, 113–14, 135
Mozi (on universal love), 34, 38, 112
Multiculturalism, xvi, 18–19, 120
  multicultural planning/design, 18–19, 120
music, 33, 36, 83, 85, 92–4, 104, 109, 115

nature, 19, 21, 23, 32–8, 47, 51, 65–6, 68, 70, 92, 109, 111, 120, 126, 135
neuroarchitecture/neuroscience and architecture, 22, 66
New York, 9, 16, 18, 21, 44, 50, 76, 88, 108, 135

occupation, 75–6, 112, 116
Ontario, see Richmond Hill (Ontario)
Oregon, see Portland (Oregon)

philosophy and religion, 91, 114, 116
Plato, 2, 94, 115, 120
plot ratio, 133–5
Portland (Oregon), 10, 21, 108
property management, 46, 71, 84, 90, 112–13
Protestant, 91–2, 114

qi, 21, 23–5, 27–32, 37–8, 60–61, 72, 105–7, 110, 116

Richmond Hill (Ontario), 14, 42–3, 45–8, 56, 58, 63–5, 77, 79, 95
roofs, 27, 39, 57–9, 110, 116, 129, 135
  roof terraces/gardens, 58–9, 110, 134

site, 11, 24–5, 27–9, 32–3, 37, 39, 41–2, 54, 61, 121, 124–5, 133–4
social cohesion, 21, 75, 90, 105–7, 112, 116
social interaction, 7, 44, 46, 52, 59, 76–8, 83, 90, 93–4, 108–9, 113, 119–21, 127, 135
social relations, 7, 19, 73, 75–6, 78–9, 113, 116

Spring Festival (Chinese New Year), xv, 100–102, 104, 115
Spruce Court Housing Co-operative, 11
Sternberg, Esther M., 6, 22, 39–40, 66, 77, 92, 94, 107, 109, 111, 113, 115, 135
study room, 50, 95–6
sunlight, 24, 39, 43, 54, 56–7, 59, 67–9, 72, 92, 109, 126, 135

Thanksgiving (North American), 101, 115
Thanksgiving to the Stove God (Chinese), 100, 115
Toronto (Ontario), xvi–xvii, 3–4, 6, 11–17, 20–21, 41–3, 52–5, 59, 68, 79–84, 86, 90, 98–9, 102–3, 108–9, 113, 116

unity, 21, 33–4, 38, 75, 106
universe, 7, 21, 23, 32–5, 37–8, 91, 110, 114

Vancouver (British Columbia), xvi, 13, 17, 21, 42, 44, 108

water, 5, 23–4, 27–31, 33, 37–40, 57, 67, 70–71, 73, 78, 82, 84, 105, 109, 111, 127, 133
wedding, 33, 52, 75, 86–7, 113–14, 116
wind, xv, 24–7, 29–30, 33, 37
WindSong Cohousing Community, 13, 83
Windward Co-operative Homes, 13, 16
window, 33, 39, 43, 50–51, 59, 63, 69, 80, 84–5, 94, 101, 109, 116, 126, 135
Winter Solstice Festival, 100, 102, 104, 115
Wolf Willow Cohousing, 13, 83

xu shi, 24, 30

yards and gardens, 39, 51, 59, 109, 116, 127, 133, 135
Yellow Emperor's Canon of Internal Medicine, 25, 30
Yellow Emperor's Canon on Houses, 32
Yi Jing, 23, 39, 91–2, 114
Yin Yang, 21, 23–4, 35, 37, 39, 59, 105–7, 116

Zhuangzi, 32, 36–7, 61